# THE ORIGINS OF VIOLENCE

# The Origins of Violence

## Religion, History and Genocide

John Docker

First published 2008 by Pluto Press
345 Archway Road, London N6 5AA

www.plutobooks.com

British Library Cataloguing in Publication Data
A catalogue record for this book is available from the British Library

ISBN 978 0 7453 2544 6 Hardback
ISBN 978 0 7453 2543 9 Paperback

Library of Congress Cataloging in Publication Data applied for

This book is printed on paper suitable for recycling and made from fully managed and
sustained forest sources. Logging, pulping and manufacturing processes are expected to
conform to the environmental standards of the country of origin.

10 9 8 7 6 5 4 3 2 1

Designed and produced for Pluto Press by
Curran Publishing Services, Norwich
Printed and bound by CPI Group (UK) Ltd, Croydon, CR0 4YY

This book is dedicated to Ned Curthoys

# CONTENTS

## CONTENTS

# PREFACE AND ACKNOWLEDGEMENTS

In 1917, Benedetto Croce's 'History and Chronicle' was published during another time of world-shaking violence. In this witty and memorable essay, so influential in the development of modern historical writing, Croce remarks that 'only an interest in the life of the present can move one to investigate past fact', for 'past fact' comes alive when it is 'unified with an interest in the present', when it vibrates in the 'soul of the historian'. Croce believes we only become interested in a particular problem in the past when:

> that problem is related to my being in the same way as the history of a bit of business in which I am engaged, or of a love affair in which I am indulging, or of a danger that threatens me. I examine it with the same anxiety and am troubled with the same sense of unhappiness until I have succeeded in solving it.[1]

I cannot say that the problem that I seek to examine, the origins of violence, is related to any bit of business or to a love affair. It is, however, related to a 'sense of danger that threatens me', and threatens, I dare to think, humanity in the new millennium: the continuing omnipresence of violence in the world. I could mention examples from early in the twenty-first century like September 11, or the London bombings, or the Anglo-American war in Iraq. I could also mention, in a longer-range sense that acknowledges the continuing power in history of settler-colonialism and genocide, the never-ending cruelty of Israel's oppression of the Palestinians. But doubtless there will be more examples of appalling violence as the century proceeds.

Disarmingly, Croce talks of examining a problem with 'anxiety' and 'unhappiness' until one has 'succeeded in solving it'. I don't think one can succeed in solving any intellectual enquiry, so anxiety and unhappiness must remain one's permanent companions, especially with a topic such as this, so often involving harsh judgement on what humanity has done, and continues to do, and perhaps will always do. In the last several years, I must recognize, my thinking and interests have indeed taken a melancholy turn. Yet, and this is what Croce is elegantly gesturing towards, and is something Ann Curthoys and I explored in our *Is History Fiction?* (2005), there is also a palpable joy in intellectual work: in research, in reading and interpreting texts, in spirited analysis, in agreement and disagreement, in establishing the contours of an argument, in arriving at what one hopes is a true interpretation.

My approach in this book reveals, I think, certain abiding interests. In particular, I have long been dissatisfied with the way a great deal of contemporary scholarship, in seeking explanations for phenomena of group violence like colonization, conquest, empire and genocide, won't in my view go back far enough in history. Explanations are looked for in the assumed essential nature of the Enlightenment, or in the nineteenth-century age of European empires. There tends, that is, to be a focus on modernity as if it is an enclosed or self-sufficient epoch, as if it will furnish the necessary insights into why such phenomena of group violence exist or take the form they do or are so salient and pervasive. To the contrary, and I'm not sure if I can say why I am so drawn, I always want to go back as far as I can or think is relevant. As the reader will see, this has involved journeys into primatology, evolution and world history: journeys that touch on the intersections of violence and gender, and speculation about the catastrophic impact on hunter-gatherer societies worldwide of agricultural-commercial society, so relatively recent in its appearance, yet always assuming it is humanity's ideal form. A question that shadows my thinking in this book is, what is the relationship between ancient and modern? Are there predispositions and tendencies and possibilities that go back to primatology and that continue in different ways and forms and interactions in all future human history? And how can one contemplate such possible enduring features of humanity without being determinist?

Another dissatisfaction I have long had with contemporary scholarship, at least since my *1492: The Poetics of Diaspora* (2001), is its secularism, to which I prefer a 'postsecular' approach that recognizes how much religious narratives, for good or ill, stimulate, inspire and shape human action. It puzzles and astonishes me not a little to see scholars attempting to understand and illuminate phenomena like colonization, conquest, empire and genocide as if religion and mythology don't matter, as if they are mere epiphenomena, worth only a side-glance. After my *1492: The Poetics of Diaspora*, I became interested, via analyses of Freud's *Moses and Monotheism*, in the historical issue of the differences between monotheism and polytheism.[2] I tended, I must confess, rather to idealize polytheism, for its pluralizing of deities, its inclusion of female as well as male principles of divinity, its internationalism and cosmopolitanism, its translatability of gods and goddesses across mythologies. Harshly, I saw, and still see, monotheism, and here I am influenced by Jan Assmann's *Moses the Egyptian*, as a religion that works by reaction against other religions, or parts of its own religion, with which it disagrees. Monotheism's historical mode of existence tends therefore to be fractious and always potentially violent, wishing or attempting to exclude, persecute, discipline, erase the non-monotheistic world or adherents of monotheism it opposes. Its history, in Europe and the West, is riven by endless splits, between Old Testament and New, Catholicism, Protestantism, and multiple Protestant groups and grouplets from Puritans, Calvinists and Lutherans onwards, and such a fissiparous mode shows no sign of lessening. In this book, however, I am also critical of polytheism. My focus is on recognizing and exploring commonalities between polytheism and monotheism in terms of sanctioning intergroup violence.

This book is a work of literary, cultural and intellectual history. I can't see why any of these activities should be sufficient unto themselves. Long ago, so long it's a little unsettling to recall, I began my intellectual life as a literary critic, before making many expeditions into other disciplinary territories, while always holding on to the importance of textual analysis. My fealty here would be to a certain 'European' tradition of interdisciplinary thinking in the humanities, in figures like Mikhail Bakhtin, Walter Benjamin and Hannah Arendt, and I try to do justice to, to continue, that tradition here.

In the last several years I have been involved with genocide studies, especially the innovative and imaginative 'new genocide studies' that developed from the late 1990s onwards. The 'new genocide studies' does not wish to be confined to a narrow or exclusive definition of genocide. Rather it has renewed interest in the thinking of the 'founder' of genocide studies, Raphaël Lemkin, who created the term in 1944, and sought, in both his published and unpublished writings, to make the concept very wide-ranging so that it could include long-term processes like colonization as well as catastrophic events or acts or episodes (which can also be part of colonization). The 'new genocide studies' seeks to be comparative, to explore relationships between genocide and situations of settler colonialism in world history, and to be open to new approaches and perspectives. I would like to acknowledge my colleagues in genocide studies for the stimulation and assistance they have provided, especially Larissa Behrendt, Tony Barta, Ann Curthoys, Ben Kiernan, Wendy Lower, Dirk Moses, Dan Stone and Jürgen Zimmerer. I would also like to thank the *Journal of Genocide Research* for publishing an earlier version of the chapter on the Enlightenment and the Holocaust.[3]

In terms of evolutionary thinking I would like to acknowledge reading and talking with Hilary Rose and Steven Rose.

I would also like to acknowledge those of us, like Hilary and Steven, as well as Ned Curthoys, Ghassan Hage, Nur Masalha and Ilan Pappé, who have critiqued Zionist Israel and work towards averting the catastrophe that Israel is trying to bring upon the Palestinians. Zionism and the modern state of Israel are part of the long history of colonization, conquest and genocide I have tried to illuminate in this book.

Much of this book explores genocide, and questioning of genocide, in the ancient classical world, an interest that grew out of the chapters on Herodotus and Thucydides in Ann Curthoys and my *Is History Fiction?* I would particularly like to thank Ned Curthoys and David Pritchard for suggesting that I reflect not only on the works of history's founders but also explore classical Greek tragedy and texts of moral and political philosophy in the Greco-Roman world. Such I have attempted in this book, and it has been a delight to do so.

I would like to thank Mark Dorrian for enjoyable discussions of what the Elizabethan English thought they were doing in sixteenth-century Ireland.[4]

I would like to thank Shino Konishi for enjoyable discussions of the notion of honourable colonization.

There are other scholars I would like to thank for discussion of ideas and encouragement: Clare Brandabur, Gavin Edwards, Julie Evans, Debjani Ganguly, Ann Genovese, Heather Goodall, Ian Higgins, Barry Hindess, Peter Hulme, Daniel Joyce, Ben Kelly, Frances Peters Little, Ida Nursoo, and Patrick Wolfe.

My thanks to the staff in the following libraries: ANU Library, the American Jewish Historical Society, the New York Public Library and the British Library.

My thanks to my colleagues in the Research School of Humanities at ANU, and especially to the director of the Humanities Research Centre, Debjani Ganguly.

While a visiting fellow at the Institute for Advanced Studies in the Humanities at the University of Edinburgh in early 2008, I did a final reading of the manuscript; I would especially like to thank Susan Manning and Anthea Taylor for providing such a tranquil and productive atmosphere for research and reflection.

My thanks to Pluto's Roger van Zwanenberg for his encouragement throughout, including bracing discussions at an early stage of why I wished to go so far back in history; also to Robin Derricourt for his encouragement.

Above all, I would like to thank Ned Curthoys: this book could not have been written but for our long walks, coffee sessions, emails and even mobile texting discussing ideas, as well as his reading of manuscript chapters. Notions like supersessionism I particularly owe to Ned.

Above all as well: Ann Curthoys.

# INTRODUCTION

> As an account of atrocities ... this book of mine ... should
> be able ... to furnish documentation for a quiet study of
> certain aspects of the human mind.
>
> (Primo Levi, *If This is a Man*)[1]

In this book I discuss violence and genocide, and questioning of
violence and genocide, as constitutive of the human condition
down the ages. My focus is not on violence between individuals,
but on intergroup violence. My aim is to evoke and explain such
intergroup violence in ways that include both physical violence
and the violence that inheres in language and culture, in ideas,
notions, concepts, narratives and images.

## I

The arguments I present here follow from my involvement in the
last several years in the field of genocide studies, in particular my
explorations of the writings of the Polish-Jewish and then American jurist and historian Raphaël Lemkin (1900–1959), who in his
1944 book *Axis Rule in Occupied Europe* created the term 'genocide'. Lemkin argued that genocide is a recurring phenomenon in
the way human groups treat each other, just as homicide continually occurs in relations between individuals.[2] For decades after the
Holocaust, it was felt that its horror would deter future genocides,
that genocide was now unthinkable. But in the latter part of the
twentieth century the genocides that occurred in Cambodia, the
former Yugoslavia and Rwanda, and the Israeli genocide of the

indigenous Palestinians that is continuing in Israel/Palestine in the twenty-first century,[3] have urgently re-opened our necessary awareness of Lemkin's insight into human history: genocide between groups, as with homicide between individuals, has always occurred and will probably keep occurring.

In this book I consider the sombre implications of Lemkin's reconceptualization of history: rather than violence being abnormal, it is an intrinsic characteristic of human activity. The history of humanity is the history of violence: war and genocide; conquest and colonization and the creation of empires sanctioned by God or the gods in both polytheism and monotheism; the fatal combination of democracy and empire; and revolution, massacre, torture, mutilation, cruelty.

Lemkin invoked a close relationship in world history between genocide and colonization. Here is the key passage in *Axis Rule in Occupied Europe*:

> Genocide has two phases: one, destruction of the national pattern of the oppressed group; the other, the imposition of the national pattern of the oppressor. This imposition, in turn, may be made upon the oppressed population which is allowed to remain, or upon the territory alone, after removal of the population and the colonization of the area by the oppressor's own nationals.[4]

Lemkin's definition has wide-ranging and explosive implications for the history of humanity. I draw on it throughout *The Origins of Violence* as a kind of guiding thread.

In retrospect, we can see Lemkin's own historical conceptions and legal thinking emerging from a 1930s and 1940s context where émigré intellectuals were attempting to reprise and develop traditions of cosmopolitanism and internationalism which they saw being engulfed by Nazism, itself a culmination of nineteenth-century European nationalism, imperialism and colonialism. Figures like Walter Benjamin, Freud, Lemkin, Hannah Arendt, Erich Auerbach, Albert Einstein and Leo Spitzer were concerned that humanity should establish a duty of care to all the world's peoples and cultures.[5] Central to Lemkin's thought were notions of world culture and the oneness of the world, valuing the variety and diversity of human cultures.[6] Lemkin believed that a loss of any one society and culture through genocide is a loss to all humanity. Such considerations will have a bearing on my approach throughout this book.

Lemkin is important to my book in terms of method. While researching his papers in the American Jewish Historical Society in New York, in a folder concerned with a projected history of genocide, Ann Curthoys and I came across, under the heading 'Revised Outline for Genocide Cases', a list Lemkin had drawn up suggesting detailed categories by which to analyse historical genocides. The history of genocide was to be explored in terms of categories such as historical background; methods and techniques of genocide, physical, biological and cultural; the attitudes of the genocidists; propaganda, that is to say, rationalization of the crime; responses of victim groups, active and passive; responses of outside groups; and aftermath.[7] In *The Origins of Violence* I have deployed Lemkin's list of categories, and detailed sub-categories, to help with the literary and cultural investigations by which much of my book proceeds, for example, in analysing classical Greek tragedies concerned with the mythological stories of the Trojan War, or, in the later chapter on the notion of the honourable colonizer, Shakespeare's *The Tempest*.

## II

In terms of analysing the inner working of texts, whether literary texts or works of historical writing or philosophy, I draw throughout on Mikhail Bakhtin (1895–1975), roughly a contemporary of Lemkin's in the twentieth century. My approach is not author-centred, as much conventional intellectual history can be, desiring to find in an author a definitive set of beliefs and values.

An author-centred focus misses out on so much in literary, cultural and intellectual history that is eccentric, wayward, contradictory and multiple in meanings and values. The writings of Bakhtin provide me with a rich repertoire of concepts, in particular notions of the dialogic, polyphony and menippean, as well as a dynamic evocation of genres and their interactions. Such notions refer to how texts work not only in modernity, but in the long cultural history descending from the ancient classical world. In particular for my purposes, Bakhtin felt that the importance of the genre of the menippea in European and world literature, from antiquity to modernity, has not been sufficiently appreciated.[8]

In his brilliant early book *Problems of Dostoevky's Poetics*, Bakhtin suggests that the menippea was and is a form of great plasticity, protean, flexible and inclusive of other genres, a carrier in literature of carnivalesque, wonderfully free in its inventiveness and use of the fantastic. The menippea of antiquity, says Bakhtin, could include the Socratic dialogue and the symposium; indeed, he comments, the menippea was sometimes formulated directed as a symposium. The menippea was hospitable to kindred genres like the utopia. It features historical and legendary figures. It is a philosophical genre where its bold use of fantasy and adventure is devoted to the 'testing of a philosophical idea, a discourse, a *truth*, embodied in the image of a wise man, the seeker of this truth'. The menippea deploys fantasy to contemplate the world on the broadest possible scale. It is a genre of ultimate questions. In order to provoke and test an idea, the heroes of a menippea might wander through unknown and fantastic lands, or might be placed in extraordinary life situations. Characters ascend into heaven or descend into the nether regions. Indeed, Bakthin writes, the menippea places great importance on the nether world, leading, in later European literature of the Renaissance and of the seventeenth and eighteenth centuries, to the special genre of the 'dialogues of the dead', in which people and ideas separated by space and time collide with one another on a dialogic plane.[9]

I wish, then, to bring together into productive conversation the fields of genocide studies on the one hand, and literary, cultural and intellectual history on the other, and so bring new dimensions to the historical study of genocide and violence. The two have so far stood apart. Claude Rawson's *God, Gulliver, and Genocide: Barbarism and the European Imagination, 1492–1945* (2001), for example, is rich in subtle nuanced readings of a wide range of texts and authors and a major contribution to the literature which sees '1492' as a key event in world history. Yet it does not engage with contemporary genocide studies. It especially misses the body of scholarship that relates, in the way suggested by Lemkin's definition in *Axis Rule in Occupied Europe*, genocide to European colonialism, a theme of his book.[10] At the same time, genocide scholars, such as those who publish in the *Journal of Genocide Research*, are rarely literary or cultural critics.

I devote a substantial amount of *The Origins of Violence* to analysis of texts in the ancient and classical worlds of the Middle East and Mediterranean: the Bible's Exodus, Joshua and Judges, and works of Herodotus, Thucydides, Aeschylus, Euripides, Plato, Cicero, Virgil and Tacitus. I am working in a tradition that looks to biblical writings and classical texts to see how much they illuminate the history of violence; I think here of René Girard's *Violence and the Sacred* (1972) and Richard Waswo's *The Founding Legend of Western Civilization: From Virgil to Vietnam* (1997). While I found that Girard focused too narrowly on sacrifice as a kind of general explanation, a key to all mythologies, Waswo's book offers profound insights into Western history, and I must pay tribute to it here as an influence on this book. Neither of these books, however, uses the concept of genocide.

# III

Throughout *The Origins of Violence* I deploy and develop a number of notions, concepts and terms by which to explore group violence. These concepts and terms include genocide, supersessionism, victimology, chosen people, promised land, culture-bringers and honourable colonization.

- *Genocide*: a theory of intergroup violence; this is the frame story for this book.
- *Supersessionism*: one of the most destructive beliefs in world history. It is the view that some peoples can be erased or removed or superseded by other peoples and groups, who see themselves as history's true heirs.
- *Victimology*: a belief and narrative that earlier bondage and persecution and suffering justifies later violence, conquest and destruction in other lands or islands and directed against peoples who had no part in the original bondage and persecutions.
- *Chosen People*: a belief held by a group which claims to be blessed by God or the gods. The view of oneself as chosen is always precarious, because chosenness may be claimed by another group, looking to other gods. It may be felt that people are only chosen for a while, that they may fall into divine disfavour, and God or the gods may elect another people to be sanctioned as chosen. In world history, there is constant competition amongst groups to be chosen and be known as chosen.[11] In *The Origins of Violence* I explore the importance of the notion of a chosen people in the biblical stories and in Cicero's *Republic*, Virgil's *Aeneid* and Tacitus' *Agricola* and *Germania*.
- *Promised land*: a concept close to and usually entwined with notions of a chosen people and victimology. In these influential narratives, a people from elsewhere, perhaps having suffered persecution and the agony of wandering and exile, are divinely assisted by a father god, whether monotheistic or polytheistic, to find final refuge by conquest and colonization in another land. This 'new' land is promised to them by the father god, even if already occupied and inhabited by indigenous or previous peoples.
- *Culture bringers*: this invaluable concept I have drawn directly and gratefully from Waswo's *The Founding Legend of Western Civilization*. It refers to those who come from elsewhere as colonizers and conquerors, who see themselves as culture-bearers in possession of what they regard as superior knowl-

edge of agriculture, cities, law and religion. Such culture-bringers regard their presence in a place as more worthy of the support of God or the gods than indigenous peoples or people already inhabiting a land or island, whom they subdue by conquest and colonization, leading, in Lemkin's terms, to genocide. Yet culture-bringers always see themselves as honourable colonizers, my next category.

- *Honourable colonization*: in possession of a high moral consciousness, honourable colonizers in effect reassure themselves of their own innocence in history. They are aware of the dangers of colonization, especially in the initial stages, in infringing the rights of the colonized and as a threat to their own morality and standing. For this awareness, they are always to be *admired* in history, whatever the actual long-term consequences of colonization. Instead of colonization being a catastrophe for those facing destruction, as evoked in Herodotus and Thucydides, or in Greek tragedy concerned with the ruining of Troy, or in aspects of Cicero's *Republic*, Virgil's *Aeneid* and Tacitus's *Agricola*, colonization becomes a celebration of the complex, ambivalent, and even anguished moral state of the colonizers.[12]

# IV

*The Origins of Violence* begins at the beginning, contemplating how much humanity is formed in its earliest stages by being a primate in common with other primates, sharing an evolutionary history, with predispositions to violence, including intergroup violence. Such evolutionary predispositions may have been formative of human history and might remain influential and salient. Genocide is one such. By working through primatology in Jane Goodall's *The Chimpanzees of Gombe*, the 'world history' arguments of Jared Diamond's *The Rise and Fall of the Third Chimpanzee* and Hugh Brody's *The Other Side of Eden*, and the questioning by the prominent Australian Indigenous leader Galarrwuy Yunupingu of who are the nomads, hunter-gatherer or agricultural peoples, we can say that genocide was widespread in the movements and migrations of humans from the beginning. We see it especially in the invasions, colonizings and expansion of agricultural-commercial societies across the globe when they appeared – relatively recently – in history. Indeed, as both Diamond and Brody stress, the coming some 6,000 to 8,000 years ago of agricultural-commercial societies massively increased intergroup violence in world history, in the constant efforts of these societies to expand, spread, conquer and supersede, efforts particularly directed against hunter-gatherer societies.

I argue in this book that genocide was a common feature of the ancient Mediterranean and near-Eastern world, the area of the world where agricultural-commercial societies developed. It was, perhaps, the genocides of the ancient Mediterranean world that set the historical precedents for the later post-1492 history of European colonization. In classical times, I discuss the many examples of genocide, both Persian and Greek, evoked by Herodotus's *The Histories* and Thucydides' *History of the Peloponnesian War*, not least in the Athenian destruction of Melos in 416–15 BCE. Yet in both Herodotus and Thucydides there are stories and episodes – often evoked with compassion and pathos – questioning violence and genocide, bequeathing to the future a divided legacy about the justice of conquest, colonization and empire. I explore this divided legacy in both the classical Greek and Greco-Roman worlds, in tragedy, moral and political philosophy, and historiography. I consider plays concerned with the destruction of Troy by Aeschylus and Euripides, the *Republics* of Plato and Cicero, epic as in Virgil's *Aeneid*, and biography and ethnography in Tacitus' *Agricola* and *Germania*. I explore how the narratives of the biblical stories, in Exodus, Joshua and Judges, highlight the terrible human costs of conquest and colonization.

## V

I see the millennia-long questioning of conquest, colonization, empire and genocide as part of the conceptualization and development of international law, constituting a continuing challenge to its troubled and sometimes frankly absurd history; a challenge taken up in modernity with great daring by Lemkin and in contemporary world courts concerned with genocide and crimes against humanity. As a jurist Lemkin, the prime mover in the 1948 UN Convention on the Prevention and Punishment of the Crime of Genocide, felt that radically new kinds of international law were necessary in order to restrain or prevent genocide. In this view, previous international law was either inadequate in focusing too much on individual rather than intergroup law, or actively facilitated and enabled intergroup violence. In notions of natural law from Roman times onwards, in the law of nations in early modern Europe and as a cumulative body of law in modernity, international law has collaborated in conquest, colonization, empire and genocide. Lemkin's epochal challenge to inherited legal thinking was influential in the latter part of the twentieth century and in the twenty-first century in new avenues of international law concerned with crimes against humanity, in the International Criminal Court and the International Court of Justice.[13]

# VI

This book also explores the ways that Thucydides' *History of the Peloponnesian War* stages an argument between rival views of democracy and empire. One abiding view, held by the Athenians themselves, is that democratic nation-states like Athens not only have the right to possess an empire but achieve greatness, the glory that will live through the ages, by the possession of empire. Empire is to be regarded as selfless, as altruistically spreading values beneficial for all those nations, states and peoples it includes, and therefore the power and might of an empire should not be opposed. In this imperial view, the doctrine of might is right – the doctrine that features in the Athenian destruction of Melos, which had wished to stay neutral in the war between Athens and Sparta – is acceptable and necessary in an empire in its dealing with subject states or states it wishes to subject. In the Melian Dialogue, Thucydides' *History* dramatizes an alternative position, prophetically suggested by the Melians themselves, that the doctrine of might is right and the imperial actions it gives authority to bestow lasting infamy on a society.

Thucydides' *History* helps us think how much in democracies – ancient and modern – hubris, with its thirst for power and glory through war, is embodied in recurring figures like the statesman, the demagogue, the parvenu and the adventurer, figures who take to the political stage with relentless enthusiasm. The *History* decisively explodes any myth that because a society (like ancient Athens) is democratic, it cannot engage in destruction, genocide and cruelty. Quite the contrary: democratic nation-states that possess a colonizing empire or work through an imperium are especially likely to perpetrate such acts.[14]

In a way that strikingly anticipates Hannah Arendt's political theory, Thucydides' *History*, then, implies that imperial domination, and especially the quelling of resistance to imperial authority, results in an ethical deterioration both towards subject peoples and within the home society itself. Such ethical deterioration, as evoked by Thucydides in antiquity and Arendt in modernity, is a motif of this book. [15]

# VII

*The Origins of Violence* alludes to Darwin's *Origin of Species* and to Arendt's works like *On Violence* and her famously titled *The Origins of Totalitarianism*. Like Arendt, and perhaps unlike Darwin, I am cautious of the implications of the term 'origins'. In her biography, *Hannah Arendt: For Love of the World*, Elisabeth Young-Bruehl reports that Arendt was never satisfied with that title because she suspected the notion of 'origin' when it implies a clear ground from which history coherently and causally unfolds (a suspicion she shares with thinkers as varied as Walter Benjamin, Foucault, Oakeshott and Derrida). Arendt, like her friend Benjamin before her, preferred a notion where origins are fluid and fractured.[16] In these terms, I do not present here a single inclusive chronology, since there are disparate 'origins' with different histories: genocide, agricultural-commercial society, polytheism, monotheism, democracy and empire, settler-colonialism. Also, with each of these themes, there are in the chapters that follow constant conversations between past and present.

In the sense of origins as fluid and fractured, I wish to write in the spirit of 'late style' as Edward Said defines it in relation to Freud's *Moses and Monotheism*: a 'willingness to let irreconcilable elements ... remain as they are: episodic, fragmentary, unfinished (i.e. unpolished)', an 'intransigence' and 'unseemliness'. Said elaborated on this theme in his posthumously published *On Late Style*.[17]

Certainly, *The Origins of Violence* does not propose an origin in ethnobiology or its successor evolutionary psychology.[18] Zygmunt Bauman wrote in the preface to *Modernity and the Holocaust* that he hoped his book would contribute to self-awareness and self-questioning. Such is the hope I entertain for my book. It explores 'moments' in history in order urgently to bring to a clarity of awareness how much disaster and catastrophe are ever-near. Only in such intense clarity of awareness can alternatives to violence be reprised and thought.

# 1 GENOCIDE AS ANCIENT PRACTICE: CHIMPANZEES, HUMANS, AGRICULTURAL SOCIETY

Since warfare involves conflict between groups of people, rather than between individuals, it has, through genocide, played a major role in group selection.

(Jane Goodall, *The Chimpanzees of Gombe*)[1]

Genocide has been part of our human and prehuman heritage for millions of years.

(Jared Diamond, *The Rise and Fall of the Third Chimpanzee*)[2]

Plato himself suggested that human beings and animals once lived a life in common, and even conversed on philosophical questions.

(Paola Cavalieri, 'The Animal Debate')[3]

Differences between hunting and gathering and agriculture are at the heart of history.

(Hugh Brody, *The Other Side of Eden*)[4]

[ 13 ]

In *History, Memory and Mass Atrocity* (2006), the Holocaust historian Dan Stone argues against approaches that suggest the mass murder of the Jews was carried out in a bureaucratic spirit without passion or emotion, thus distinguishing its mass murder from other mass killing, or that the Nazis were bestial and psychopathic in a way that set them apart from those who inhabit modern, rational, liberal, postwar societies. What is involved here, Stone observes, is a false distinction between the modern and the pre-modern. Because of this false distinction, we have failed to recognize, Stone contends, that the perpetrators, even in the use of technology for industrial-like mass killing, acted primarily with their hearts, in passion and emotion. In this failure to recognize our common humanity, we have tried to 'conceal from view the unnerving similarity of the perpetrators to ourselves'.[5]

In this spirit, I explore here intergroup violence like genocide in relation to the common history of humanity, a history shared in its early stages between humans and other primates, and which also includes the coming of agricultural societies and their impact on hunter-gatherer communities worldwide.

## RAPHAËL LEMKIN

I'll begin with Raphaël Lemkin's view of human history as the history of genocide. Given how much genocide will feature in this and other chapters, it is very important to emphasize that Lemkin's originating definition of genocide was very wide-ranging. I stress this, because many later definitions of genocide, in the light of the horror of the Holocaust as it was recognized in the 1960s and 1970s, narrow 'genocide' down to state-directed mass killing. Lemkin conceived his definition, expressed most fully in the now famous Chapter 9 of *Axis Rule in Occupied Europe* (1944), in the midst of the Second World War, when he himself had had to flee Poland in 1939 and during which most of his European family died.[6] Lemkin arrived as an exile in the United States in 1941, and revealed remarkable energy and dedication in writing what became *Axis Rule in Occupied Europe* and in agitating in fledgling UN committees to have the notion of genocide legally recognized and proscribed; he was the prime mover in the discussions that led to the 1948 UN Convention on the Prevention and Punishment of the Crime of Genocide. The Convention, while it represented a narrowing of Lemkin's definition in *Axis Rule in Occupied Europe*, was nevertheless still wide-ranging and was certainly not confined to mass murder.

When Lemkin in *Axis Rule in Occupied Europe* proposed his new concept of 'genocide', deriving the term from the Greek word *genos* (tribe, race) and Latin *cide* (as in tyrannicide, homicide, fratricide), he took great care to define genocide as composite and manifold. Not only is genocide for Lemkin not confined to mass killing – though it certainly includes mass killing – it is also not necessarily directed by a state body or power. In Lemkin's view, genocide signifies a coordinated plan of different actions aiming at the destruction of the essential foundations of life of a group. Such actions involve considerations that are cultural, political, social, legal, intellectual, spiritual, economic, biological, physiological, religious, psychological and moral. Such actions involve considerations of health, food and nourishment, of family life and care of children, and of birth as well as death. Such actions involve consideration of the honour and dignity of peoples, and the future of humanity as a world community.[7]

In the 1940s and 1950s, Lemkin wrote many essays in manuscript form, and kept research notes and cards for a book he was writing on the history of genocide, a project that kept expanding, taking in examples from antiquity to modernity, and sadly remained unpublished when he died in 1959. When, with Ann Curthoys, I read this archival material at the American Jewish Historical Society in New York in December 2003,[8] what I felt particularly stood out were the many ways Lemkin was expanding on his linking of genocide with colonization made in Chapter 9 of *Axis Rule in Occupied Europe*. In the manuscript essays and notes he deploys genocide as a framework by which to understand and illuminate European colonizing around the world, including of the

Americas, by the Spanish from 1492 and later in North America by the English, French and post-independence Americans. He is highly critical of Columbus as an egregious genocidist (Lemkin's own term) who set the historical example for the future of Spanish colonization in the Americas, instituting slavery and catastrophic loss of life. He develops a sophisticated methodology that permits the possibility of multifaceted analyses of settler-colonial histories in relation to genocide: in Lemkin's formulations, 'genocide' as concept and method is certainly not, as it used often to be considered, merely a blunt instrument. He carefully distinguishes between cultural change and cultural genocide, and believes cultural genocide to be very important in the processes of genocide. He points out that the relationship between oppressor and victim in history is always unstable, and that in world history there are many examples of genocidal victims transforming into genocidists, the formerly persecuted into the persecutors of others. He outlines recurring features in historical genocides: mass mutilations; deportations under harsh conditions often involving forced marches; attacks on family life, with separation of males and females and taking away of the opportunity of procreation; removal and transfer of children; destruction of political leadership; death from illness, hunger and disease through overcrowding on reserves and in concentration camps.[9]

Lemkin's views on humanity and violence were double-edged, both pessimistic and optimistic. He did not regard human history as a narrative of progress, since he saw genocide as following humanity through history. Yet he also hoped that international law could restrain or prevent genocide. It may be worth at this point reminding ourselves of the key clauses of the 1948 UN Convention definition, set out in Article II, which constitute a narrower version of Lemkin's definition:

> In the present Convention, genocide means any of the following acts committed with intent to destroy, in whole or in part, a national, ethnical, racial or religious group, as such:

Killing members of the group;
Causing serious bodily or mental harm to members of
the group;
Deliberately inflicting on the group conditions of life
calculated to bring about its physical destruction in
whole or in part;
Imposing measures intended to prevent births within
the group;
Forcibly transferring children of the group to another
group.[10]

Genocide, the concept unhappily conceived by Lemkin as necessary to comprehend the wide sweep of human history and in the
hope of international agreement to prevent or at least punish its
occurrence, has proven increasingly influential as a perspective
and frame story for our species from its beginnings; a concept that
inspires thought at the limits of what humanity might be and
become.

## JANE GOODALL

Lemkin's insight into human history, that genocide between
groups, as with homicide between individuals, has always
occurred and will probably keep occurring, finds support in primatology, with its interest in shared ancestors between humans and
other primates. I'll focus on a celebrated text of primatology, Jane
Goodall's *The Chimpanzees of Gombe* (1986), which at one point
mentions genocide, as I record in my opening epigraphs above,
though Goodall seems unaware of Lemkin's definition. Goodall
doesn't define what she means by genocide and is more interested
in the question of warfare and its relation to the activities and
thinking of both chimpanzees and humans. For many decades,
Goodall has been the worldwide 'face' of primate studies in
Africa, though her work has not escaped questioning and criticism. In *Primate Visions* (1989), Donna Haraway sceptically

probes the complex interplay between gender, science and race, and especially the curious prominence of Western white women like Goodall and Dian Fossey in the conduct and shaping of primate research in Africa amidst pressing contexts of imperialism and colonialism, and, from the early 1960s, decolonization; contexts where their writings have been marked by their own histories and cultures and an overarching narrative of relating primate behaviour to humanity conceived as ultimately Western. Haraway is critical of Goodall's claim, in the Introduction to *The Chimpanzees of Gombe*, that the spirit of her research is similar to that of Colombus discovering America, as if Colombus were to be considered an innocent and disinterested figure in world history. Here, Haraway suggests, Goodall appears to be naively disowning any situating contexts of colonialism and decolonization.[11] Haraway doesn't, however, discuss in detail *The Chimpanzees of Gombe* as a text, which is what I will do here, especially the chapter 'Territoriality'. My perspective will be that of genocide scholarship.

*The Chimpanzees of Gombe* is an engaging and beautifully written study, not least because Goodall conversationally introduces her own life story, research experience and uncertainties and speculations as vital to her analyses of chimpanzee behaviour. In her Introduction, Goodall tells us how she came to be in Gombe in Tanzania on the forested shores of Lake Tanganyika for 25 years studying the chimpanzees of the Kasakela Valley. It had, she confides, been a childhood dream of hers to study animals in Africa, and she finally was enabled to do so by Louis Leakey, who found funding for her expedition: 'And so it was that in July 1960 (accompanied by my mother and an African cook) I set foot, for the first time, on the sandy beach of Gombe on Lake Tanganyika.' Goodall says Leakey was interested in her research because he was particularly curious about chimpanzees, our closest living relatives today in biochemical terms, brain anatomy and uncanny similarities in social behaviour. Leakey asked Goodall to consider, in a sustained longitudinal examination, the evolutionary argument that since 'man' and chimpanzee once diverged from common stock, behaviour patterns that exist in modern humans and modern chimpanzees were probably present in that common ancestor, and therefore in 'early man' as well. Leakey's evolutionary argument and vision, Goodall contends, has been 'more than justified', and indeed Goodall believes that the argument can be taken a step further, particularly if we are to understand the place of aggression in both chimpanzees and humans.[12]

Leakey had anticipated, Goodall recalls, that her study might last for ten years, but, given that chimpanzees may live for as long as 50 years, even 25 years is, she feels, not long enough. Because Goodall and her fellow field observers continued beyond the initial decade of research, they could, she is able to say, document many remarkable things about chimpanzees: there may be enduring, affectionate bonds between family members, sometimes lifelong; close kin will aid and support each other; adult males cooperate in hunting, patrolling territorial boundaries, and protecting their females and young. Above all, Goodall believes, observation over many years revealed that the chimpanzees have advanced cognitive abilities accompanied by sophisticated social interactions, the development of cultural traditions, and individuality. Yet sustained longitudinal study also revealed disturbing aspects of chimpanzee behaviour in terms of relations between groups, including the 'violent aggression' that broke out when the Kasakela community, the particular social group she is studying (who are habituated to human presence), divided into two groups: 'We discovered that in certain circumstances the chimpanzees may kill and even cannibalize individuals of their own kind'.[13]

Chapter 17, 'Territoriality', is devoted to the aggression and violence that occurred when a group from the Kasakela community split away and began to live in a different valley, raising issues of desire for land and territory, genocide, warfare and violence towards stranger females and, sometimes, their infants. Goodall tells us the premise of this unsettling chapter: that a group is best studied not in isolation but in its interactions with other groups. She also regards certain facets of chimpanzee social organization as relevant to what occurred when the Kasakela group divided, with the remaining Kasakela community retaining a larger number of warrior males, while the new Kahama community to the south, now their neighbours, had fewer males. Unlike many primate groups (such as the baboons of Gombe), chimpanzees do not travel in stable groups nor do they follow predictable paths, so that a lone male may suddenly encounter several males of a neighbouring group, or a party of males may surprise a single female. While male chimpanzees remain in their natal group, females may transfer out, though young immigrant females may face violent hostility from resident females. And females may also travel relatively often in the overlap zones between communities, in a situation where there are no well-defined boundaries. In general, Goodall feels that observation has established that interactions between males of neighbouring communities are typically hostile. She also observes, and remains puzzled by, severe attacks on older females, leaving them badly injured, to the point where they might disappear and presumably die. Chimpanzees may even hunt a stranger female. Female chimpanzees may also join in attacks on stranger females and cause considerable injury.[14]

In the 1970s Goodall and her fellow field workers recorded the assaults on and dispersal of the breakaway Kahama Valley community by the Kasakela group, their relatives, with whom they had had affectionate relationships. It was in 1972 that Goodall's observers recognized that a new community, the Kahama group, had come into existence at Gombe, but it would only last for five years. In 1974 the Kasakela males initiated a southward movement of violent aggression that culminated in the complete destruction of the Kahama community and annexation of the Kahama community range. Goodall describes in detail the 'consistently brutal and protracted' attacks on members of the Kahama group: the vicious attacks on Godi, then Dé (with the female Gigi joining in the attack), Goliath (one of the attackers being Jomeo, who had been friendly with Goliath in the past – there is a photo of Goliath being groomed by Jomeo), Charlie and finally Sniff, the only remaining Kahama male. The crippled older

Kahama female Madam Bee and her daughters Little Bee and Honey Bee were subject during 1974–75 to a series of attacks by the Kasakela males and also Gigi, though only the mother, Goodall records, was hurt. In mid 1975 Madam Bee was fatally attacked by Kasakela males, watched by four Kasakela females, including Little Bee, who had by this time transferred into the Kasakela group. Goodall is sure that two other Kahama females, Mandy and Wanda, also suffered fatal attacks. In 1978 the Kasakela community then began to sleep as well as feed in what had been Kahama territory, though they themselves soon had to retreat when the powerful Kalande community further to the south of the Kahama Valley began to push northwards, the Kahama group no longer being a buffer between the Kalande and Kasakela groups.[15]

In a concluding discussion to this chapter, Goodall ponders the meaning and possible purposes of such aggressive intergroup violence in Gombe's chimpanzees. Goodall is especially puzzled by assaults on older stranger females, at times accompanied by the death of their infants, including by being cannibalistically eaten or partially eaten. Goodall reflects, however, that the aggression was clearly directed at the mothers, not the infants, who are at other times not harmed; infanticide, that is, was not the object of the assaults. It is noteworthy, Goodall suggests, given chimpanzees' characteristic aversion to strangers, that the victims were all members of neighbouring communities, usually encountered in overlap zones where the chimpanzees, aware that neighbouring males might be nearby, are nervous. She also wonders if those older females who are mothers travelling with daughters are attacked as a way of weakening mother–daughter bonds, which are very strong, so that the daughters can be recruited into the community. Nevertheless, Goodall remains unsure of the adequacy of these explanations: 'For the present, this whole area must remain speculative. More facts are badly needed.'[16]

Chimpanzee violence towards older stranger females may recall aspects of the dreadful history, also problematic to explain, of torture and killing of witches in European Christian history, given blunt biblical warrant in Exodus xxii, 18: 'Thou shalt not suffer a witch to live.' In an eerily resonant analysis, Lyndal Roper writes in *Witch Craze: Terror and Fantasy in Baroque Germany* (2004), her study of witches in sixteenth and seventeenth-century southern Germany, that the 'cruelty shown to older women is one of the more disturbing aspects of early-modern German culture'. Anyone could fall prey to Satan and become a witch, and people were especially vulnerable to Satan's temptations while in a state of depression, despair, melancholy, or excessive sadness and sorrow. It was, however, predominantly older women who became known as witches, and older women were in any case held to be prone to the attacks of melancholy that might permit Satan to seduce them. Older women who were menopausal or post-menopausal, and over the age of 50, were consistently over-represented; most of these women had been mothers, but now were no longer fertile. Hatred of old women – often depicted as horrifyingly sexually rapacious but unable to give birth to children and envying younger women who could – was evident throughout German art, literature, medicine and popular culture. Often they were accused of cannibalism. At witch trials, the bodies of accused old women were subject to 'vicious aggression'. Roper suggests that while witches were not hunted everywhere in Europe, there was a powerful cultural current of hatred of elderly women in early modern societies, linked to deeply held fears and fantasies concerning mothers and wombs: fears and fantasies that clustered around death of babies and older women's physical decay and lack of fecundity; witches would confess (under sustained interrogation and gruesome torture) to having sex with the Devil and eating the flesh of dead babies.[17]

There was also, Roper tells us, a story that involved apes. The witch craze, she points out, intersected with and was intensified by the centuries-long history of anti-Semitism (including massacres, expulsions and the myth of Jewish ritual murder of Christian children). In one particular tale, a Jewish woman criminal is deported to a desert island where she is captured by a tribe of apes and forced to become the wife of one of them; she gives birth to several children and lives on the island for some time in this state of degradation, until rescued by Portuguese sailors on a passing ship. When the ship arrives back at port, the woman is condemned to be burnt as a sodomite.[18] Here, it would appear, in the dehumanizing of the outcast Jewish woman, primatology meets early modern European Christian fantasy. Goodall mentions a similar phenomenon amongst chimpanzees, in relation to strangers. If chimpanzees, adult and infant, are recognized as not belonging, they may be attacked as if they are prey animals, as if no longer to be considered as fellow chimpanzees, or, as she wryly puts it, they are *dechimpized*.[19]

What notions of territory, Goodall asks, do chimpanzees seem to work on? She notes that much of the literature on non-human territorial behaviour, widespread in the animal kingdom, is authored by ornithologists, where among many bird species territory owners are a single male or a male–female pair. Chimpanzee behaviour, however, differs in important ways from territoriality based on bird behaviour, which is relatively peaceful and ritualized. For chimpanzees, it is often the size of the patrol that determines an encounter, not the possession of territory. Furthermore, chimpanzees are (like hyenas and lions) violently hostile towards neighbours to a degree that differs from traditional territory owners of the animal kingdom. Chimpanzees don't simply chase trespassers away, they assault them, leaving them perhaps to die; they may also mount aggressive raids into the core area of a neighbouring group, and Goodall and other primatologists have observed in their long-range studies, not only at Gombe but also Mahale, three major invasions, during which adult males, and some females, were killed or disappeared.[20]

In the chimpanzee, territoriality functions not only to repel intruders from the home range, but sometimes to injure or eliminate them; not only to defend the existing home range and its resources, but to enlarge it opportunistically at the expense of weaker neighbours; not only to protect the female resources of a community, but to actively and aggressively recruit new sexual partners from neighbouring social groups.[21]

Goodall poses a question highly relevant to the study of genocide: do chimpanzees show intent to kill? Goodall first declares that 'we can tell nothing about the "intentions" of the aggressors' in the case of the Kasakela group when they made victims of the Kahama group. Nevertheless, she reports that the 'observers, all thoroughly experienced in chimpanzee behaviour, *believed* that the aggressors were trying to kill their victims'. She asks the field assistants why they think this is so, and they reply that the attacks revealed patterns also evident during the killing of large prey, with assaults continuing until the victims were incapacitated; such patterns, they said, are not characteristic of intracommunity fighting. Goodall summarizes these discussions: 'the Kasakela males were making determined attempts, through wounding and battering, to incapacitate the Kahama chimpanzees.' She then adds that if the Kasakela males had had 'firearms and had been taught to use them, I suspect they would have used them to kill'.[22]

Mention of firearms leads Goodall to another speculative question: can such intergroup aggressive violence in chimpanzees be seen as a precursor to warfare? War, she notes, is usually defined as uniquely human behaviour, a universal characteristic of human groups, involving organized armed conflict. Here she introduces the term 'genocide': because war amongst humans has involved genocidal destruction of certain groups and not others, it became part of evolution, of 'group selection'. Goodall also refers to the speculative literature which postulates early forms of warfare in hominids, sometimes referred to as *dawn warriors*, as very important in developing valued human qualities, for example, altruism, courage, intelligence and increasingly sophisticated cooperation among group members, qualities which would have to be matched by other groups if they wished to survive. Warfare may even have been the principal evolutionary pressure that created, according to such evolutionary thought, the huge gap between the human brain and that of our closest living relatives, the anthropoid apes.[23]

Goodall disagrees with, or at least wishes to complicate, the notion of warfare as unique to humans. She points out that destructive warfare amongst humans required 'preadaptations' that are also possessed by chimpanzees: not only an inherent fear of, or aversion to, strangers, revealed in aggressive attacks on them, but also group living, group territoriality, cooperative hunting skills, weapon use and the intellectual ability to make cooperative plans. Chimpanzees also, she continues, reveal other 'inherent characteristics' that would have been useful for the 'dawn warriors in their primitive battles'; the young male chimpanzee, for example, is 'inherently disposed to find aggression attractive', even to the extent of risking approaching potentially dangerous neighbours on his own. In similar terms, Goodall feels, early human males may have been inherently disposed to look forward to or enjoy aggression, a shared trait of humans and chimpanzees that may have 'provided a biological basis for the cultural training of warriors' as in the later glorifying of the warrior or soldier, condemning cowardice, rewarding bravery and battlefield skill, and the practising of so-called *manly* sports in childhood.[24]

Again, chimpanzees develop a strong sense of group identity, of differentiating between those who belong and those who don't. Goodall, however, is critical of the notion of 'xenophobia': 'This sense of group identity is far more sophisticated than mere xenophobia.' Xenophobia is too unsupple a concept, particularly if we consider that the members of what became the Kahama community had, before the division into two groups, enjoyed close and friendly relations with those who would become their aggressors. By seceding, Goodall reflects, they lost their right to be regarded as group members, instead being treated as strangers. The stranger, that is, is a shifting and uncertain category.[25]

Cannibalism and cruelty are further questions to consider. Goodall points out that cannibalism, reported in humans from all over the world and as existing far back in history, had until recently been treated as a trait that distinguished humans from other primates. Yet, she reports, her research has revealed that amongst chimpanzees cannibalism of infants may accompany intergroup conflict with neighbouring females. Again, Goodall reminds us, it used to be thought that human destructiveness and cruelty, especially the acts of great cruelty shown in warfare, distinguished humans from other animals; in this view, only humans were capable of cruelty because only humans had the intellectual sophistication, in terms of understanding what pain is and empathizing with the pain of the victim, to enjoy or be indifferent to another's pain. Such a distinction between humans and other primates is doubtful, Goodall believes, because chimpanzees do perform cruel acts and they are capable to some extent of imputing desires and feelings to others and of feelings akin to sympathy. Nevertheless, Goodall readily concedes, chimpanzees are 'intellectually incapable of creating the horrifying tortures that human ingenuity has devised for the deliberate infliction of suffering'.[26]

Goodall brings this chapter of *The Chimpanzees of Gombe* to a close on a perturbed and pensive note. She observes that when humanity's remote ancestors acquired language, they could then expand intergroup conflicts into the organized, armed conflict that defines warfare. Nonetheless, she submits, the chimpanzee has reached a stage where 'he stands at the very threshold of human achievement in destruction, cruelty and planned intergroup conflict'; and given that the chimpanzee is close to learning language, perhaps, she wonders, he is close as well to waging war 'with the best of us'.[27]

For a genocide scholar, reading Goodall's evocation of the violence of the Gombe chimpanzees is very interesting. Her analysis is consonant with Lemkin's argument that genocide signifies a coordinated plan of different actions aiming at the destruction of the essential foundations of life of a group. The Kasakela group, it would appear, conducted planned and coordinated operations that aimed to destroy the foundations of life of the Kahama group so that it could no longer function as a group. In terms of Lemkin's observations of recurring features of genocide, there was mutilation of the victims, and an attack on

Kahama family life, taking away continuing opportunities of procreation within the Kahama community. Lemkin also writes that those who have been victims and persecuted may turn around if given historical opportunity to be the genocidal victimizers and persecutors of others; from Goodall's analysis, it is clear that the Kahama group, if they had been stronger than the Kasakela, might have genocidally attacked them.

There is another resonance with genocide theory, in terms of perpetrator enjoyment of violence and being drawn to risk, even extreme risk. Goodall observes that when the Kasakela males attacked the Kahama male Sniff, they were in a 'state of considerable excitement'. In the attack on the Kahama male Goliath, they became 'incredibly excited'. Most adult male chimpanzees, particularly young prime individuals, appear strongly motivated to travel to peripheral areas, finding encounters with strangers highly attractive, not least the 'frenzied rush' toward stranger females. Chimpanzees, she notes, actually go out of their way to create opportunities, by visiting peripheral areas (on average, once every four days) in order to encounter intruders at close range.[28] In 'Genocide as Transgression', the essay I quoted from earlier, Dan Stone proposes that modern genocides and massacres, as in Cambodia and Rwanda, the Rape of Nanjing and My Lai, share, in anthropological terms, a transgressive violence: the enjoyment of violence, including killing and anticipation of killing, and the theatre of violence itself. The perpetrators enjoy the acts of violence to a degree that can be called orgiastic, and together, in the act of killing, the perpetrators form temporary ecstatic communities, experiencing a heightened sense of belonging to their own group in the act of performing violence, which may also be erotically charged; a collective effervescence in belonging, often involving as it were ordinary people.[29]

Goodall's evocation of the combination of contradictory qualities of Gombe chimpanzee society and external relations, frequently affectionate and caring within the circle of those who belong to a group, violently aggressive towards those who are perceived as not belonging, is intriguing and possibly illuminating in terms of a shared history between chimpanzees, 'early man' and continuing human history. We can think immediately here of Walter Benjamin's familiar dictum suggesting the permanent co-presence within human history of the civilized and barbarous ('There is no document of civilization which is not at the same time a document of barbarism'), or the great historian of the Middle East, Maxime Rodinson, reflecting that all peoples 'have been victims and executioners by turns, and all peoples count among their number both victims and executioners'.[30] Dan Stone makes a similar observation, referring to Georges Bataille's contention that the same peoples can be alternately barbarous and civilized in their attitudes and actions; so called ordinary or normal people, says Stone, commit genocide and massacres.[31]

In terms of long-running debates about biological determinism in primate – including human – behaviour, I agree with the sophisticated anti-determinism of Hilary Rose and Steven Rose which allows a powerful space for plasticity of brain and mind, the capacity not to be predetermined, the talent to be transformative, to be able to change and reverse and invert, to be unpredictable.[32] In these terms, while there may be shared characteristics between chimpanzees and early humans, these may act in human history as potentialities, as possibilities, rather than as inevitable or binding; and they may not be carried through at all.

A final irony from the perspective of genocide studies: Jane Goodall's presence at what became the large Gombe research station was initially enabled by British colonial control and occupation in Africa; a colonialism not too dissimilar from that of the Gombe chimpanzees, though on a vastly greater and worldwide scale. It's sobering to reflect that not that far away in Africa, throughout the 1950s, British colonial officials had been brutally repressing the Mau Mau independence movement and in effect imprisoning the entire Kikuyu population, accompanied by the torture, mutilation and death of many thousands of Kenyan people.[33]

## JARED DIAMOND

Lemkin's insight into genocide as an enduring aspect of human history finds support in ornithologist Jared Diamond's *The Rise and Fall of the Third Chimpanzee* (1991). Though Diamond like Jane Goodall seems unaware of Lemkin's definition, genocide nevertheless features in his largely pessimistic narrative. He devotes Chapter 16, 'In Black and White', to its persistence and pervasiveness, not least in the colonial genocides of Aboriginal peoples in Tasmania and Australia generally, and of Native Americans in the United States. In an appendix to this chapter, Diamond assembles some chilling quotes where various famous Americans enthuse on the desirability of extermination of the Native Americans: President George Washington, Benjamin Franklin, President Thomas Jefferson, President John Quincy Adams, President James Monroe, President Andrew Jackson, Chief Justice John Marshall, President William Henry Harrison, President Theodore Roosevelt, ending with a quote from General Philip Sheridan: 'The only good Indians I ever saw were dead.'[34] This is a passionate chapter indeed.

While he considers there is no simple way of defining genocide, Diamond nevertheless argues that 'collective killing' is its 'essence'. He does not think that genocide is necessarily state-directed, because such a formulation would entail that genocide is a primarily modern phenomenon. Rather, Diamond argues that genocide amongst human groups probably began millions of years ago, when the human species was just another big mammal. He believes that perhaps the commonest motive for genocide in history occurs in disputes over *lebensraum*, when a 'militarily stronger people attempt to occupy the land of a weaker people, who resist'.[35]

Genocide, he also notes, is quite common among animal groups, especially in social carnivorous species like lions, wolves, hyenas and ants, taking the form of coordinated attacks by members of one troop on members of a neighbouring troop. Genocidal behaviour can also be observed in two of our closest relatives, gorillas and common chimpanzees. Diamond reports on Jane Goodall's research, especially calling attention to what I've highlighted in *The Chimpanzees of Gombe*, the episode when one chimpanzee band exterminated another. Chimpanzees share with humans, Diamond feels, a 'xenophobia' in relation to other bands and groups.[36] (We might, however, recall here Goodall's reservations about the concept of xenophobia in her analysis of the Gombe chimpanzees.)[37] What especially interests Diamond in Goodall's evocation of the chimpanzee genocide is that the Gombe chimpanzees, lacking weapons, are, compared with humans, largely inefficient in their killing, Diamond referring to how by contrast Australia's settlers, heavily armed, 'often succeeded in eliminating a band of Aborigines in a single dawn attack'. Diamond suggests that human group living probably came about as a way of defending against other human groups. In history, the main danger to human life comes from other humans.[38]

In the chapter 'Agriculture's Two-Edged Sword', Diamond questions the conventional 'progressivist' view that situates agriculture as a sacred milestone in humanity's march towards civilization. On the contrary, says Diamond, we should return a mixed report card on the introduction of agricultural society into history, with some gains and many losses for humanity. Agriculture began to emerge only relatively recently, and it arose not because of its evident civilizational superiority, but because of its practical advantages in producing food. For most of human history, humans were, in Diamond's view quite sensibly, hunters and gatherers, and they did not take to agriculture, from its origins in the Near East around 8000 BCE, with any noticeable alacrity or enthusiasm at all. Agriculture reached Greece around 6000 BCE and Britain and Scandinavia some 2,500 years later. Even in the nineteenth century, he is interested to observe, the Indians of California preferred to hunt and gather, though they knew of agriculture through trade with farming Indians in Arizona. Amongst surviving hunter-gatherers, and contrary to the progressivist view, the Kalahari Desert Bushmen have a great deal of leisure time, sleep a lot and do not devote excessive time to obtaining food, perhaps working only 12–19 hours per week. Extant hunter-gatherer groups are healthy, do not suffer from much disease, and enjoy a diverse and nourishing diet.[39] (Diamond could also have mentioned the traditional life of Australian Aboriginal groups; we might also think here of the 2006 film *Ten Canoes* set in the past of Australia's Arnhem Land.)

Indeed, archaeology, Diamond contends, is helping to demolish the view that hunter-gatherers in the pre-agricultural past were worse off in terms of diet and health, or inferior in art and culture, than those who came to live in agricultural societies. Agricultural society certainly did bring in increased food production and practices of food storage, but it also introduced as well many features that are the 'curse' of modern human existence, and Diamond devotes much of the chapter to detailing what these are. The staple high-carbohydrate crops like rice, potatoes and corn produced by farmers are lower in protein, vitamins, minerals and general nutrient value than the food enjoyed in the hunter-gatherer diet. Because hunter-gatherers eat a wide range of edible plants, they are not susceptible to starvation when a farming crop, as with potatoes in Ireland in the 1840s, precipitately fails. Then there are comparative height levels, indicative of health and nutrition. Paleopathologists, studying ancient skeletons from Greece and Turkey, have concluded that the average height of hunter-gatherers in that region towards the end of the Ice Age was something like an impressive 5 foot 10 inches for men, and 5 foot 6 inches for women. With the adoption of agriculture, however, the height of people lessened dramatically, descending by 4000 BCE to only 5 foot 3 inches for men, 5 foot 1 inches for women. In classical times, people's height was rising again, but modern Greeks have still to regain the height of their hunter-gatherer ancestors.[40]

The coming of agricultural society was, Diamond argues, ruinous for human health. When paleopathologists studied American Indian skeletons in the Illinois and Ohio River valleys, they realized that the introduction of corn there, around 1000 CE, led to tooth cavities, tooth loss and abscesses; enamel defects in children's milk teeth suggested that the mothers were severely undernourished; people now lived shorter lives and suffered more from anaemia, and tuberculosis became established as an epidemic disease; half of the population of these valleys suffered from yaws or syphilis, and two-thirds from osteoarthritis and other degenerative diseases. Malnutrition and infectious diseases killed off almost a fifth of children between the ages of one and four. Diamond tells us that in the transition from hunter-gathering to farming elsewhere in the world, evidence from studies of skeletons emerges of similar public health disasters, which were also intensified by a major feature of the coming of agriculture: people living together in crowded, sedentary populations which can constantly reinfect each other. Diseases like cholera and measles could not survive and persist in small, scattered bands of hunters and gatherers who often shifted camp. But such 'crowd epidemics' are coincident with the rise of agriculture: 'Tuberculosis, leprosy, and cholera had to await the rise of farming, while smallpox, bubonic plague, and measles appeared only in the past few thousand years with the rise of cities.'[41]

Farming, and the storage of food which accompanies it, also introduced, Diamond believes, more curses for humanity, breaking with the patterns of egalitarianism that generally characterize hunter-gatherer societies. Who can appropriate stored food, who can control it, led in farming societies to class divisions, often between disease-ridden and malnourished masses and healthier elites as in distinctions between commoners and royals. Sexual inequality may have intensified with the advent of agriculture, with women's health drained by frequent pregnancies. By contrast, 'nomadic' hunter-gatherers limited their number of children by infanticide and other means, since a mother in such communities has to carry her child until it is old enough to keep up with the adults. The coming of farming permitted the presence of full-time craftsmen and artists, yet, for all the great art and architecture that has been achieved in the last few thousand years, we should also recall, Diamond observes, the great paintings and sculptures, if on a smaller scale, of the hunter-gatherers of Cro-Magnon times and the work of Eskimos and Pacific Northwest Indians in the present era. (Again, Diamond could have mentioned the great art of Australian Indigenous people, past and present.) Furthermore, the specialization afforded by agricultural societies also introduced 'standing armies of professional killers'. Agricultural societies have brought humanity 'starvation, warfare, and tyranny'.[42]

Diamond concludes his reflections in this chapter by suggesting that at the end of the Ice Age, the choice by some hunter-gatherer groups, in no position to anticipate the 'evils of farming', to adopt agriculture led to a new global force for destruction. Such farming bands, now sedentary, outbred and then drove off the bands that had chosen to remain hunter-gatherers, and were able to do so because 'ten malnourished farmers can still outfight one healthy hunter'. Hunter-gatherers were forced out of all areas of the world that farmers wanted, and persist now only in the Arctic, deserts and some rainforests.[43]

In *Guns, Germs and Steel* (1997) Diamond developed in greater detail many of the motifs and themes of *The Rise and Fall of the Third Chimpanzee*. In his prologue, Diamond writes on a personal note that living in Europe from 1958 to 1962, 'among European friends whose lives had been brutally traumatized by twentieth-century European history', had made him think hard about the chains of causes that operate in history. Also in the prologue, Diamond repeatedly raises the question of genocide as shaping, along with conquest and epidemics, the interactions between disparate peoples that have constituted the modern world. In Chapter 11, 'Lethal Gift of Livestock', Diamond amplifies on the dubious benefits of agricultural society in terms of health. Many germs that afflict modern humanity were transferred from livestock to people living in crowded conditions. Smallpox, flu, tuberculosis, malaria, plague, measles and cholera are infectious human diseases that evolved from diseases of animals. Furthermore, such diseases played a major role in the colonization of the Americas that began with

Columbus's voyage of 1492. The germs brought by the 'murderous Spanish conquistidores' devastated the Native Americans, for while Europeans had to some degree become habituated to such germs, their introduction was new in the Americas and the Native Americans had neither immunity nor genetic resistance, leading to catastrophic population decline.[44] *Guns, Germs and Steel* is a work of anxious concern for the fate of humanity, from its earliest history to the present.

Diamond's observations of the dangers and deleterious aspects of the coming of agricultural societies, in a continuum that stretches from antiquity to the present, remain pertinent and disturbing. In terms of agricultural society and animal–human transfer of germs in the past, John M. Wilkins and Shaun Hill note in *Food in the Ancient World* (2006) that recent studies of Minoan Crete of the late Minoan III period (fourteenth century BCE) suggest the presence of infectious diseases in the population, including 'osteomyelitis, brucellosis (transferred to humans from infected cow's milk), tuberculosis ... and nutritional diseases such as osteoporosis, scurvy, rickets and iron-deficiency anaemia'.[45] The danger of avian flu and other possible animal–human transfers in an overpopulated world – brought directly on by the coming of agricultural society – continues to be a frightening possibility.

## GALARRWUY YUNUPINGU

In the latter 1990s, Ann Curthoys and I were fortunate to attend a speech given by the central Australian Aboriginal leader, Galarrwuy Yunupingu, to the National Press Club in Canberra (on 13 February 1997). Yunupingu said he was continually astonished by the way the European colonists of Aboriginal lands always referred to themselves as the settlers while designating his people by contrast as nomads. Such a characterization, he observed, was historically preposterous. The European colonists and migrants, he pointed out, were the inveterate wanderers on the face of the earth, they were the ones who had travelled to distant places, across oceans and far from their own homes, and now constantly roamed within the Australian continent. European politicians in the Northern Territory, where his people lived, constantly boasted that they were the settlers and belonged to the Territory. Yet, he noted with irony, those same white politicians some years later could be observed living elsewhere in Australia. Meanwhile the Aboriginal peoples, who stay on their own lands as far as they are permitted by the colonizers to do so, to look after their country and because they belong to it, are always referred to as nomads!

We discussed Yunupingu's speech many times afterwards, for it changed much of our thinking about colonization, migration and world history, in particular his highlighting of such pervasive colonizer and migrant reverse narratives. Ann explored Yunupingu's insight in relation to the persistent ways settler colonists in Australia always see themselves as victims and so incapable of being the victimizers of others.[46] In *Is History Fiction?* (2005) we related Yunupingu's thinking to Herodotus's *Histories* in our discussion of the hubris of colonizers from agricultural societies in regarding themselves as the settlers wherever they restlessly roam, concluding that it is the supposedly settled and urbanized peoples who are the nomads of world history.[47]

## HUGH BRODY

A number of years after hearing Galarrwuy Yunupingu's questioning of a key Western mythology, I was fortunate to learn of Hugh Brody's *The Other Side of Eden: Hunter-Gatherers, Farmers, and the Shaping of the World* (2000), and immediately recognized a convergence in hunter-gatherer perceptions of world history between Australian Aboriginal peoples and the peoples of the Canadian Arctic.[48] Indeed, what startled me was the similarity between Galarrwuy Yunupingu's thinking about who are the settlers, who the nomads in Australian history, and Brody's thinking concerning who are the nomads inspired by his experience of living, as he evokes it, in breathtakingly beautiful snow and icescapes alongside Arctic hunter-gatherer peoples:

> a crucial difference between hunter-gatherers and farmers is that one society is highly mobile, with a strong tendency to both small- and large-scale nomadism, whereas the other is highly settled, tending to stay firmly in one particular area or territory. This difference is established in stereotypes of 'nomadic' hunters and 'settled' farmers. However, the stereotype has it the wrong way round. It is agricultural societies that tend to be on the move; hunting peoples are far more firmly settled. This fact is evident when we look at these two ways of being in the world over a long time span.[49]

In this eloquent and passionate work, Brody shares Jared Diamond's questioning of history as a narrative of progress.[50] He calls on Diamond's analysis of the fatal effects of the animal-to-human diseases that are transferred in agricultural societies, and emphasizes that the 'microbes that came with the conquerors and settlers to the Americas killed far more indigenous peoples than did European weapons'. In some parts of North America, 75 per cent of the indigenous population was wiped out by such introduced illnesses: 'In all areas, weakness and fear remained for those who survived.'[51]

Brody shares an interest with Diamond in the shaping force of genocide in history. When agricultural societies meet hunter-gatherer societies, a clear pattern emerges: 'One kind of economy and culture overwhelms another.' Above all in this genocidal process, the new settlers from Europe wanted for their own purposes the land the hunter-gatherers occupied: 'Any opposition to farming had to be checked, made impossible. The enemies of settlement had to be silenced or removed. This is the story of the United States, Canada, Australia and much of southern Africa.' Such genocide by incoming settlers involves land primarily, but is also associated with other kinds of dispossession and suppression of hunter-gatherer peoples and their culture, for example the loss of indigenous languages enforced by Canada's residential schools.[52]

Like Diamond, Brody argues that a major force for genocide, violence, destruction and cultural loss in world history is the relentless movement of agricultural-pastoral societies, so recent in their appearance, into the areas of the world where hunter-gatherer groups had lived for many thousands of years.

Primates such as chimpanzees and humans have always practised intergroup violence including genocide, so that intergroup violence and genocide remain permanent possibilities. In human history, such violence and genocide were immensely and disastrously intensified with the coming of agricultural societies. Such has been the world we have lived in for the past 6,000 years. Such, I will now also argue, was certainly very much in evidence in the ancient classical world.

# 2 GENOCIDE, AND QUESTIONING OF GENOCIDE, IN THE ANCIENT GREEK WORLD: HERODOTUS AND THUCYDIDES

… the misery of war …

(Homer, *The Iliad*, Book Five)[1]

Your king is not a just man – for were he so, he had not coveted a land which is not his own, nor brought slavery on a people who never did him any wrong.

(Ethiopian king to the Persians, in Herodotus, *The Histories*, 3.21)[2]

The reason why Athens has the greatest name in all the world is because she … has spent more life and labour in warfare than any other state, thus winning the greatest power that has ever existed in history, such a power that will be remembered for ever by posterity.

(Pericles in Thucydides, *History of the Peloponnesian War*, 2.64)[3]

Massacres of whole peoples are not unprecedented. They were the order of the day in antiquity, and the centuries of

colonization and imperialism provide plenty of examples
of more or less successful attempts of that sort.
(Hannah Arendt, *Eichmann in Jerusalem*)[4]

In this chapter, I investigate instances of intergroup violence
including genocide, and questioning of such violence, in the classical Greek world, as evoked in Herodotus and Thucydides, the
founding figures of Western historical writing. Both created their
great works *The Histories* and *History of the Peloponnesian War*
in fifth-century Greece BCE, when Athens went from a city-state
successfully resisting Persian invasion early in the century to the
powerful possessor of an empire as the century went on. In both
texts we can, I argue, discern allegorical 'Gandhian' moments of
profound questioning of the value of war, violence, conquest,
empire and colonization.

As in Chapter 1, my framework will be that of genocide studies. Because genocide was once thought to be a blunt instrument of
analysis, an aim of this and succeeding chapters is to show, especially when deploying Lemkin's wide-ranging definition, how intri-
cate and multi-faceted it can be. This is especially so when we apply
the concept to the ancient world. Lemkin had planned to do so: one
of the contents lists for his unfinished book on the history of genocide, held in the New York Public Library, includes a proposed
chapter on genocide in Ancient Greece.[5] In this chapter I will also
be agreeing with Hannah Arendt's comment in the epigraph that
genocide was 'the order of the day in antiquity'. In particular, if a
city lost a siege which it had resisted, it was likely that the men of
fighting age would all be slain, while the women and children would
be taken separately into slavery, followed by colonization of the
defeated city by the victors. Genocide occurred in the ancient classical world during war, conquest, extensions of empire, colonization
and also civil war, the slaying of those perceived as political
enemies. In this last sense, while political genocide was excluded as
a consideration in the 1948 UN Genocide Convention, it was
certainly part of Lemkin's original 1944 definition in *Axis Rule in
Occupied Europe*.

## HISTORICAL WRITING

What, I think, is truly remarkable about Herodotus and Thucydides is that they established history as cosmopolitan and international in spirit. Their writings were engagingly anti-nationalist and anti-ethnocentric. They could be extremely critical of Greek no less than of other societies, and they certainly did not exempt democratic Athens from harsh judgement.[6]

The proliferating stories of Herodotus's *The Histories*, whose frame story is the war between Persia and Greece early in the fifth century and the subsequent gaining by Athens of a powerful and resented empire of allied and subject states, work emblematically as fables, parables, allegories of world history. Thucydides' *History of the Peloponnesian War* is also cast in a literary form, suggesting a tragic or at least highly problematic and fraught relationship between democracy and empire. Like Herodotus's *The Histories*, Thucydides' *History* explored what might be recurring or enduring or persisting features of history and humanity through the ages.

In both Herodotus and Thucydides there is an interesting play of perspectives concerning violence, including stories of protest at and criticism of the intergroup violence and genocide involved in war, colonizing and empire, as unworthy of what humanity should be. Herodotus and Thucydides establish history as a mode of ethical reflection with which all future thinking about empire, conquest and colonization in the European classical and neo-classical tradition had to engage: no easy task, given the moral weight of their reflections is opposed to empire and colonization.

In the second half of the twentieth century and in the twenty-first, it is the anti-empire and anti-colonial spirit in Herodotus and Thucydides, with its appeal to international humanitarian protection as laws all people should hold in common, that has resurged strongly in critical thinking about empire and colonialism. The same spirit is also evident in new forms of international law that have seriously challenged older international law, which appeared always to assist and enable colonization and empire.

It is in this light that Thucydides' *History* in particular has been invoked for its contemporary significance by a judge dealing with cases of genocide in the Balkans. In the International Tribunal for the Prosecution of Persons Responsible for Serious Violations of International Humanitarian Law Committed in the Territory of the Former Yugoslavia since 1991 (1999), Judge Shahabaddeen gave a separate opinion in which he directly quoted from the *History*:

> Some time ago, yet not far from where the events in this case happened, a 'breakdown of law and order' occurred. There 'were savage and pitiless actions into which men were carried not so much for the sake of gain as because they were swept away into an internecine struggle by their ungovernable passions'. The turmoil saw 'the ordinary conventions of civilized life thrown into confusion'. Sadly, it seems, people took 'it upon themselves to begin the process of repealing those general laws of humanity which are there to give a hope of salvation to all who are in distress, instead of leaving those laws in existence, remembering that there may come a time when they, too, will be in danger and will need their protection'.

Justice the Hon. Mohammed Shahabaddeen, an eminent jurist who has been a judge also of the International Court of Justice (elected in 1987) and would later be a judge in the International Criminal Tribunal for Rwanda (2005), reflected that the 'general laws of humanity' that the ancient chronicler spoke of had taken over 2,000 years to become binding norms applying worldwide with legal force.[7]

## HERODOTUS

In Herodotus's remarkable array of stories, covering a vast geography in the ancient world from the Black Sea and beyond to

Mesopotamia to Egypt to Africa to Greece and environs, amidst evocations of unceasing war, colonization and attempted extensions of empire, there are egregious examples of genocide and population transfer or ethnic cleansing as a common practice, eerily anticipatory of those blood-soaked centuries the twentieth and now the twenty-first.[8]

Herodotus tells us about the practice of netting by the invading Persian naval forces on their way to war with Athens, a practice that would now be described as ethnic cleansing. The Persians attacked Ionian islands like Chios, Lesbos and Tenedos, which were 'reduced without difficulty'. Whenever they became masters of an island, Herodotus says, the Persians 'netted' the inhabitants: 'Men join hands, so as to form a line across from the north coast to the south, and then march through the island from end to end and hunt out the inhabitants' (6.31); an activity that anticipates what British forces infamously tried to do to the indigenous people on the island of Tasmania over two millennia later.[9] The Persian land forces also captured Ionian towns upon the mainland, 'not however netting the inhabitants, as it was not possible'. Here they 'chose out all the best favoured boys and made them eunuchs, while the most beautiful of the girls they tore from their homes and sent them as presents to the king', at the same time 'burning the cities themselves, with their temples'. The Ionians were reduced to 'slavery' (6.32).

Herodotus relates many instances of colonization. These could be examples not of invasion and displacement, but of desperate or invited migration (1.94, 6.18–22). However, colonization also, especially when part of a desired expansion of empire, often involved injury or attempted injury to those peoples already living in the area, and in recounting these situations Herodotus's sympathies lie with the colonized, not the colonizers; those facing conquest, not the conquerors.

Early in *The Histories* there is a striking ethical confrontation between the Persian King Cyrus and Tomyris Queen of the Massagetae, a people living on a vast plain east of the Caspian Sea. In an exchange of messages, Tomyris questions the imperative of imperial expansion: 'Be content', Tomyris has a herald say to Cyrus, 'to rule in peace thy own kingdom, and bear to see us reign over the countries that are ours to govern', though she (rightly) doubts that Cyrus will 'choose to hearken to this counsel, since there is nothing thou less desirest than peace and quietness' (1.206) (recall Dan Stone's thought that a constant possibility in human violence is an anticipated joy in war and killing).[10] As it turns out, Cyrus should have listened to Tomyris' counsel. In the ensuing war, after 29 years as king and regarding himself as invincible, he is killed (1.206, 214). Tomyris has Cyrus's body brought to her, and mournfully intones to the dead king that while she has defeated him in battle, yet he has ruined her life in the death of her son, who had been captured by Cyrus and died by suicide in captivity. In this sad and tragic speech, Tomyris highlights the hubris of male rulers in history pursuing the misery of war, in wars of conquest that always put nations and peoples under threat of loss of liberty and death of loved ones (1.204–14; also 2.102).[11]

A similar ethical duel occurs between the Persians and Ethiopians. King Cambyses, son of Cyrus, decides to attack Ethiopia, first sending messengers to the Ethiopian king, offering gifts, friendship and alliance. But the king realizes that they are spies and that Cambyses is bent on conquest. He tells the messengers:

> Your king is not a just man – for were he so, he had not coveted a land which is not his own, nor brought slavery on a people who never did him any wrong. Bear him this bow, and say, – 'The king of the Ethiops thus advises the king of the Persians – when the Persians can pull a bow of this strength thus easily, then let him come with an army of superior strength against the long-lived Ethiopians – till then, let him thank the gods that they have not put it into the heart of the sons of the Ethiops to covet countries which do not belong to them' (3.21).

When Cambyses' spies return and report the Ethiopian king's speech, Cambyses is so angered that he forthwith sets out on a march against the Ethiopians without making any proper provisions for his army or reflecting, Herodotus dryly comments, that he was 'about to wage war in the uttermost parts of the earth'. Before he has gone but one-fifth of the distance, the army's provisions fail and the soldiers begin eating anything they can, including the 'sumpter beasts' and then grass and herbs, until finally, arriving at 'bare sand', they cast lots and slay one of their own for food. Cambyses, hearing of 'such cannibalism', at last gives up and retreats, having lost vast numbers of his men: 'And so ended the expedition against Ethiopia' (3.25). In relation to this story, we might think of the primatological observation of Jane Goodall in *The Chimpanzees of Gombe* that human beings have through time and all over the world practised cannibalism.[12]

Again and again, Herodotus evokes the destructiveness of colonization. *The Histories* tells of a Greek colony in Libya and its consequences for the Libyans. A man called Battus, born with a stammer and lisp, goes to Delphi to consult the oracle about his voice; the pythia, however, reports that Phoebus Apollo bids Battus to 'establish a city in Libya, abounding in fleeces'. In the event, Battus and other Greeks go out to 'colonize Libya', though at first the colony, established on an island off the Libyan coast, fares poorly. Consulted again, the oracle tells Battus and his fellow colonizers to settle on the Libyan mainland itself. The Libyans induce them to leave the place where they first attempt to settle, and lead them elsewhere, bypassing in the night 'the most beautiful district of that whole country'. The colonists establish the city of Cyrêné, beside a spring, on pleasant and fertile land. After many decades, and in the reign of a new king, it transpires that the advice of the oracle 'brought Greeks from every quarter into Libya, to join the settlement', for the 'Cyrenaeans had offered to all comers a share in their lands'. When this 'great multitude' of Greeks came, the 'Libyans of the neighbourhood found themselves stripped of large portions of their lands', so they and their king, 'being robbed and insulted', sent messengers to Egypt to intervene on their behalf. This was an ill-fated entreaty, for subsequently the Egyptian army which came to support the Libyans was 'routed with such slaughter that but a very few of them ever got back home' (4.154–159).

In a similar vein, Herodotus tells a story of the coming of the Scythians into the land of Cimmeria. The Scythians had once dwelt in Asia, but decided to move after warring, with ill success, against the Massagetae. As they approached Cimmeria, 'the natives', hearing how numerous are the Scythians, found themselves divided on what to do, some urging flight as otherwise they would be destroyed, others urging that the people stay and fight 'the invaders' for their soil to the last. As it turned out, according to this account, the two factions of the Cimmerians warred with each other, with the side urging they stay and fight being slain; the other Cimmerians then departed, and the Scythians, 'on their coming, took possession of a deserted land' (4.11).

*The Histories* does not, however, create an ancient world that is lawless, that operates only by invasion and conquest. Throughout *The Histories* Herodotus notes many instances of accepted international conventions concerning the protection and kind treatment of strangers, travellers, messengers, ambassadors, heralds, supplicants, refugees and exiles. Herodotus tells of King Xerxes' outrage at instances of cruel Athenian and Spartan treatment of some Persian messengers that had occurred in King Darius's time: Xerxes declares, with 'true greatness of soul', that such killing of heralds and messengers broke the 'laws which all men hold in common'. Herodotus himself suggests that such international law concerning kindly reception of strangers was divinely sanctioned; breaking it would incur the wrath of the gods in the form of various calamities, in which was manifest the 'hand of Heaven' (7.133–137).

There are also in Herodotus 'Gandhian' allegorical moments of non-violence, stories of societies that eschew war and violence, stories that challenge the usual course of history. In particular, Herodotus tells of a community beyond the Scythians, the Argippaeans, who possess no warlike weapons, and are so special and gentle a people that their neighbours look upon them as sacred. When their neighbours fall out, the Argippaeans make up the quarrel; and when a neighbour flies to them for refuge, he is safe from all hurt (4.23).[13] In this parable, sacredness is associated with non-violence, rather than with war, conquest and empire that are held by various peoples to be sanctified by the gods or God. And sacredness is associated not with a bellicose masculinity, but with its reverse.

In the frame story of *The Histories*, after the defeat of the Persian fleet at Salamis, the Athenians, now the dominant Greek naval power, set about forging an empire in the Ionian islands and city-states east of Athens, which the Persians had formerly controlled as part of their empire. Herodotus observes in the victorious Athenians values that accompany the acquisition of new subject states, especially visible in predatory commanders like Themistocles, as he extracts, or attempts to extract, tribute from Greek island peoples: rapacity, greed, arrogance and willingness to betray one's own (8.111–12). Here is a new historical situation for democratic Athens, gaining and possessing an empire, and almost immediately, as he notes in Themistocles, there is a rapid deterioration in morality and ethics that bodes ill for Athens' future, let alone the future of its new subjects, as well as presenting ominous problems for the other nations of the Greek world that have to deal with Athens and its new imperial status and self-image.[14]

As we shall now see, Thucydides takes up the frame story of Athens and the ethical consequences of possessing an empire from the point where Herodotus ceases his narrative.


## THUCYDIDES

The misery of war, civil war, colonization and attempted extensions of empire are features of *The History of the Peloponnesian War*, with egregious examples of genocide and population transfer or ethnic cleansing, examples so appalling in their implications that Thucydides' *History* has forever afterwards shadowed the claims of democracies to be superior in history. Let's reprise for a moment the story of the near 30-years' war, fought intermittently from 431 to 404 BCE, between democratic Athens and its empire, and monarchical Sparta and its league of oligarchic allies, as Thucydides' *History* constructs it for us; a war that Athens would lose, along with its empire.

In Thucydides' *History*, we witness the Athenian statesman Pericles as foremost among those, Athenian or Spartan, who incite the war to begin. A brilliant orator in the Sophist tradition, Pericles in his speeches to the assemblies assures them that Athens will quickly win the war, if it follows his strategy. The Athenians, he recommends, should leave the countryside, their homes, farms and temples in Attica, and come to reside in Athens and between the Long Walls that lead down to the port of Piraeus, and in Piraeus; because of their seamanship and experience as soldiers landing from ships, they enjoy naval superiority (and can always import food and supplies from Ionia to the east); they must not, however, attempt to acquire any new territory, rather they should steadfastly hold on to what they already possess. Pericles' plans, however, are almost immediately thrown off course. A devastating plague – suggested by the *History* to be a divine judgement on Pericles and Athens' desire for war (2.54)[15] – breaks out in the crowded conditions that his strategy creates in Athens and between the Long Walls and Piraeus, and in subsequent speeches Pericles has to tell assemblies of his fearful and resentful fellow citizens why they must continue to fight this war. Athens, Pericles says, has become a great city, perhaps the greatest city ever known, because of the warfare practised by their forebears that established their empire. Whatever the feelings of the peoples of the subject states, the empire is the means of making Athens great, to be remembered for all time for its civilized achievements: democracy, equality before the law, advancement by merit, relaxed freedom and tolerance in private life, laws protecting the oppressed, the beauty and good taste of Athenian homes, an excellent education system and Athens as an open city (2.35–42).

In his Funeral Oration held for those Athenian men first to die in the war, Pericles says it is part of Athens' greatness that it acts in relation to others with a 'free liberality', doing kindness to others out of friendship and not out of calculation: 'We make friends by doing good to others, not by receiving good from them.' And, says Pericles, Athens is 'unique' in this: 'When we do kindness to others, we do not do [it] out of any calculations of profit or loss.' He feels no hesitation in declaring that 'our city is an education to Greece'. Athens' empire reveals mighty monuments left for posterity: 'Future ages will wonder at us, as the present age wonders at us now.' And part of the reason for the success of Athens is 'our adventurous spirit', which has 'forced an entry into every sea and into every land'. Everywhere, Pericles declares, 'we have left behind us everlasting memorials of good done to our friends or suffering inflicted on our enemies.' Such disinterested virtue, along with valour, adventurousness and 'manliness', have made Athens 'splendid' (2.40–42).

Yet along with such altruism, Pericles' speeches also reveal the kind of nationalist and ethnocentric values and imperial hauteur and arrogance that were increasingly alarming the other Hellenic nations, including Athens' own allies and subject states, who more and more tried to revolt and break away. Pericles' long-term concern, it is evident, is with Athens itself, its survival and continuance as an imperial power. In the stress of the plague, he urges his fellow Athenians to recall their 'superiority' that accompanies Athens' 'imperial dignity'. Such superiority and imperial dignity are dependent on their possession of empire, and they must hold onto their empire even when they know that they have incurred the 'hatred' of its subject peoples in administering it. Pericles even admits that it may have been wrong to have taken the empire in the first place, because it has become a 'tyranny'; but, if the Athenians wish to continue as a great society, they must not let their empire go (2.62–3).

Here, for a fleeting and perhaps horrified moment, Pericles concedes that Athens' cultural treasures are dependent on tyranny and hatred, radically putting into question his and Athens' own self-image of moral and ethical superiority. In effect, Pericles is here anticipating Walter Benjamin's observation, in his 'Theses on the Philosophy of History', that one can only contemplate 'cultural treasures', the cultural treasures prized by the victors and rulers in history, 'with horror'.[16]

In these terms, Pericles admires in Athens what we would now recognize in modernity – if we think of settler colonial states like apartheid South Africa or Zionist Israel – as a *herrenvolk* or ethnic democracy.[17] There is an elite group who compose Athens' participatory citizens: the Athenian males, but not the subject peoples of the empire. Thucydides' *History* suggests that democracies, and this is especially so when democracies seek to acquire empires, will always be *herrenvolk*; they are never wholly inclusive, citizenship is always restrictive or conditional, and the morality that excludes will always undermine the high values proclaimed as the sign of greatness of the democracy.

The kind of ethical deterioration that Hannah Arendt perceived in late nineteenth and early twentieth-century European imperialism[18] is evident in Pericles' disdain for non-Athenians, his sense of Athenian superiority, his lack of moral concern for the victims of Athens' 'tyranny' and his acceptance of double standards – that it is morally unobjectionable in his view that Athens be a democracy while the subject states of the empire are denied their freedom and independence, since the only criterion that fundamentally matters is what is good for Athens.

## GENOCIDE AND THE HONOUR OF NATIONS

In the artistic design of the *History of the Peloponnesian War*, as the war goes on the Athenians' ethical deterioration, an increasing heartlessness, a lack of sympathy and empathy with others subject to Athens or those who should in their view be subject to Athens, is chillingly evident. Such heartlessness is particularly prominent in two scenes involving a near genocide and an actual genocide, as evoked in the *History*: the Mytilinean Debate and the Melian Dialogue.[19] In the Mytilinean Debate, the demagogue Cleon distinguishes himself by declaring to the assembly that to feel pity and compassion for a conquered people like the Mytilineans, who have tried to revolt, is against the interests of an imperial power like Athens, which must accept that it is a tyranny and act accordingly; for Cleon, the rights and wrongs of why Mytilene attempted to revolt are irrelevant (3.37–40). Cleon recommends mass death for the Mytilineans, though this is averted at the last moment, Mytilene just escaping, as Thucydides' *History* puts it, a 'massacre' (3.49).[20]

In the Melian Dialogue, presented in Book Five, the people of the island of Melos, originally a colony of Sparta, wish to preserve their long-standing independence and to stay neutral in the war between Sparta and Athens. The island, however, is visited by an Athenian force, sure of their superior military strength, whose leaders tell the Melians, with brutal directness, that Melos has to come within the Athenian empire; if the Melians refuse they and their city will face devastation. The Athenians declare that they are not interested in any considerations of justice, for example, that the Melians have not joined Sparta in the war nor done any harm to Athens. The Athenians insist that the only morality that is relevant is not justice, but practical matters of self-interest, force and power: 'the strong do what they have the power to do and the weak accept what they have to accept' (5.89).

Athenians: It is for the good of our own empire that we are here and … it is for the preservation of your city that we shall say what we are going to say. We do not want any trouble in bringing you into our empire, and we want you to be spared for the good of yourselves and of ourselves.

Melians: And how could it be just as good for us to be the slaves as for you to be the masters?

Athenians: You, by giving in, would save yourselves from disaster; we, by not destroying you, would be able to profit from you.

Melians: So you would not agree to our being neutral, friends instead of enemies, but allies of neither side?

Athenians: No, because it is not so much your hostility that injures us; it is rather the case that, if we were on friendly terms with you, our subjects would regard that as a sign of weakness in us, whereas your hatred is evidence of our power.

(5.91–95)

The Melians, after discussing the Athenian threat among themselves, then tell of their decision, that they 'are not prepared to give up in a short moment the liberty which our city has enjoyed from its foundation': 'we invite you to allow us to be friends of yours and enemies to neither side, to make a treaty which shall be agreeable to both you and us, and so to leave our country' (5.112).

The Athenians refuse, immediately commence hostilities, and eventually (in 416 BCE) succeed in what they had threatened to do:

Siege operations were now carried on vigorously and, as there was also some treachery from inside, the Melians surrendered unconditionally to the Athenians, who put to death all the men of military age whom they took, and sold the women and children as slaves. Melos itself they took over for themselves, sending out later a colony of 500 men.

(5.116)

If the Athenians had shown hesitation, and worried about being cruel and engaging in mass slaughter in relation to the Mytilineans, no such hesitation is revealed in the case of the Melians. The description of the destruction of Melos fits exactly the concept of genocide as defined by Lemkin, of an attack on a group followed by reduction of its population and replacement of the original population by colonization. In this process, enslavement was an instrument of ethnic cleansing, as we would now call it, in the ancient classical world.

The probing questions put to the Athenians by the Melians anticipate a famous work of post Second World War moral philosophy, Isaiah Berlin's *Historical Inevitability* (1954), where Berlin argues that in the past individuals could have chosen to act otherwise than how they did; they could have avoiding acting in the ways they did act.[21] The Melians warn the Athenians that they are making a choice that is concerned only with short-term advantage, which they may regret in a longer view. The Athenians, say the Melians, are being unwise; they 'should not destroy a principle that is to the general good of all men – namely, that in the case of all who fall into danger there should be such a thing as fair play and just dealing': 'this is a principle which affects you as much as anybody, since your own fall would be visited by the most terrible vengeance and would be an example to the world' (5.90). One day, the Melians are suggesting, when the Athenians are themselves in danger of being harmed or destroyed, they will not be able to appeal to a general human principle of 'fair play and just dealing' for protection. Their fall will be 'an example to the world' of the consequences of ignoring international humanitarian law 'that is to the general good of all men' and which could possibly protect the Athenians themselves in their own inevitable time of weakness and vulnerability. Few would come forward to defend them, the Melians imply, because by their brutality the Athenians have dishonoured themselves among the nations; dishonoured themselves in history.

## ATHENS INVADES SICILY

The Athenian destruction of Melos is only one amongst other examples of genocide, of which there are many throughout the *History*. Indeed, in his introductory remarks in Book One, Thucydides reflects that extreme intergroup violence characterized the Peloponnesian War as a whole. Such violence had begun much earlier in the century when, the Persians having been defeated, the Athenians conquered their former possessions, as in the siege of Eion, where they made slaves of the inhabitants, and the island of

Scyros in the Aegean: 'They enslaved the inhabitants and colonized the island themselves' (1.98). During the Peloponnesian War, while total destruction of the Mytilineans was at the last moment averted, the Athenians nevertheless 'divided all the land' into 3,000 holdings, 300 of which 'were set apart for the gods, while the remainder was distributed by lot to Athenian shareholders, who were sent out to Lesbos', the Mytilineans now becoming 'subjects' of Athens (3.50).

In the *History* it is clear that the sympathies of Thucydides as narrator are with those who dislike and protest at empire and the subjugation of subject states that accompany it. A common theme is that the Athenians, in taking over part of Persia's empire, had become like the very Persians the Greeks had thought they were fortunate in expelling. Perhaps the most powerful denunciation of such Athenian/Persian identity was voiced by Hermocrates of Syracuse, during the ill-fated Athenian invasion of Sicily; Thucydides refers to Hermocrates as 'in every way a remarkably intelligent man' (6.72). Hermocrates told the assembly that the Athenians are attempting 'to take away from us what is ours':

> The fact is that just as they won an empire in Hellas, so they are trying to win another one here, and by exactly the same methods. The alliance of Ionians and others racially connected with Athens voluntarily accepted Athenian leadership in the war to get their own back from Persia; but the Athenians deprived them all of their independence, accusing some of failure to fulfil their military obligations, some of fighting among themselves, bringing forward, in fact, any plausible excuse to fit each particular case. So, in making this stand against Persia, Athens was not fighting for the freedom of Hellas. … What Athens wanted was to substitute her own empire for that of Persia.
>
> (6.76)

In the event, the Syracusans' desire to maintain their independence overwhelmed the Athenian hubris of wishing to extend their empire to the west.

By the campaign's end, the Athenian navy had been destroyed and their military forces were facing complete humiliation, degradation and slavery: 'Indeed, they were like nothing so much as the fleeing population of a city that has surrendered to its besiegers' (7.75). Certainly they did not receive sympathy or leniency from the Syracusans – whose lands had been attacked by Athens for no other reason than to advance Athens' imperial ambitions – who had defeated them so utterly (7.85–87).

## THE CHALLENGE TO ATHENS

Herodotean and Thucydidean anti-nationalist cosmopolitanism was certainly a challenge to the image Athenians held of themselves and by which they wished to be remembered, a self-admiring image we've already witnessed in Pericles' Funeral Speech in Thucydides' *History*.

In *Theseus, Tragedy and the Athenian Empire* (1997), Sophie Mills suggests that Thucydides' critical attitudes towards war, conquest and empire were sharply at odds with the usual or conventional view that most Athenians in the classical age would have maintained of themselves and their city.[22] In this idealized self-image, Mills relates, Athens claimed Theseus as its guiding mythological hero, to be honoured for triumphing over the Minotaur in Crete, where he faced danger for the sake of others, and freed Athens from King Minos' control. Theseus' heroic prowess, Mills argues, was held to symbolize Athenian national virtues, at home and abroad – Athens as the city of justice and mercy, opposing all forms of tyranny, always altruistic, always a civilizer and liberator, a benefactor to humanity. Just as Theseus in his heroic exploits combined physical strength with intelligence and moral wisdom, so did Athens in all its actions, including its foreign policy. In this self-image, which became part of its imperial ideology, Athenian military might was always used in the generous service of civilized values; Athens was loyal to its friends and selflessly intervened for the common good on behalf of the weak and vulnerable. In this Periclean view, as Mills says, Athens should be admired as the only truly Greek city, an example to all the others; its duty was to educate Greece in ideal Athenian values.[23]

Yet Mills also notes that the sanitized and domesticated portrait of Theseus adopted by Athens in the sixth and fifth centuries was not necessarily shared by non-Athenians, who could readily think of stories descending from the eighth and seventh centuries where Theseus can be observed as a far more ambivalent figure. Certainly he conquers the Minotaur, but then, in a notorious act of ingratitude and treachery, he abandons King Minos' daughter Ariadne on the way back to Athens, Ariadne who has helped him to escape the laybyrinth. In such stories, Mills reflects, Theseus can also be considered a parricide, if indirectly, for on his return he breaks his promise to his father Aegeus that he will change the sails of his ship from black to white if he has succeeded against the Minotaur, leading to his father's suicide. In other unfavourable stories, Theseus disastrously abducts Helen and hides her in Aphidna in Attica, causing an invasion by the Dioscuri (Helen's brothers) to recover her, during which Theseus' mother is captured; there was a tradition that Theseus was not present to save his defenceless mother from suffering and humiliation. On another occasion, Theseus assists his friend Peirithous in a failed attempt to abduct the queen of the underworld; in one common story, the two abductors are tricked into sitting down and then, as punishment for their hubris, are bound fast for eternity, Theseus having to be rescued by Heracles. Increasingly in Athenian retellings, however, Mills observes, Theseus was remade as a representative hero of Athens, portrayed as the humane democratic king who stood firm against all forms of tyranny, his apparent failings explained away. Mills suggests that for non-Athenians Theseus was nonetheless exceedingly unlikely material as a hero representing all that was to be revered in a city.[24]

In Thucydides' *History*, the Melian Dialogue is dramatically at odds with the Athenian self-idealization that Sophie Mills evokes. The Melians suggested – and such I feel is the view of the *History* as a whole – that the Athenians would be judged harshly in history for their enthusiasm for war and their imperial morality, or amorality.[25] They would suffer an eternal loss of historical prestige.[26] And indeed the episode of the destruction of Melos, as created by Thucydides in his remarkable dialogue, has become a 'classic' of genocide literature.[27]

## CONCLUSION: SPEAKING TO THE FUTURE

When Judge Shahabaddeen in his separate opinion in 1999 on cases of genocide in the Balkans in the former Yugoslavia fulsomely praised Thucydides' *History*, he was referring to the evocation in Book Three of the terrible civil war in Corcyra in 427, between the democratic and oligarchic parties, each side appealing either to Athens or Sparta, part of a more general pattern of civil wars during the Peloponnesian War as a whole. The leaders of these parties in cities like Corcyra, Thucydides' *History* comments, had rival programmes which appeared admirable: 'on one side political equality for the masses, on the other the safe and sound government of the aristocracy'. But such programmes became quickly confused by love of power, greed and personal ambition, followed by 'violent fanaticism' once the struggle had broken out, accompanied by the destruction of any citizens who held moderate views (3.82) – a remarkable anticipation of the civil war that broke out in Jerusalem in the revolt against Rome that had begun in 66 CE, as evoked by Josephus in *The Jewish War*.[28]

In the civil war in Corcyra, both sides were guilty of appalling atrocities, including the killing of suppliants (with other suppliants, seeing their companions being killed, choosing to commit suicide, either by killing each other or hanging themselves from trees). There were massacres of those considered enemies: 'There was death in every shape and form. And, as usually happens in such situations, people went to every extreme and beyond it.'

[ 57 ]

Fathers killed sons; people were killed not for political reasons but on grounds of personal hatred or else by their debtors because of the money they owed; men were dragged from temples or butchered inside 'on the very altars'; some were walled up and died in the temple of Dionysus (3.81). The civil war in Corcyra presaged a general convulsion during the extreme stress of war that would engulf the Hellenic world; in city after city there were revolutions and revolutionary zeal, with seizing of power and 'unheard-of atrocities in revenge' (3.82).

As a result, there was a 'general deterioration of character throughout the Greek world' (3.83). What was now threatened was the universal 'idea of justice' (3.84). And, as would the Melians speaking to the Athenians in the Melian Dialogue, Thucydides' *History* here, as Judge Shahabaddeen sagely notes, urges the necessity of international humanitarian law: in Thucydides' words 'those general laws of humanity which are there to give a hope of salvation to all who are in distress' (3.84). It is surely clear from this intervention that Thucydides supported the appeal to universal justice by the Melians, and opposed the pitiless imperial actions of the Athenians.

In the wake of the horror and destruction of the Second World War, the newly established United Nations crafted a new body of international law, in the UN Declaration of Human Rights and the UN Convention on the Prevention and Punishment of the Crime of Genocide, both enacted in 1948 within a day of each other.[29] New courts were established, as in the International Court of Justice and later in the twentieth century the International Criminal Court. (The ICC was established by the Rome Statute of the International Criminal Court on 17 July 1998; the Statute setting out the Court's jurisdiction, structure and functions entered into force on 1 July 2002.) International law now judged that territory could not be won by conquest, ethnic cleansing was a crime against humanity, and children should be protected.

It's interesting to contemplate Thucydides' *History* in terms of Article II of the 1948 Genocide Convention, which regards as a crime the forcible transfer of children of a group to another group

(Article II, clause 5). As the *History* evokes the war, children in the ancient classical world along with women were routinely sold into slavery after a siege lost by a city's defenders. Children could also be moved in and out of societies in situations of crisis. In Book Five, after a battle between Sparta and its allies and democratic Argos and its allies (including Athenians), the Spartans are victorious. In the following winter they send to Argos proposals for a settlement whereby Argos would become pro-Spartan, a settlement which includes the giving back of children on all sides. Sparta too would observe this injunction: 'If the Spartans have any children in their power, they shall give them back each to his own city' (5.73, 76–77).

Contemporary international law is, as Judge Shahabaddeen observed, a reprise and fulfilment of the anti-colonial and anti-empire conceptions and protests of Thucydides over 2,000 years before. Thucydides famously wrote in his *History* (1.22) that he wished to write not for his contemporaries but for future generations: truly he did so!

# 3 GENOCIDE, TRAUMA AND WORLD UPSIDE DOWN IN ANCIENT GREEK TRAGEDY: AESCHYLUS AND EURIPIDES

Do not with these soft attentions woman me,
Nor prostrate like a fawning Persian mouth at me
Your loud addresses.
> (Agamemnon to Clytemnestra in Aeschylus'
> *Agamemnon*)[1]

I implore you, do not tear my child from me, do not
Kill her. There is enough death. In her lies my joy,
In her I forget troubles, and find comfort for
All I have lost. She is my city now; my nurse,
My staff, my guide. The strong ought not to use their
strength
To do what is not right; when they are fortunate
They should not think Fortune will always favour them.
I once was fortunate, and now I am so no more;
One day has taken happiness, wealth, everything.
Then be my friend. Let awe, and pity, move your heart.
Go to the Achaean army; talk them round; tell them
What odium will fasten on you, if you kill

Women whom first you did not kill, but pitied, when
You dragged them from the altars.
>(Hecabe to Odysseus in Euripides, *Hecabe*)[2]

If men, to settle each dispute,
Must needs compete in bloodshed, when
Shall violence vanish, hate be soothed,
Or men and cities live in peace?
>(The Chorus in Euripides, *Helen*)[3]

In this chapter, I continue my investigations of intergroup violence including genocide, and questioning of such violence, in the classical Greek world, this time as evoked in tragedy. My key texts are Aeschylus' *Agamemnon* and Euripides' *Hecabe, Andromache* and *The Women of Troy*, with some side glances at Euripides' *Helen*. I reflect on the consequences of genocide both for perpetrators like Agamemnon and Odysseus, and for victims, especially conquered women and their children consigned to slavery in faraway lands.[4] As in the previous chapter in relation to historical writing, I argue that in these powerful texts there are discernible allegorical 'Gandhian' moments of profound questioning of the value of war, violence and vengeance. Orientalism, too, figures in these plays, as a spur to violence; yet Orientalism is also profoundly questioned.

In this chapter, then, genocide studies meets classical Greek drama, where plays about the mythological age perform as a theatre of fundamental values, of interpretation and reinterpretation, questioning and contestation, disaster and lament.

In general terms, I argue that these tragedies, along with Herodotus and Thucydides' histories, present a foundational challenge to how we conceive Western cultural history.

## LEMKIN'S ANALYTIC METHOD

I have referred before to Lemkin's diagrammatic outline for analysing cases of genocide. It's time to look at the outline more closely. I reproduce it here, as follows, including its spelling.[5]

**Revised outline for genocide cases**

1. Background – historical

2. Conditions leading to genocide – Fanaticism (religious, racial)
   Irredentism (national aspirations)
   Social or political crisis and change
   Economic exploitation (e.g. slavery)
   Colonial expansion or milit. conquest
   accessability of victim group
   evolution of genocidal values in genocidist group
   (contempt for the alien, etc.)
   factors weakening victim group

3. Methods and techniques of genocide
   **Physical:**
   > massacre and mutilation
   > deprivation of livelihood (starvation,
   > exposure, etc. – often by deportation)
   > slavery – exposure to death

   **Biological:**
   > separation of families
   > sterilization
   > destruction of foetus

   **Cultural:**
   > desecration and destruction of cultural symbols
   > (books, objects of art, religious relics, etc.)
   > loot
   > destruction of cultural leadership
   > destruction of cultural centers (cities,
   > churches, monasteries, schools, libraries)
   > prohibition of cultural activities or codes of behavior
   > forceful conversion
   > demoralization

4. The Genocidists – responsibility
   intent
   motivation
   feelings of guilt

demoralization
attitude towards victim group
opposition to genocide within genocidist group

5.  Propaganda – rationalization of crime
    appeal to popular beliefs and intolerance; sowing discord
    (divide and rule)
    misrepresentation and deceit
    intimidation

6.  Responses of victim group
    **active:**
    submission; polit. subordination
    escape (suicide, hiding, etc.); assimilation
    disguise; resistance
    emigration (planned); demoralization
    **passive (emotional, mental)**
    terror
    conceptions of genocidist and his crimes

7.  Responses of outside groups – opposition to genocide
    indifference to        ”
    condonement of     ”
    collaboration in      ”
    demoralization (exploitation of genocide situation)
    Fear as potential victims

8.  Aftermath – cultural losses
    population changes
    economic dislocations
    material and moral deterioration
    political consequences
    social and cult. changes

This outline can be found in Folder 11, Box 8, Subseries 2 of the
Lemkin papers in the American Jewish Historical Society
Museum in New York. In the next folder, number 12, Lemkin puts
into practice and continuously deploys the categories of analysis

of the diagrammatic summary in his consideration of post-1492 America. In 'Spanish Treatment of South American Indians Essay, n.d.', Lemkin, drawing in particular on the observations of Las Casas, successively evokes 'Methods of Genocide – Physical', which include massacre, slavery and deprivation of livelihood.

Family life was disregarded, bread made of root-meal was often the only food; when the slaves fell sick, they were left to die or at best sent home. The treatment of Indian women consti-tuted an aspect of biological genocide, the 'death of the race'. Slave mothers, exhausted with hunger and fatigue, could not nurse their babies. Children were not infrequently carried off by the Spanish; some Indian women were not only violated indis-criminately but also taken to 'fill the Harems of the Spanish colonists'. In terms of physical genocide, the population of the islands fell catastrophically. There was also a 'subtle kind of cultural genocide' committed by the Spanish missions which abounded in Mexico, California, Louisiana and elsewhere. Continuing to apply his method, Lemkin evokes and gives exam-ples of other categories of genocide, from looting and pillaging of Indian wealth to destruction of cultural centres and devasta-tion of Indian leadership in the murder of one chief or king after another. Under the heading of 'Responsibility', Lemkin argues that with few exceptions the Spanish colonists of New Spain were guilty of genocide: 'the colonists were guilty on all counts'.[6]

Here I will deploy the outline as a method for analysing some Greek tragedies.

## GENOCIDAL CONSCIOUSNESS IN AESCHYLUS'S *AGAMEMNON*

Let's think now of the features of genocide that Lemkin regards as recurring through history as they might bear on Aeschylus's *Agamemnon*, a play that is precious to humanity's heritage. In terms of Lemkin's opening heading, 'Background – historical', we can think of the various mythological stories that concern and curse the House of Atreus. Agamemnon, the son of Atreus, older brother of Menelaus and husband of Helen's sister Clytemnestra, leads the Greek expedition against Troy, commanding 100 ships, the largest force in the fleet. In the outline, under 'Conditions leading to genocide', Lemkin lists 'Colonial expansion or milit. conquest'. Agamemnon, King of Argos, and Menelaus, King of Sparta, sail eastwards not to conquer and then colonize the Asian city of Troy, but to enact revenge on Priam its king by military defeat. Priam's city is to be overrun, its fighting men slain, including Paris who abducted Helen from Sparta and her husband Menelaus, its women and children captured as trophies of war and enslaved, the city burnt to ashes, and Helen either to be killed or brought home to Greece. Yet almost immediately, at the beginning, before the avenging fleet can sail, Agamemnon risks and earns disapproval both divine and human. While hunting, the king catches a stag, and then unwisely boasts that he is a better hunter than Artemis; offended, the goddess holds the fleet wind-bound at Aulis, and the Greeks, upon the advice of the army seer Calchas, decide to appease Artemis by sacrificing to her Iphigenia, Clytemnestra's beloved daughter; Iphigenia is sent for on the pretext of her marrying Achilles, and once she is sacrificed by the Greeks the fleet can sail with favourable winds. After a ten-year siege, the destruction of Troy will occur consequent upon the Trojans being deceived by the Wooden Horse harbouring Greek soldiers.

In Aeschylus's *Agamemnon* (performed 458 BCE), the first of his Orestes cycle of plays, Agamemnon himself kills Iphigenia, for which he is never forgiven by Clytemnestra, who nurses her desire for revenge until her husband returns. In the play, Agamemnon, triumphally coming home to his palace as conqueror of Troy, enters in his chariot, followed by another chariot loaded with the spoils of war, including Cassandra the daughter of King Priam and his wife Queen Hecabe. The extraordinarily formidable Clytemnestra, who will shortly put to death both Agamemnon and Cassandra, welcomes home the king her husband; she instructs her maids to carpet the way into the palace with crimson tapestries and invites her husband to walk on them into his home. Agamemnon in cold reply suggests to Clytemnestra that her welcome is inappropriate: a woman should not engage in public praise of a warrior and conqueror; and, as we can see from our epigraph, he regards with disdain the crimson cloth as 'soft attentions' which will 'woman' him in an Asian way, as if Clytemnestra is a 'fawning Persian'.[7]

After a vigorous exchange during which he accuses her of going beyond her sex ('It does not suit a woman to be combative'), Agamemnon gives in, gets an attendant to untie his shoes and begins to walk his silken way inside. He advises Clytemnestra that she should treat Cassandra well, for his new slave is the 'army's gift' to their leader, the chosen jewel of 'Troy's wealth' that has been taken by the victors. He betrays no consciousness that while he returns with the daughter of a foreign king as concubine, he had killed his and Clytemnestra's daughter ten years before, and indeed he appears to have forgotten that her death had ever occurred. Cassandra 'the prophetess', the ever unfortunate foreteller of fate, never to be believed, at first refuses to leave the loot-chariot as we might call it, fearful of what might happen. Cassandra soon realizes that like Agamemnon she will be killed once inside the palace, home of a family doomed by generations of gruesome violence and vengeance. Cassandra also prophesies that in her turn Clytemnestra will be killed in revenge for Agamemnon's death by their son Orestes, currently living in exile.[8]

When, however, Clytemnestra exultantly declares to the chorus that she has killed Agamemnon by netting him in his bath and then stabbing him (the 'crimson rain' of his blood falling on her, she says, like 'the dew of heaven when buds burst forth in Spring'), she is confident that Justice has been served, her daughter's cruel sacrifice has been avenged, and she in turn will not suffer revenge for what she has done.[9]

Now to the Powers that persecute
Our race I offer a sworn pact:

> With this harsh deed and bitter fact
> I am content; let them forget the past,
> Leave us for ever, and oppress
> Some other house with murderous wickedness.[10]

It is a recurring motif of the ancient Greek tragedies – and perhaps such is an insight into a general pattern of history – that those enacting revenge for a perceived great wrong believe that they themselves will not experience revenge. Vengeance, they feel, stops with them, because in their view, as Clytemnestra says, justice has been fulfilled.[11] The cycles of revenge, they feel sure, will now cease.

In 'Conditions leading to genocide', Lemkin refers to the 'evolution of genocidal values in genocidist group (contempt for the alien, etc.)'. In *Agamemnon*, the returned conqueror Agamemnon in his tone towards Clytemnestra clearly valorizes masculine warrior values above all others; in warfare, a man can attain everlasting fame, fame he himself has earned by his victory over Troy. Agamemnon has contempt for women as not warriors, and for Trojans who in a 'Persian' way are given to 'fawning' to power and who, as it were, unman themselves in their love of luxury. When Clytemnestra asks him to imagine what Priam would have done if he were the conqueror, Agamemnon disdainfully replies: 'Walked on embroidered satin, I have little doubt.' When Lemkin refers to 'intent' under the heading 'The Genocidists', we can think that Agamemnon is profoundly pleased that his intent to destroy Troy, its city and people, its world and its cosmos, has been resoundingly fulfilled. As a genocidist, his bearing is one of pride and arrogance as he coldly converses with his wife whom he hasn't seen for ten years and instructs her to accept Cassandra as part of their household; he is not afflicted by any doubts, any uncertainties concerning his actions, which in his view were amply justified by the crime of Priam's son Paris against Menelaus, an insult to the Greeks as a whole; he does not question war, violence or revenge; as victor he is certain that the immortal gods were fully supportive of what he has done, and that he was 'pious' in carrying out his task, which was to doom 'Troy's walls to dust, her men to the sword's edge'. Lemkin lists 'separation of families' under the heading 'Methods and techniques of genocide – Biological': Cassandra the child of Priam and Hecabe has been torn from her home, enslaved, and is to be sexually available for her captor. In terms of those suffering genocide, Lemkin, listing 'Responses of victim group – active', refers to 'submission' and also 'escape (suicide, hiding, etc.)'. Cassandra escapes her captivity by choosing death at the hands of Clytemnestra, in effect suicide; when the chorus asks her why she is entering the palace knowing she will die, Cassandra despairingly tells them that she will submit to the comforting embrace of death. In his outline's final section, 'Aftermath', Lemkin refers to 'cultural losses', and here we can recall that immediately upon his return Agamemnon tells the chorus of his satisfaction in destroying an oriental city, its 'wealth and luxury' now 'dead'.[12]

## PERPETRATOR AND VICTIM CONSCIOUSNESS IN EURIPIDES' *HECABE*: TERROR AND TRAUMA

If female figures in Aeschylus's *Agamemnon* like Clytemnestra and Cassandra stand out in their eloquence, proud bearing and some-times terribleness, especially in seeking revenge, there are also, famously, striking female characters in Euripides' tragedies later in the century, after the Peloponnesian War has begun. *Hecabe* (425 BCE) was produced two years after Mytilene was saved at the last moment from Athenian destruction. In the play, Troy having been conquered and its men and warriors massacred, including Priam, Hecabe experiences unbearable levels of suffering.

We can begin applying Lemkin's categories of analysis to this play by interpreting Hecabe's multiple sufferings as a victim of genocide. Lemkin's outline, under 'Methods and techniques of genocide – Physical', lists 'deprivation of livelihood (starva-tion, exposure, etc. – often by deportation)'; and under 'Methods and techniques of genocide – Biological', there is 'separation of families'. Hecabe, once a great queen, learns she is to be enslaved, having been allotted to Odysseus, one of the commanders supervising and managing the devastation of the city; she is to become a humble and humiliated servant in his household on his return home. In this dramatic situation, enslavement is, then, very much like deportation: Troy's remaining population of women and children is to be transferred, as in ethnic cleansing in modernity, from Troy to cities in Greece. It is a tiny comfort to Hecabe that she and her remaining family members will still be alive even if enslaved, but it turns out not to be quite so, and as news of what is to happen reaches Hecabe, agony is heaped upon agony, shock upon shock, bearing down on her so that on stage she can barely walk, or she lies down or crawls in anguish as she learns of fresh deaths or threats that will mercilessly turn into deaths. Here is genocide as bodily and mental trauma of the victim.[13]

In *Hecabe* Hecabe herself, as her woes multiply, appeals to Agamemnon at one point to see her suffering as if with a painter's eye: 'here you see the face of misery; / Stand back and view it like a painter. Pity me.'[14] Hecabe is suggesting that we can be more moved by art's representations of suffering than by direct witnessing of it. The aestheticizing of suffering and violence is an interesting aspect of the play.

When we first see Hecabe, supported by two younger women, leaning on a stick, she confides her hope that her one remaining son, Polydorus, too young to fight in the war and who has been sent to Thrace to be looked after by a supposedly friendly neighbouring king, is still alive and is being given continued protection; all her other sons have been killed. Hecabe has also just learnt that the ghost of Achilles is demanding 'a maiden's blood in sacrifice', and she desperately hopes that her 'darling daughter Polyxena' will not be chosen. The chorus, however, composed of Trojan women held prisoner by Agamemnon and allotted to various Greek warriors as slaves, as 'spoils of war', have to tell Hecabe that her daughter Polyxena will indeed be sacrificed to Achilles' ghost.

The Greeks, the chorus has heard, had argued over whether she should be sacrificed, with 'two Athenians, the sons of Theseus', distinguishing themselves by insisting that she should be killed, her throat to be cut over Achilles' tomb in the presence of the Greek army. In the event, the matter is decided by Odysseus, a figure who, in contrast to the portrait of Odysseus as wanderer and trickster in the *Odyssey*, is decidedly not admired in *Hecabe*, the chorus referring to him as a 'cunning, honey-tongued quibbler', a 'pleaser of the mob'.[15] In the discussion among the Greeks, the chorus reports, Odysseus urges the army not to 'dishonour the bravest of all the Greeks' for the 'sake of a slave's throat'; to sacrifice Polyxena is, Odysseus tells them, a patriotic duty. It should not be said, he avers, that 'Greeks forget their debts to Greeks', that the Greeks 'came away from the plains of Troy / Neglecting those who died there for our country'. Odysseus' view is agreed to, and he takes it upon himself to request that Hecabe give Polyxena up for sacrifice. When Polyxena and Hecabe learn of the army's decision and that Odysseus is approaching, Polyxena herself tells her mother that she is resigned to die, for that way her life will avoid 'shame and misery' as a slave: in the terms of Lemkin's outline, she chooses escape by death, in effect by suicide.[16]

Odysseus appears and tells Hecabe that he has come to take Polyxena to Achilles' tomb where she will be slain, an act to be overseen and performed by Achilles' son. There follows a remarkable dialogue – anticipating in many ways the Melian Dialogue in Thucydides' *History* – between Odysseus and Hecabe; between genocide perpetrator and victim. Hecabe questions Odysseus on the morality of his actions as if in a courtroom scene. As would the Melians to the Athenians at Melos in Thucydides' later narration, Hecabe attempts to appeal to Odysseus's compassion and humanity, but finds only mercilessness and indifference. Hecabe reminds Odysseus that she had once saved his life, when he had come as a spy into Troy; Helen had recognized him, and told only Hecabe; he had clung to Hecabe's knees as a 'humble suppliant', and 'invented 20 arguments to save' his life. Hecabe had sent him back unharmed from Troy. She suggests to Odysseus that it would be more appropriate to sacrifice a bull to Achilles' tomb, rather than shed a 'child's blood'. She reminds him that in his own 'country's law' killing is killing: no distinction is made between the killing of a slave or a free person, so to do what he is proposing to do to Polyxena would be judged as murder in his society. Hecabe also pleads that she be sacrificed in place of Polyxena. To this last plea, Odysseus's answer is short: 'Achilles asked for your daughter, Hecabe, not you.'[17]

Odysseus' replies to Hecabe are curiously dull and mechanical, to a degree where we can certainly think of Hannah Arendt's description of Eichmann as an impersonal functionary, indifferent to any suffering, banally efficient in his genocidal consciousness. Odysseus in these exchanges with Hecabe and Polyxena, who also makes moving speeches in this scene, emerges as one who has a rational bureaucratic task to perform, to collect Polyxena from her mother and take her to be sacrificed as part of the overall series of actions that are required to organize and complete the destruction of the conquered city. Indeed, at the beginning of their conversation, Odysseus had warned Hecabe that when 'things are worst, it's still wise to be rational'.[18]

Powerless to prevent her daughter's death, Hecabe exclaims: 'O gods! How wretched is the condition of a slave, / Forced to endure the wickedness of conquerors!' Odysseus' banality of evil can be understood as also part of the general ethical deterioration in those who conquer that Arendt talked of in *The Origins of Totalitarianism*, referred to in previous chapters. Such ethical deterioration – what Lemkin in his outline lists under the heading 'The Genocidists' as 'demoralization', and under the final heading 'Aftermath' as 'moral deterioration' – is evident here in the Greeks engaging in human sacrifice, with Achilles' son enjoining that his dead father in his tomb 'drink this maid's dark untainted blood', as an offering of the 'whole army'. The assembled 'whole army' observes the scene of Polyxena's death with keen interest, as if it is occurring on stage, a spectacle to be savoured and remembered. As Achilles' son is about to cut her throat, Polyxena tears her dress to her waist, 'and showed her breasts, and all / Her body to the navel, like the loveliest / of statues'. Polyxena dies, taking care to fall becomingly, 'hiding what should be hidden from men's view'. The assembled Greeks feel exalted by the once noble Polyxena's honourable and almost erotic death, in a kind of pornography of violence reminding us of the carnivalesque and ecstatic perpetrator enjoyment of killing in group situations that Dan Stone has commented on.[19] The young princess Polyxena has been delivered to her aestheticized public death by Odysseus' unmoved and indifferent, bureaucratic and impersonal, banal perpetrator consciousness.[20]

Hecabe's sufferings, though she already feels that no woman could suffer more, that she has already died ('of all women I am the most miserable'), have not come to an end. Now occurs in the drama a kind of peripeteia, a turning point, when Hecabe goes from suffering victim to a victim seeking revenge, initially against Helen. One suggestion Hecabe makes to Odysseus is that Helen, not Polyxena, be sacrificed to Achilles, for hadn't Achilles come to Troy and lost his life because of Helen? (The chorus of enslaved Trojan women also call down a curse on Helen and hope that she will be drowned on her way back from Troy to Hellas.) Then Hecabe learns from an attendant that her youngest son, Polydorus, is no longer alive. Hecabe can now understand a dreadful dream she has had, that her son has been killed by the Thracian king Polymestor whom Priam had thought a friend. The Thracian king, to whom Priam secretly sent his son for protection, has in fact taken advantage of the siege of Troy to kill Polydorus, cast his body into the sea and purloin Priam's gold. In terms of Lemkin's categories, under the heading 'Responses of outside groups' with its further categories 'collaboration' and 'demoralization (exploitation of genocide situation)', the neighbouring Thracian king has cynically taken advantage of the destruction of Troy to collaborate in the genocide for his own benefit. Hecabe now asks permission from Agamemnon to enact 'vengeance on a murderer', on the Thracian king, and from this point on in the play sympathy ebbs away from her, as she undergoes in Lemkin and Arendt's terms an ethical deterioration. With Agamemnon's permission and connivance, Polymestor is lured to Troy, where Hecabe and her women stab and blind him and kill his two sons with their brooches. Enraged and stumbling about, Polymestor swears there are no monsters like women on the earth, only to be rebuked by the chorus: 'Because you suffer, why should you so arrogantly / Include all women in one general reproach?'[21]

In his turn, Polymestor warns Hecabe that the Thracian prophet Dionysus has told him that Hecabe will not reach Greece by ship. She will fall headlong into the sea from a masthead, then be transformed into 'a dog with glaring tawny eyes', thence to die and be buried at 'Cynossema, the Dog's Grave', as a sign for passing sailors. Hecabe replies that she does not care, for she has been 'avenged'. Polymestor then adds that the Thracian prophet has foreseen that both Agamemnon and Cassandra will die when they return to Argos, at the hands of Agamemnon's wife, raising her axe on high. Neither Hecabe nor Agamemnon believe Polymestor, Agamemnon in his closing speech hoping now that Heaven will grant the Greeks a 'prosperous voyage, and peace and happiness at home'.[22] In his perpetrator consciousness, Agamemnon, his genocidal destruction of Troy completed, cannot believe he himself could now be subjected to murderous violence.

As a perpetrator of the violence of revenge, Hecabe, feeling that justice has been met in the blinding of Polymestor and the death of his sons, also cannot believe the cycles of revenge will continue, that Cassandra will be murdered in Argos. Indeed, the chorus, just before Polymestor is blinded and his sons killed by Hecabe and the Trojan women, confidently declare that once Justice is done, the cycles of revenge and violence end:

> There is a debt to Justice, and a debt to the gods;
> Where these two coincide,
> The payment is final and complete.[23]

Yet in pursuing violent revenge, Hecabe has done what Lemkin in his manuscript history more generally evokes, become an example of how often in history the formerly persecuted can become cruel and brutal persecutors themselves.[24] And, Gandhi would have added, such will always lead to further violence.[25] Recall also the opening stories in Herodotus's *Histories* where violence and revenge leading to further violence is created as unending.[26]

## *ANDROMACHE*: THE SLAVE AS THE STRANGER WHO DISTURBS

In his outline, Lemkin includes under 'Responses of victim group' a variety of possibilities that include 'submission', 'escape' by 'suicide', and 'terror'. In *Hecabe*, the leader of the chorus of Trojan women about to be enslaved, cries out in anguish:

> Oh, my children, my children!
> My poor father! My country!
> Every house a smouldering ruin,
> Every soul a prisoner,
> Spoils of war for the men of Argos!
> And I, in a foreign country,
> Bearing the name of slave,
> Transplanted far from Asia
> Into a European home,
> Shall live the life of the dead in Hades.[27]

In Greece, in Europe, the enslaved Trojan women fear they will be the living dead, the undead, ever demoralized, existing in a kind of terror of nothingness, of loss of identity, status, bodily integrity, culture and respect.

Euripides' *Andromache*, its date uncertain, somewhere between 430 and 424 BCE, concerns the enslaved life of one of these Trojan women, wife of the great Trojan warrior Hector, son of Hecabe and Priam. Hector had been slain by Achilles, and now his widow Andromache is allotted to Achilles' son Neop-tolemus. Andromache is taken to Greece, where she becomes the concubine of Neoptolemus and has a son, Molossus, by him. Her position worsens when she becomes the slave and servant of Hermione after Hermione and Neoptolemus marry; Hermione is the daughter of Helen and Menelaus. We do not see Helen in *Andromache*, but we do see quite a lot of Menelaus, who is created in the play as unworthy and despicable. The play opens with Andromache reporting that Hermione, fearful of her slave as competitor for her husband's attentions, is threatening to kill her, with the assistance of Menelaus who has come from Sparta for this purpose, Neoptolemus being away at Delphi (where we later learn he has been killed by Orestes). To save her life and the life of her son, Andromache has come as a supplicant seeking sanctuary to the nearby shrine of Thetis the immortal sea-nymph, at the same time sending Molossus into hiding, though he will be found by Menelaus; as with Hecabe, her situation becomes ever more dire.[28]

During the play Andromache recounts her sufferings in Troy, her evocation bringing to mind Lemkin's category of 'deportation' under the heading 'Method and techniques of genocide – Physical':

> I saw Troy crumble in the pitiless flames. Men held
> Me by the hair, and hauled me to the Argive ships.
> When I came here, it was to live as concubine
> To the man whose father killed my husband.[29]

She recalls that she wore about her head the 'hateful hood of slavery' as she went with the other women to the 'crowded shore' ready to be deported. In Greece, 'my city gone, / Hector my husband dead', Andromache feels that her 'griefs' clamour for unending lamentation, her life 'harsh and joyless', an existence to be dragged out amidst unceasing tears. Now in fear of her life, her only desperate hope is that the goddess Thetis might hear and help her.[30]

Yet while Andromache like Hecabe experiences extremes of terror and trauma, she strikingly reveals a victim response to genocide identified by Lemkin under the heading 'Responses of victim group – active': 'resistance'. In *Andromache* we see figured a different kind of consciousness for women deported as slaves to be concubines and servants. Yet how can she resist? Addressing her, the chorus of local women, though Greek while 'you are an Asiatic', express sympathy for her plight; nevertheless they also feel that her attempt at revolt against her situation by taking refuge at Thetis' shrine is hopeless. Andromache should realize that she is 'nothing', that as a slave from Troy she belongs to Hermione, who is a Spartan princess. How, they ask, can 'you fight against her?'[31]

Here we can think of the brilliant early twentieth-century essay 'The Stranger' by the German sociologist Georg Simmel. The stranger, Simmel writes, is the wanderer who comes today and stays tomorrow; while s/he belongs to a spatially defined group, s/he always remains a potential wanderer. The stranger exhibits towards the group a kind of abstraction, a detachment, which is not to be confused with passivity. Such detachment gives him or her a kind of freedom, in terms of perception, understanding and evaluation of what others in the group take as given. Simmel offers as an example the trader in history, and he also cites European Jews as a classical instance.[32] Leopold Paula Bloom, wandering in Dublin in James Joyce's *Ulysses*, is a kind of embodiment of Simmel's stranger.[33] We could also think of the character of Rebecca in Sir Walter Scott's *Ivanhoe* (1819), spirited, learned and wise, a trader along with her father Isaac; Rebecca as representative of the Jewish–Muslim–Christian social, intellectual, cultural and trading world of the medieval Middle East, North Africa and Moorish Spain. In *Ivanhoe*, Rebecca disturbs the Saxon–Norman convergence of English national identity of late twelfth-century England; a convergence that excludes her as an oriental stranger and nearly leads to her being burned to death as a witch.[34] The life of the stranger can be precarious, threatened by violence, as it is for both Bloom and Rebecca.[35]

In the drama of *Andromache*, Andromache is a high-born slave brought by force from Troy, yet in her 'Asiatic' difference and her eloquence, dignity and powerful rationality she disturbs and challenges the mundane Orientalist assumptions and values of those who oppress and wish to kill her, Hermione and her father Menelaus. When Hermione appears at the shrine, she immediately launches into a volley of insults, in a language of almost grotesque ethnic hatred:

> As for you – a slave-woman, a prize of war –
> You want to own this place; to get rid of me;
> Your witchcraft makes my husband hate me; for your gain
> My womb is barren, dead. You oriental women
> Are expert in such devilry – but I'll stop you.
> You'll find no help in Thetis, neither temple nor
> Altar will save you; you shall die.[36]

In Lemkin's outline, in the category 'Propaganda – rationalization of crime', there is mention of 'appeal to popular beliefs and intolerance'. It is in this spirit that Hermione continues her verbal assault: 'You Orientals are all alike', practising incest between father and daughter, brother and sister, mother and son; oriental law countenances murder; in such 'foreign morals', polygamy is acceptable. Andromache will have to cast off her 'queenly airs' and learn to bow low, kneel humbly to her mistress and sweep the floors. During this confrontation, this agon, Andromache refuses to submit: 'No one shall say that I don't stand up for my rights'; she demolishes Hermione's arguments and replies to all her fears. In particular, she scorns Hermione's claims to possess a supposedly exclusive Greek and European quality of being 'self-controlled'. It is Hermione, says Andromache, who lacks 'common intelligence'. Hermione's threats become hysterically violent: 'I'll scar your flesh, I'll mangle you and torture you'; Andromache is a 'brazen foreign beast'.[37]

Menelaus meanwhile has found where Andromache's son Molossus has been hidden, and now tells Andromache that unless she leaves the sanctuary, 'This child's throat shall be cut instead of yours.'[38] How contemptible Menelaus is in *Andromache*! In their agon, Andromache easily proves superior to the Spartan king in wisdom, insight, perceptiveness and humanity, her speeches to him a riposte to the Orientalist view that Orientals lack reason and self-control. Not that Andromache conceals her contempt for Menelaus and his daughter:

> You! Did a coward like you lead the picked fighting-men
> Of Hellas against Priam to conquer Troy? And has
> Your childish daughter talked such spirit into you
> That you dare challenge a defenceless slave-woman?[39]

Andromache then says to Menelaus, 'come now – let us reason the matter out,' and as with Hermione, she demolishes all his attempts at argument. The chorus of Greek women, however, are scandalized by what they see as an unacceptable overturning of the established Greek gender order: 'You have said more than a woman ought to say to a man,'[40] recalling Agamemnon's similar attempt to reprove and silence Clytemnestra in Aeschylus's play.

The character of Andromache here in relation to Menelaus, woman to man, slave to king, intersects with a long cultural history of World Upside Down, of the kind Natalie Zemon Davis refers to in her famous essay 'Women on Top' about male–female inversion in carnival, festive practices and pictorial representation in early modern Europe. Davis offers as an example the medieval affection for a story from antiquity involving Alexander, the old philosopher Aristotle and Phyllis, one of Alexander's new subjects in India, who persuades Aristotle before Alexander's eyes to get down on all fours and, saddled and bridled, carry her round the garden.[41]

In their agon, Andromache accuses Menelaus of cruelty, murderousness, deceit and treachery: 'And this, with Spartans, passes for intelligence?'[42]

As it turns out, Andromache and her son's lives are saved by the intervention of Peleus, Achilles' father and Neoptolemus' grandfather, who shares her disdain for Menelaus as 'contemptible'. Menelaus retreats from the angry old man and leaves the scene; Hermione breaks down in fear of the return of her husband, revealing the lack of reason and excess of emotion she has ascribed to oriental women. When, however, Peleus learns that Neoptolemus has been killed by Orestes, he feels his life is over, he now has lost both his son and grandson. Peleus is rescued from despair by Thetis the sea-nymph, the goddess who had formerly been his wife, and who now promises to accept him again as her husband and make him into a god. The goddess also foretells a fortunate fate for Andromache, who will become the 'lawful wife' of Helenus, while her son Molossus will beget a prosperous dynasty of kings ruling over the land of Molassia to which they are now headed. At the play's end, Thetis reflects that even though the goddess Pallas (Athene) had demanded the fall of Troy, the gods overall have not entirely abandoned the Trojans: 'even to Troy the gods extend their kindly care.'[43]

Through the opinions of various characters, *Andromache* ponders the perennial question of who is to blame for the Trojan War. Andromache, like Hecabe and the other Trojan women, is sure that Helen is to blame, for when Paris brought Helen back to 'share his home and bed', the Fury of revenge followed: 'For Helen Greece vowed vengeance'; it was because of Helen that in the subsequent war Greeks like Achilles and Trojans like Hector died, Andromache saying to Hermione: 'Helen killed Achilles.' In his agon with Menelaus, Peleus offers a different view. Peleus charges that both Helen and Menelaus are at fault, are the prime causes of the war, though the more he expostulates, the more it is Menelaus whom he sees as primarily responsible. Helen, Peleus froths, is more wicked than any woman who ever lived, though such wickedness is owing, he adds, to her disgusting Spartan upbringing, for Spartan girls never grow up modest, they never stay at home, they go out with 'bare thighs and loose clothes' and they 'wrestle and run races' alongside the young men. 'I call it intolerable,' says Peleus.[44]

It is no surprise, then, in Peleus' scornful opinion that with such an immodest girlhood Helen should gad off with her young man to foreign parts, abandoning her home and 'all sacred ties'. Peleus tells Menelaus that he was a fool to have been away from his house while Paris was visiting, and it is no wonder he was cuckolded. Yet knowing the kind of loose Spartan woman Helen was, Menelaus should not have declared war on the Trojans, he should not have 'stirred a single spear for her'; rather he should have let Helen stay in Troy, indeed he should have paid her money never to ask to be taken back. Menelaus, then, for no good reason sent 'brave men by their thousands to their deaths', including Achilles. It is Menelaus who is responsible for the sadness of so many old men and women in Greece, now childless. To cap it all, Peleus charges, Menelaus, when he did conquer Troy, showed himself to be an amorous weakling; instead of immediately killing Helen, she 'had only to bare her breast' and Menelaus threw down his sword and accepted her back. Unsurprisingly, Menelaus's view of why the war began differs. He cannot, he says, blame Helen for leaving him, because what she did occurred by 'divine volition, not from her own choice'. In any case, by being a cause for war, Helen conferred great benefits on Hellas, for formerly, he feels, weapons and fighting were unknown to the Greeks; the war brought out their 'manly qualities' and also brought 'different kinds of Greeks together'. As for not killing Helen as soon as he set eyes on her, that, he tells Peleus, was simply admirable 'self-control'.[45]

Menelaus's reference to Helen being somehow divinely guided in her leaving him for Paris brings to the fore the question of the gods and how much they influence human actions, in particular, the possibility that responsibility for the war lay ultimately with the Judgement of Paris, involving the goddesses Hera, Athena and Aphrodite. The chorus laments what occurred when the 'three lovely goddesses' visited Paris, then a young shepherd, on Mount Ida, each wishing to be judged by him the most beautiful. Paris chooses Aphrodite (her reward being that he would love the world's most beautiful woman), so setting in motion the sequence of events – Paris finding Helen in Sparta and leaving with her for Troy – that caused the war. Here, then, in the divine interference of the three goddesses, might be the primary cause for the Trojan War that doomed Troy and its people to eventual destruction and ruin.[46] Certainly Cassandra thought so, as the chorus recalls. Foreseeing all that would later happen if Paris when small remained alive, Cassandra had pleaded with every elder and councillor in Troy, 'Kill that child!', 'Kill him!'[47] But Cassandra was never listened to.


## WAR, GENOCIDE AND FEMALE AND CHILD SUFFERING: *THE WOMEN OF TROY*

Euripides' *The Women of Troy* (415 BCE) was performed when memory of the Athenian destruction of Melos (416–415 BCE) during the Peloponnesian War, with the killing of all the male inhabitants of military age and enslaving of the women and children, would still have been vivid. Set in the ruins of Troy, two days after the city's capture, the play revisits the misery of Hecabe and her daughter Cassandra and daughter-in-law Andromache, and once more we will analyse their sufferings and responses in terms of Lemkin's outline. New and horrific details are added to what we earlier know from Hecabe and Andromache, in particular, what the victorious Greeks decide to do with Astyanax, Andromache's infant son from her marriage with Hector. Early in the play, Andromache knows that, humiliatingly, she will be taken to Greece as the slave of Achilles' son, but she does not yet know what will be the fate of her small child. When Talthybius the Greek herald approaches, he tells Andromache that he has terrible news for her. Andromache wonders if the news concerns herself and her son, that they will be 'assigned to different masters': recall the category in Lemkin's diagram, under the heading 'Methods and techniques of genocide – Biological', of 'separation of families', here child from mother. Later in the play, the chorus of captive Trojan women evoke the scene at Troy's gates, where the Trojan 'children / Cling and cry by hundreds', calling out for their mothers.[48] Hundreds of mothers and children, it would appear, are to be separately enslaved.

The herald, however, confesses that he can barely bring himself to say what his news is.

Andromache: At least you show some scruple, if you bring no joy.
Talthybius: Then know the worst: the Greeks are going to kill your son.
Andromache: Oh, no, no! This is worse than what they do to me.
Talthybius: Odysseus in a full assembly made his point –
Andromache: But this is horrible beyond all measure! Oh!
Talthybius: That such a great man's son must not be allowed to live –
Andromache: By such a sentence may his own son be condemned!
Talthybius: But should be thrown down from the battlements of Troy.[49]

Talthybius advises Andromache to be 'sensible' and accept the decision. When Andromache looks at her crying child clinging to her fingers and tugging at her dress, about to be thrown on Odysseus' advice from the city walls, we might think here of Lemkin's category, under the same heading referring to biological genocide, of 'destruction of foetus'. With justice does Andromache cry out against such child sacrifice as a 'Greek ritual of murder': 'Hellenes! Inventors of barbaric cruelties!'[50]

Hecabe's bodily and mental trauma is once more featured in *The Women of Troy*; indeed we are first made aware of Hecabe lying on the stage as, in the words of the god Poseidon, once the chief god of Troy, a 'prostrate figure', pitiable, 'drowned in tears / For a world of sorrows'. When Hecabe learns of what is to happen to her grandson, she calls the Greeks 'murderers' and wonders if the Trojan women like Andromache and herself have reached the 'abyss of pain'. The death of the child intensifies Hecabe's torment and desolation close to madness. Cassandra in *The Women of Troy* does go to the edge of madness, singing and dancing in so demented a way (reminding us perhaps of Ophelia in *Hamlet*) that the chorus pleads with her mother: 'Queen Hecabe, she is out of her mind.'[51] Genocide is here entwined with the possibility of psychological damage of an extreme kind.

Helen makes an appearance in *The Women of Troy*, excoriated by the Trojan women, who seek revenge on her, desiring that she be killed immediately by Menelaus, again reminding us of Lemkin's categories of 'demoralization' and 'moral deterioration' in victims of genocide. The play, however, takes an almost comic turn with the entry of Menelaus, created as a buffoon, blustering that he will kill Helen either on the spot or after he has taken her back to Hellas; he orders his soldiers to drag her out by the hair, the 'bloodthirsty murderess', she will pay with her blood for all his friends who have died at Troy. Hecabe applauds his plan to kill Helen. But when Helen appears with the soldiers, her calm, dignity and steady reasoning puncture Menelaus's risible threats. Helen argues that she did not cause the war, for a number of reasons. Priam, she says, echoing Cassandra, should have heeded the prophecy about her and Paris and killed Paris at birth. When, because of the goddess Aphrodite, Paris sought out Helen famed for her beauty, Menelaus sailed off to Crete leaving her alone with Paris; she had then fallen in love with Paris, finding love an irresistible force, just as Zeus, she reminds her former husband, had on occasion found love irresistible. Finally, she makes it clear that she did try to leave Troy and rejoin the Greek ships so that the war could end, but had been thwarted by Paris's brother Deiphobus (this was after Paris's death), who took her 'by force' and kept her as his wife.[52]

The plea of Hecabe and the chorus that Helen be killed instantly, in the interest of 'noble vengeance', is ignored by Menelaus, who insists, convincing no one, that he will certainly kill Helen, perhaps by stoning, when they have returned to Sparta.[53]

If Menelaus is a weak, clownish figure in *The Women of Troy*, the portrait of another genocidist, Odysseus, is chilling, as it had been in *Hecabe*. The herald Talthybius reports that it was Odysseus who persuaded the full Greek assembly that Andromache's child has to be disposed of, because as Hector's son he might one day become powerful. As in *Hecabe*, Odysseus is glimpsed in *The Women of Troy* as Eichmann-like in the passionless banality of his evil, rationally taking care of every necessary detail of the genocide. When Hecabe learns that she has been assigned as a slave to Odysseus, to be taken to Ithaca to become servant to Penelope, she expresses her contempt for him as a 'perjured impious outcast, who defies / Man's law and God's'. In her lamentation speech over her little grandson's body, she condemns Odysseus as a 'cunning coward'. Soon after Hecabe attempts suicide: 'Now! Into the fire! There is a royal way to die – / Wrapped in the flame that swallows my beloved city!' Hecabe is saved, however, by the Greek soldiers, because she must be kept alive as 'prize' for Odysseus, to whom she now 'belongs'.[54]

At play's end, we are left with images of the final destruction of Troy and its imminent disappearance from the world.

Hecabe:  Dust mingled with smoke wings to the sky,
          I can see nothing, the world is blotted out!
Chorus:  Earth and her name are nothing;
          All has vanished, and Troy is nothing![55]

Here are images that will haunt all subsequent world history, the genocidal spectre that what happened to Troy could happen to any other city, society, country, land, people.


## CONCLUSION

In these great tragedies, from Aeschylus's *Agamemnon* earlier in the fifth century to the Euripides plays during the Peloponnesian War, the Greeks who destroyed Troy were, in Lemkin's terms, guilty of genocide on all counts. In relation to Lemkin's category in his outline of 'Aftermath – cultural losses', the devastation of Troy clearly answers to the technique of cultural genocide, of the desecration and destruction of cultural centres and symbols (objects of art, religious relics, etc.); destruction of cultural leadership; and prohibition of cultural activities or codes of behaviour. Loss of culture occurs during looting, for Lemkin lists 'loot' under

'Methods and techniques of genocide – Cultural'; Poseidon at the beginning of the play observes the measureless gold 'and all the loot of Troy' that is going down to the Greek ships.[56] Loss of culture would also apply to the children sent away from Troy to be enslaved, and such taking away would be considered a crime under Article II of the 1948 UN Genocide Convention, which condemns: 'Forcibly transferring children of the group to another group'.[57] The enslaved children would inevitably be assimilated into the host society into which they would be sold.

Near the end of *The Women of Troy* the chorus laments the loss of their beloved city. No longer will there be:

> Music of prayer, sweet singing, mystic nights
> Of darkness and of vision, the dear forms
> Of golden gods we knew …

Nor will they ever again be able to see its beautiful surroundings, including Mount Ida where 'steep snow-swollen rivers foam and fall / Through ivied forest glades'.[58] In Lemkin's terms, the destruction of Troy represents a genocidal disappearance of one of the world's cultures, a permanent loss to humanity, a narrowing of its heritage, an assault on humanity itself.

The tragedies raise the question of religious genocide. What is the attitude of the gods towards the way Troy is destroyed? Are the gods on the side of the apparent victors in history, the genocidists Agamemnon and Menelaus and Odysseus, or of the victims of the genocide, the women and children, some but not all of whom survive? In *The Women of Troy* Andromache is sure the gods have been against the Trojans ever since Paris was spared at birth 'to live and destroy his country / For the sake of accursed Helen'. Near the end of the play, facing catastrophe, the chorus concludes: 'So, Zeus, our God, you have forsaken us,' and they demand of him, as the 'Monarch of all that lives', that he answer their challenge, 'What does this mean to You?'[59] At the play's end, as Troy burns in a holocaustal fire, Hecabe finally loses her lingering faith that the gods will save her:

> Gods! Gods! Where are you? – Why should I clamour to
> the gods?
> We called on them before, and not one heard us call.[60]

Yet, unbeknownst to the women, the play in its overall movement makes it clear that the gods have not entirely abandoned
the Trojans. *The Women of Troy* opens with Poseidon sorrowing
for what is happening to Troy, as he watches it being stripped,
sacked and left smouldering. 'Troy and its people', he laments,
'were my city.' He acknowledges his defeat by Athene, with
whom he has feuded in the past, and who had planned the
Wooden Horse ruse, so he is surprised when the goddess appears
and seeks his help on 'behalf of Troy'. Athene admits that she
had once hated the Trojans and had helped the Greeks to win, but
now confides that she is 'disposed to favour the Trojans'. When
Poseidon asks why her change of heart, Athene replies that she
is appalled by the Greeks' impiety, not least their insult to her
own temple, when Cassandra was dragged from its sanctuary.
Athene's new plan, she tells him, is to make their homeward
voyage by sea disastrous for the Greeks. Zeus, she says, has
already agreed to visit upon the Greek ships flooding rain, inces-
sant hail and tornadoes; she asks Poseidon to assist by stirring up
the sea with waves and whirlpools, so that the ocean becomes
thick with floating corpses and the 'Greeks may learn in future /
To respect my altars and show humility before the gods'. Poseidon readily agrees, for he too, he tells her, feels that punishment
should attend those who, during the general destruction of a city,
devastate the temples of the 'high gods and tombs that honour
the dead'.[61]

The audience knows, and we in the future know, that in the
mythological stories the Greek ships are scattered by the actions
of the gods with many becoming lost for long periods on the
return voyage. In *Helen*, when Menelaus appears as a 'wretched
castaway' washed up on the shores of Egypt, he explains that for
years he has been an 'unhappy wanderer upon the stormy wastes
of the grey ocean': 'I long to reach my own country; but the

[ 87 ]

gods have not thought me worthy.' He tells Helen that since Troy he has been voyaging 'seven summers and seven winters'.[62] In the many stories in the ancient Greek world of the post-Troy dispersal of their fleet, the gods can be witnessed severely punishing the Greeks for their religious genocide of the Trojans, as a warning to all those who might wish to do the same.

# 4 UTOPIA AND DYSTOPIA: PLATO AND CICERO'S *REPUBLICS*

Your advantages are the disadvantages of others. Hence building an empire involves expropriating other people's territory and enriching yourself at their expense. Aggressive generals are held to be the embodiment of valour and excellence. Teachers of philosophy give the cloak of tradition and authority to folly and crime.

> (Philus in Cicero, *The Republic*, Book Three)[1]

Now the earth itself seemed so small to me that I felt ashamed of our empire, whose extent was no more than a dot on its surface.

> ('The Dream of Scipio' in Cicero, *The Republic*, Book Six)[2]

Classical Athenian culture bequeathed a dual, uncertain and ambivalent legacy in relation to war, conquest, empire, colonization and Orientalism.

On the one hand, as we can see in Pericles' speeches to Athenian assemblies evoked in Thucydides' *History of the Peloponnesian War,* and as Sophie Mills has outlined in *Theseus, Tragedy and the Athenian Empire* (1997), Athens enjoyed an idealized self-image. Athens was to be historically wondered at as an example to humanity, for it was the city of justice and mercy, opposing all forms of tyranny, a civilizer and liberator.

In the view of Periclean Athens, there was a positive and productive relationship between democracy and war, because Athenian military might was always used in the service of enlightened values, of loyalty to friends and selfless intervention in defence of the weak and the vulnerable. Furthermore, in regarding Theseus as its mythological hero, Athens could claim a degree of divine support for its military actions and altruistic ethos which, as in the remarkable feats of Theseus himself, combined strength and skill with intelligence and wisdom.[3] In this seductive self-image, Athens was always honourable in its conduct of war and as a creator and builder of empire. Athenians felt they had the right to be supersessionist (they would educate Greece to be like them and they would represent Greece for the future, superseding as inferior all other Greek societies), and to believe (because of Theseus' semi-divine ancestry) that they were a chosen people blessed by gods.

Yet such self-admiration was shadowed by powerful questioning and contrary images and representations, not least in historiography and tragedy, as we have noted in previous chapters. Herodotus and Thucydides' histories, as well as Athenian tragedy concerned with the genocidal destruction of 'Asiatic' Troy, allegorically challenged those in the Athenian present as well as those in the future of the West who would wish to endorse empire and colonialism as a historical project. Part of the classical legacy, too, was a fear that empire is always insecure: the Persians could be defeated by a much smaller force of Greeks, the Athenians would lose their empire after defeat in the Peloponnesian War. Furthermore, there was always the danger that empire could lead to a marked ethical deterioration in those who conducted its policies. In view of Herodotus and Thucydides' cosmopolitanism, anti-ethnocentrism and internationalism, and the powerful denunciations of and protests at empire, colonization and genocidal destruction in their histories and in Euripides' Trojan plays, how could empire, colonization and destruction of other societies continue to be unproblematically promoted by those trained in the Greek classical tradition? In Thucydides' *History*, the Melians warned that the Athenians would

be judged harshly in history for their desire for war and their imperial amorality; they would suffer an eternal loss of historical prestige.[4] How could such judgments and passionate reflections be
avoided by those who nonetheless wished to participate in, establish
and justify empires and found colonies?

Such a legacy of doubt, of foundationally conflicted
thought, of competing perspectives, has haunted Western history
to the present. Most immediately, it would haunt the Roman
world, which was so profoundly influenced by and in constant
conversation with Greek philosophy and culture.

In this and following chapters, I discuss attitudes and values in
relation to empire, conquest, war, colonization and Orientalism in
some famous texts of Greco-Roman antiquity, in political philosophy, epic, and historical writing: *The Republic* of Cicero (106–43
BCE), the *Aeneid* of Virgil (70–19 BCE), and the *Agricola* and
*Germania* of Tacitus (c.56–117 CE). I choose these texts because
their attempts to negotiate the troubling legacy of classical Greek
thought, pro-war and anti-war, pro-empire and critical of empire,
were so important in subsequent thinking about colonization and
empire in early modern Europe and later Western history, in ways
that are still salient, of continuing and contemporary significance.

The questions I explore are: given the challenge posed by
Herodotus and Thucydides and Greek tragedy set in the mythological era to those who favour colonization and empire, how could
one be a honourable colonizer? Can one be a honourable colonizer? Do empires and colonizers bring death and dispossession
and destruction, or are they admirable bringers of culture and law?
Do they genocidally destroy the cosmos of other peoples, or do
they include other peoples in an overarching cosmos that is
divinely approved? Do they act according to natural law that is
universal and applies to all humanity and which all humanity
should observe, or does a claim to universal natural law always
work in favour of specific interests, that is to say, the powerful
states and nations?

There are immediate differences in historical situation
between the two great Greek historians in particular and these

Roman writers. Herodotus was an outsider to any settled ethnic and national identity in the Greek world, while Thucydides was exiled from Athens for much of the Peloponnesian War; they were accused in later antiquity of being too harsh towards Greeks in general (Herodotus) and Athens in particular (Thucydides).[5] Cicero, Virgil and Tacitus were in varying ways much closer to the centre of their society, though in an imperial Roman state where times were always dangerous. My focus, however, will be on the texts themselves. In deploying the critical and cultural theory of modernity, especially of Mikhail Bakhtin as I outlined in the Introduction, as well as Walter Benjamin, I explore the play of genre, textual tensions, ambivalences, unresolved differences in attitudes and viewpoints, singularities, oddities, extremes. Such constitute their legacy to the future, not presumed essentialized intellectual positions held by 'Cicero', 'Virgil' and 'Tacitus'.

The *Nachleben*, the afterlife, of the classical Greek and Greco-Roman writings are far more complicated and contradictory, and far more interesting, than such sterile intellectual history can allow.

One more introductory note: while the focus in this chapter is on the Greco-Roman world, I will be including some comparative discussion of Greco-Roman texts and Jewish and Christian religious histories. Greco-Roman polytheistic, and Jewish and Christian monotheistic, histories increasingly intersected in the ancient world; and concepts and historical processes that I am arguing throughout this book are important in world history, in particular genocide, supersessionism, victimology, chosen people and culture-bearers can be perceived crossing the monotheism–polytheism divide. In these terms, I will be comparing aspects of the relationship between the Old Testament and the New Testament to features of Cicero's *Republic*.

## PLATO

Cicero was an important political and intellectual figure in Roman history during the collapsing world of republican politics, as a barrister, orator, high official (holding the consulate among other offices), political philosopher and writer; he was well travelled and profoundly versed in and familiar with Greek learning, including as a student of philosophy and rhetoric in Athens and Rhodes. *The Republic* is clearly in intimate conversation with Plato's *Republic*, both being concerned with the nature of political wisdom and the ideal character of the state, and sharing aesthetic features of literature as philosophy, philosophy as literature. Each proceeds by question and rejoinder between a number of interlocutors. Yet such conversations relate to wider cultural histories, of genre and carnivalesque. To understand aesthetic and rhetorical features of Cicero's *Republic*, we have to have some sense of Plato's *Republic* and how its generic features relate to and contrast with other Plato texts, especially *The Symposium*.

Bakhtin's comments in his *Problems of Dostoevsky's Poetics* on the serio-comic literary-philosophical genres of antiquity such as the Socratic dialogue, the symposium and the menippea, which infuse, help shape and interact in both Plato's and Cicero's *Republics*, are illuminating here.[6] Bakhtin regards the Socratic dialogues as a genre of great vitality in literary, cultural and philosophical history. As he explains in *Problems of Dostoevsky's Poetics*, which seeks to evoke the long and rich generic history that informs the polyphonic novel and finds a summit in Dostoevsky, the genre of the Socratic dialogue grew out of carnivalistic folklore, with a dialogic method of investigating ideas and searching for truth. In the Socratic dialogue, says Bakhtin, an idea is organically combined with the image of a person, the carrier of the idea; the person in the text, the character, becomes in effect an image of the idea. In these terms, Bakhtin admires Plato's Socratic dialogues, where truth is not ready-made but is born between people as they collectively search for it. Socrates, says Bakhtin, called himself a pander, someone who brought people together and made them collide in a quarrel; Socrates also referred to himself as a midwife, assisting in the birth of an emergent truth.[7]

Nevertheless, Bakhtin distinguishes between Plato dialogues featuring Socrates as pander and midwife, and other Plato dialogues where Socrates has become a monologic teacher. Here the Socratic dialogue reduces itself, Bakhtin laments, to a simple mode for expounding ready-made truths, ultimately degenerating into a question and answer form similar to a catechism, in danger of losing all connection with a carnival sense of the world.[8]

In such Bakhtinian terms, we can say that in Plato texts like *The Symposium* Socrates is created as but one character amongst others putting forward theories. A brilliant dialogic philosophical and historical novel (written early in the fourth century but set in 416 BCE), *The Symposium* explores the meaning of love. Its scene is one of after-dinner relaxation between (male) friends and acquaintances, including Aristophanes as well as Socrates, where the entertainment is the art of conversation itself. In *Problems of Dostoevsky's Poetics*, Bakhtin observes that the symposium is a banquet dialogue:

> Dialogic banquet discourse possessed special privileges (originally of a cultic sort): the right to a certain license, ease and familiarity, to a certain frankness, to eccentricity, ambivalence; that is, the combination in one discourse of praise and abuse, of the serious and the comic. The symposium is by nature a purely carnivalistic genre.[9]

In *The Symposium* multiple representations of love glance off each other as in a kaleidoscope, ranging from Aristophanes' fascinating burlesque images, a highlight of the novel, to mystical interpretations of homosexual desire and love in Socrates' contribution to the discussion, highly curious in its mode. Walter Benjamin, talking in the prologue to *The Origins of German Tragic Drama* of the kind of philosophical history that he preferred, wrote of its critical method that the representation of ideas should move sideways, should constitute itself as digression (*Darstellung als Umweg*), and such is a feature of Socrates' elliptical procedure in *The Symposium*.[10] When asked for his opinion by his companions, Socrates doesn't answer directly but instead recounts a conversation he once had with a female philosopher, Diotima, 'the woman from Mantinea', who taught him, he says, his method of proceeding by question and answer; she was also, he confides, 'my instructress in the art of love'. Socrates then relates to his listeners a long question and answer session with Diotima where she treats him at times quite roughly for his philosophical ignorance and inadequacy while leading him to see the sacredness that ideally inheres in the desire for beauty, goodness and truth. What features in their exchange, as happily reported by Socrates himself, are male–female inversions of knowledge, wisdom and rigour of argumentation.[11]

In terms of Bakhtin's contrast, however, between dialogic and monologic Plato texts, in Plato's *Republic* Socrates is far more the acknowledged authority in the conversation, explaining, explicating, expounding, the text's node of truth. With Socrates too much in control, the question and answer sessions are close to catechism, his interlocutors reduced to passivity, assenting to whatever he as master thinker declares to be so.

Nevertheless, Plato's *Republic* presented world history with a most remarkable utopia, always challenging and certainly influential. *The Republic* explores questions of lasting interest to humanity: for example, the immortality and transmigration of souls, who should ideally govern a society, what do we think of the multitude, how should men and women relate, which is the best form of government, democracy or oligarchy. There are the wonderful parables, of the Sun, the Divided Line and the Cave.[12] *The Republic* is especially controversial for its view that the ideal state should be governed by the Guardians, an elite of philosopher rulers, who are eugenically bred to be educated and knowledgeable above anyone else, and who are held to be superior by a very wide margin to the despised multitude in history.

We can contrast Plato's *Republic* with Thucydides' *History* in this regard. In *The Republic*, the spectre of political violence inheres in its recommendation of an authoritarian, not to say totalitarian state, a mode of governance with a long and appalling history, culminating in twentieth-century totalitarian societies that took advantage of precisely what Plato's *Republic* points out, the willingness of the multitude not to think for itself, to be submissive before power and leaders. Thucydides had already observed such dangerous submissiveness and lack of critical reason in the multitude in his *History*; but he had also pointed out that authoritarian regimes, based on notions of superiority of a particular group, would necessarily be dependent on political violence for their establishment and maintenance.

Yet how contradictory a text Plato's *Republic* is! For example, the constitution of the Guardian elite bears on the position of women in history. Socrates tells his interlocutors that the elite men and women must be equal, though it should be remembered that males are stronger than females. Women should receive the same education and be as free as men to engage in a variety of occupations, skills and activities (administrative work, medicine, music, athletics, soldiering, philosophizing). What of exercising together, Socrates is doubtfully asked, for don't Greek men always exercise naked? Yes, says Socrates, women of any age should exercise naked alongside men of any age in the gymnasium, as part of women's physical training and education which fits them to carry arms and join in hunting and military service. How, Socrates is asked, are children conceived and brought up in the community of Guardians? Socrates' view, which anticipates notions of collective rearing of children and abolition of the private family in the science fiction and utopian social thought and experiments of modernity,[13] is that the Guardians are to have partners and children in common.[14]

In the community of the ruling elite the family and private property have been abolished. The Guardians will have mating festivals, leading to couples breeding, but the children will be brought up in state nurseries. Men and women Guardians will be forbidden by law to live in separate households. Children will be held in common, and no parent should know its child, or child its parent. Guardian officers, who may be men or women, will take the children bred to be the best to another part of the city, so that Guardian stock can be kept 'pure', and the Guardians are to be restrained from too close an association and attachment which may lead back to a desire for the private family.[15] The remarkable passage on breastfeeding is well worth quoting:

> They [the officers] will arrange for the suckling of the children by bringing their mothers to the nursery when their breasts are still full, taking every precaution to see that no mother recognizes her child; if the mothers have not enough milk they will provide wet-nurses. They will see that the mothers do not suckle children for more than a reasonable length of time, and will hand over all the sitting up at night and hard work to nurses and attendants.[16]

In this way, child-bearing will be made easy for the Guardian mothers, so that they can devote themselves to their occupations. Children, however, who are judged inferior in some way, for example if they be born 'defective', will be 'quietly and secretly disposed of', a formulation that has raised the troubling question ever since of whether or not *The Republic* supports infanticide.[17]

While the bulk of Plato's *Republic* is monologic, it closes with the beautiful witty parable, 'The Myth of Er', evoking the varied journeys involved in the transmigration of souls.[18] 'The Myth of Er' anticipates the genre of the menippea so admired by Bakhtin – I very much admire it myself![19] – and which he saw, along with the Socratic dialogues and the symposium, as significantly contributing to the development of novelistic notions of polyphony and the dialogic.[20]

We can think of 'The Myth of Er' in Bakhtin's terms as a menippea, exploring in fantastical situations the idea of immortality and transmigration of souls. 'The Myth of Er' relates the observations of a soldier, Er, killed in battle, but who comes to life again on the funeral pyre and can then tell the story of what his soul had seen in 'the other world'. His soul came to a place where there were gaping chasms in the earth, and, opposite, gaping chasms in the sky; between the chasms sat Judges, who delivered verdicts on the destinations of the unjust, to go downwards into the underworld, and the just, to ascend into heaven. When Er comes before them, the

Judges order him to listen to and learn all that goes on, so that he can report back to the living about what awaits them. Er sees the souls in their travels and travails choosing future lives, sometimes crossing between humans and animals. The soul of Orpheus the great singer, for instance, was unwilling to be born of a woman because Orpheus hated all women after his death at their hands (he had been torn to pieces by Maenads, female followers of Dionysus), and so chose the life of a swan. Agamemnon, 'because of his sufferings hated humanity', and so his soul decided on the life an eagle. Odysseus's soul, because the 'memory of his former sufferings had cured him of all ambition', settled on the 'uneventful life of an ordinary man'.[21]

Later in this chapter I will look at 'The Dream of Scipio', modelled on 'The Myth of Er', though treating of different subjects.

## CICERO

In contrast to Plato's, Cicero's *Republic*, as we have it, is in its ideas a far more sober text, but it is also more polyphonic and contrapuntal in its juxtapositions of attitudes to fundamental questions, especially in relation to how much humanity should value the creation and possession of empires. It was originally composed of six books, but only survived antiquity in incomplete and fragmented form.[22] The complete text was lost after about 600, though portions were preserved by other writers, including Augustine, and became widely known in the Middle Ages and Renaissance, not least 'The Dream of Scipio', which, like 'The Myth of Er' in Plato's *Republic*, closes the final book. (Early in the nineteenth century, in 1819, a portion of *The Republic* was also brought to light as part of a palimpsest in the Vatican library.) In dialogue form, *The Republic* was set in a previous time, in 129 BCE at the home of the ex-general and public figure Scipio Aemilianus. Scipio is prominent in the conversations, as is his friend, Gaius Laelius. Another friend of

Scipio's who participates, in very interesting ways, is Lucius Furius Philus, sometimes as one who willingly agrees with Scipio, at other times as one who advances contrary positions in the manner of classical rhetoric. The dialogue occurs over a number of days, and Cicero provides prefaces to the books by which to frame the conversations.[23]

Like Plato's, Cicero's *Republic* is a philosophical and historical novel, where the characters refer to actual figures in the past. To those in genocide studies, however, the choice of figures is very strange. In his *Scipio Aemilianus*, A.E. Astin tells us that Cicero admired, to the point of idealizing, Scipio as somewhat of a political giant, a great man of public affairs, who in Republican Rome had enacted what for Cicero was an ideal combination of success in action with enjoyment of learning, an exemplar, along with his friend Laelius, of traditional Roman virtues that were becoming increasingly rare, in Cicero's view, in his own time. Astin also warns that figures like Scipio and Laelius are characters and there is no necessary relationship between the views that Cicero's *Republic* imputes to them and the actual opinions they might have held.[24] This is a warning to be closely heeded, for it suits my own approach to *The Republic* as, in Bakhtin's terms, a text working by counterpoint and agon, much more so than the main part of Plato's *Republic*.[25] Cicero's *Republic* reveals an aspect of the menippea concerned with the adventure of philosophical ideas where no character possesses any final truth or position that is uncontested, and where the author as narrator is one character amongst others, his opinions, even when they attempt to frame the discussions as with Cicero's prefaces, only one view amongst others. Characters function as author-thinkers, taking philosophical positions that are to be considered in their own right.[26] In these Bakhtinian terms, neither Cicero's historical admiration for Scipio nor his framing prefaces control the text; characters have the dialogic right to answer back, to present alternative views. We will analyse the *Republic* as polyphonic and menippean in a moment.

While granting that Scipio is indeed a character in a text, it is nonetheless difficult not to feel very uneasy as a modern reader in knowing that his name refers to a historical personage – Cornelius Scipio Aemilianus Africanus (Numantinus) – who, in the terminology of Raphaël Lemkin, was an egregious genocidist, infamous for the destruction not only of Carthage in 146 BCE, but also of Numantia in Spain in 132; a serial genocidist, we might say. In *Axis Rule in Occupied Europe*, Lemkin refers to the destruction of Carthage as an example of wars of extermination waged in classical times in which nations and groups were completely or almost completely destroyed.[27]

Laelius was with Scipio in the siege of Carthage. Astin relates that in the spring of 146, the siege entered its last agonizing phase as Scipio launched his final assault against Carthage's starving defenders. A force under Laelius captured a section of the wall, and after a week of what Astin describes as continuous and horrifying street fighting, there was a surrender from the central citadel of many thousands of wretched survivors, destined to be sold into slavery. Scipio cursed anyone who might wish to resettle there. However, as victor, Scipio reminded those around him of the mutability of fortune and the folly of presumptuous words and deeds. Some time after the capture of the city, Scipio gave the order to set fire to those parts of it which still stood, to complete its devastation. It is reported that Scipio, watching the conflagration, turned with tears in his eyes to his friend Polybius, the Greek historian, confessing his dread that the same thing might happen to his beloved home city of Rome. On his return to Rome, the destruction of Carthage was celebrated in a triumph, conferring on Scipio great glory and making him a powerful figure in the political life of the imperial capital.[28]

When he took command of the war against Numantia, Astin tells us, the organization of the siege of the Spanish hill-town was relentless and efficient from the outside, full of horror and agony for those within. Numantia suffered the same fate as Carthage; those who survived were enslaved, and it was razed to the ground.[29] Again, Scipio returned in triumph to Rome.

Let's return to Cicero's *Republic*, observing the Bakhtinian convention that we are dealing with characters who are independent author-thinkers. *The Republic* is a menippea where ultimate questions are entertained.

There are differing unresolved attitudes in the dialogues, tensions between supersessionism and questioning of supersessionism, teleology and scepticism of its hubris, utopia and anti-utopia, war and anti-war, the importance of empire and belittling of empire, natural law and questioning of natural law, should cities be coastal or inland, and ethnocentrism and dislike of cosmopolitanism as against interest in human diversity. From the fragments we have, it is Scipio who pronounces conventional views concerning Rome and its history. Scipio emerges as an arch-supersessionist, exalting in utopian spirit the supremacy of Rome as humanity's ideal future, history's telos. In the early part of the text his interlocutors, Laelius and Philus, keep rather obsequiously agreeing with Scipio, as if we are reading a monologic text like Plato's *Republic*. Scipio's listeners assent to whatever he says, treating the general as a teacher of ready-made truths.

Indeed, in Scipio's view, Rome is to be considered blessed in all fundamental aspects of a society and polity. Scipio makes it clear that in the production of political theory, concerned with the supervision and management of a society, Romans, the 'toga-wearing people', are not to be considered inferior to even the wisest and foremost of the Greeks. The Roman constitution, a carefully proportioned mixture of monarchy, democracy and rule by a select group (aristocracy), is incomparable.[30]

There is another way that Rome supersedes Greece and societies like it. What kind of society is superior in history, the coastal or the inland? By the divine Romulus' careful foresight, Rome, Scipio judges, is ideally situated away from the coast, as an inland settlement, thus giving it the best chance of permanence and power. The disadvantage of a coastal city is that a maritime, naval enemy can be suddenly upon one, whereas with an inland settlement we are given advance warning of an enemy's approach. Also, the moral character of coastal cities is prone to corruption and decay, by reason of what we might refer to as the threat of cosmopolitanism. In the coastal city, people are exposed to a 'mixture of strange talk and strange behaviour'; foreign customs are imported along with foreign merchandise; ancestral institutions cannot persist unaffected; the inhabitants of coastal cities do not stay at home, either dashing off to foreign parts 'full of airy hopes and designs', or, even when they stay put, wandering abroad in their imaginations. Such restlessness and dispersal of their citizens were primarily responsible for the ultimate overthrow of Carthage and Corinth, for they failed to attend to their land and their army. The sea brings enticements to luxury in the form of booty and imports; the attractiveness of a coastal site 'represents many temptations to sensual indulgence', whether through extravagance or idleness. Scipio is sure that what applies to Corinth applies to 'Greece as a whole', for the Peloponnese is largely surrounded by the sea, and the Greek islands 'almost float on their surface along with the customs and institutions of their cities'. Seafaring, therefore, Scipio concludes, was 'clearly the cause of Greece's misfortunes', including her political instability, which resulted from the characteristic vices of coastal cities. Scipio also mentions the Phoenicians as barbarians who sailed the seas in order to trade.[31]

In Scipio's view, what Romulus achieved, by founding Rome on the banks of a river whose broad stream flowed down to the sea, was a combination of the advantages of a coastal city in terms of trade, with the advantages of being an inland settlement. Due to such foresight, Rome would eventually form, says Scipio, 'the site and centre of a world empire'. Rome was also endowed, following the example of Romulus, with an intense interest in military pursuits that led to brilliant success in war, yet its military tradition was tempered by religious ceremonies, and 'mild and civilized behaviour' as in fairs and games. By such means, longevity was ensured, because Rome came to be characterized by 'two factors which, above all others, ensure that states will last, namely religion and humane behaviour'. Not only was its mixed constitution history's best practice, but its education and culture were also unsurpassable, for Rome absorbed into itself the 'rich flood of moral and artistic teaching' that flowed into it from Greece.[32]

The relation of Rome to Greece is one of supersession, evidenced in Scipio himself. Laelius assures Scipio that his method of exposition is superior to any Greek treatise, indeed superior to Plato's Socrates. [33] Scipio the Roman, then, supersedes Socrates the Greek. In his preface to Book Three, Cicero himself enthuses that in the art of 'governing and training peoples', good and able men like Scipio, Laelius and Philus have produced an 'almost incredible and superhuman kind of excellence'. Statesmen such as these combine in themselves experience in the management of great affairs, an art in itself, with other arts, such as the pursuit of wisdom that history usually associates with Socrates; they are therefore superior to Socrates, who practises only one art, that of philosophy. Such eminent, almost godlike, Roman men, therefore, combining action with study, attain the highest distinction in life, adding 'foreign learning derived from Socrates to the native traditions of their forefathers'.[34]

We can think here of a comparable supersessionist teleology in Jewish and Christian history in the Middle Eastern and Mediterranean world of antiquity. The biblical scholar Robert P. Carroll writes, in *Wolf in the Sheepfold: The Bible as a Problem for Christianity* (1991), that so much of the religion of the Hebrew Bible belongs to Canaanite belief and practice that we should now understand the strictures against the Canaanites as a way of distancing the new religion from its antecedents. Similarly, Carroll goes on to observe, the Christian churches distanced themselves from being Jewish while clearly taking over some of the beliefs and practices of the Jewish communities of their time. Carroll exclaims of the historical irony involved in both situations that 'what the Jews did to the Canaanites in the Hebrew Bible, the Christians did to the Jews in the New Testament!'[35]

In like terms, Rome absorbed Greek culture into itself, while regarding itself as historically superior to Greece; in this double movement, Greece is both included and transcended, just as the Hebrew Bible is included within Christianity as the Old Testament, with Judaism transcended in the New Testament. (There are perhaps similarities in this kind of process with Hegel's notion of *Aufhebung*, or sublation, indicating a forward movement in history, including and preserving that which it overcomes.)

## DEBATING THE VIRTUES OF EMPIRE, ROME, NATURAL LAW

Yet in the drama of Cicero's *Republic* as a text of polyphony and counterpoint, supersessionist discourse comes to be opposed, especially, by Philus's later interventions. Asked to take contrary views for the sake of rhetorical argument, Philus eloquently proceeds to question any conventional view which might suggest that whatever is Roman is ideal.

There is, for example, a juxtaposition of opposing arguments presented by Laelius and Philus concerning natural law.

In Book Three, Laelius asserts the universal truth of natural law, that it is the basis of all human societies, and that Rome and its empire have been created in its terms. Laelius contends that law is 'right reason in harmony with nature', and that it spreads throughout the whole human community in a way that is 'unchanging and eternal, calling people to their duty by its commands and deterring them from wrong-doing by its prohibitions'. Indeed, says Laelius in high-flown language, 'all peoples at all times will be embraced by a single and eternal and unchangeable law', supervised by god, the 'one lord and master of us all'. There are leaves of *The Republic* missing, but it would appear from quotations in other ancient authors that Laelius expands on what he considers are the foundational truths of natural law: for example, when it is just for a state to pursue war. Thus, 'the best kind of state never resorts to war except in defence of its honour or its security.' Laelius is also quoted in another ancient source as stating, again high-mindedly, that:

> wars are unjust when they are undertaken without proper
> cause. No just war can be waged except for the sake of

punishment or repelling an enemy. ... No war is deemed
to be just if it has not been declared and proclaimed, and
if redress has not previously been sought.

He then goes on to argue that it is just for superior to rule over
inferior.[36]

In Book Three, Philus's views are in this context refractory,
dissident and irreverent. As a rhetorical exercise, and because it is
known that he likes to argue both sides of a case, Philus is asked
to offer arguments why injustice is necessary and advantageous.
There are quite a few leaves missing from Book Three, and in
places what Philus may have said (as with Laelius) has had to be
reconstructed by later scholarship where *The Republic* has been
quoted by other authors in antiquity. But what fascinating things
Philus does say! For he presents powerful arguments questioning
much of the supersessionist confidence in Roman superiority in
history that shines forth in Scipio's earlier expositions, Cicero's
prefaces and now Laelius's arguments in Book Three. Since, in
Bakhtin's terms, Philus is appearing in Book Three very much as
an independent author-thinker, what he says is salient and
challenging, not merely a rhetorical exercise. What, Philus asks,
constitutes justice in the puzzlingly contradictory history of
humanity?

Let's take attitudes to the notion of natural law, that it is natural for humanity to do certain just things, a notion that is extremely
important in the long history of European and Western colonizing
and empire-building. In his preface to Book One, Cicero is sure of
a 'basic fact' of existence, that 'nature has given to mankind such
a compulsion to do good, and such a desire to defend the well-
being of the community, that this force prevails over all the temptations of pleasure and ease'; nature spurs humanity on to fulfil a
purpose, which is to increase the wealth of the human race and to
make men's lives safer and richer.[37] In Book One, Scipio also
refers to 'the universal law of nature', which is that 'nature decrees
that nothing belongs to anyone except the person who can handle
and use it.'[38] Scipio is formulating a natural law that anticipates
the mythos of agriculture that we will soon find in the *Aeneid*, and

also the doctrine of *res nullius* that became part of international law, the law of nations, drawn on to justify colonizing and empire from early modern European times to modernity.

In Book Three, Philus reprises the relativizing and pluralizing play of perspectives in Herodotus and Thucydides' histories questioning classical Greek ethnocentrism and Athenian self-admiration. He proceeds by undermining Roman certainty that they are putting in practice in their state and empire what is universally natural for human communities to do. It should follow from the notion of natural law, Philus points out, that if nature has laid down the Roman system of justice, then every other country would have the same laws, and would always have had them through time. However, the notion of natural law, the argument from nature, cannot hold for all humanity, not least in the case of justice; if, he points out, justice were a part of nature, like hot and cold, or bitter and sweet, then 'just and unjust would be the same for everyone'. But what we see is that people's customs are 'vastly different'. Quite clearly, Philus reflects, given humanity's extraordinary variety of peoples and societies, justice is not an element of nature but a political phenomenon that changes from society to society. The 'varieties of laws, institutions, customs and habits' are so diverse among the nations, and have in any case changed so much even within any one nation, that the doctrine of natural law cannot hold.[39]

After all, Philus points out, it is clear that there is constant change among societies, nations, cities and laws, including within the history of Rome itself, and there is therefore no reason to think present Roman law is necessarily just or ideal. For example, referring to the 'rights of women', Philus points out how unfair Roman law, 'passed in the interests of men', is against women in regard to bequests and legacies. 'Why', Philus asks, 'shouldn't a woman possess money of her own?' Here, he says, is a 'serious injustice'.[40]

Bakhtin writes of the menippea that, in its experimental fantasticality, there is the possibility of observation from some unusual point of view, from on high, for example, resulting in a radical change in the scale of the observed phenomena of life.[41] Let's imagine, Philus says to his interlocutors, that we are on high, as if in a chariot in the sky. Looking down and surveying many different cities and countries, what would the onlooker see? He would see the most diverse of attitudes, where what is just in the view of one society is unjust in the view of another. In the land of Egypt, the bull Apis and many other beasts are worshipped as gods. In Greece, the onlooker would notice splendid temples consecrated to statues in human form, a practice followed by the Romans as well, but which the Persians regarded as sacrilegious. Indeed, did not Xerxes order the temples of Athens to be burnt, believing it was 'impious to confine within walls gods whose abode was the whole universe'?[42]

Recalling the ethnographic sweep of Herodotus's *Histories*, Philus asks his friends to think of a range of nations and rulers, from the Taurians on the Black Sea to Basiris, King of Egypt, to the Gauls and Carthaginians, who have regarded human sacrifice 'as a holy act, most welcome in the sight of the immortal gods'. As for we Romans, says Philus, we imagine ourselves to be 'paragons of justice', yet don't we 'forbid the tribes beyond the Alps to plant olive-trees and vines, in order to enhance the value of our own products'? How can this be considered just? What of Lycurgas the great law-giver, didn't he give the land of the rich to the common people, for the latter 'to work as slaves'? There is, then, Philus observes, 'nothing natural about justice'.[43]

In passages that appear in other ancient authors, Philus presents an alternative to natural law theory, choosing instead a mode of historicizing the notion of justice, a comparative sociology, stressing features in history like expediency, self-interest, mystification of motives, war for gain and dubious claims to divine support. In this alternative view, Philus certainly does not spare his fellow Romans, as we can see in our epigraph to this chapter, as well as in the following quotations:

> The Romans themselves illustrate the difference between justice and expediency. By declaring war through the

fetial priests they have given a specious legality to lawless behaviour; and by seizing other people's land they have acquired a world empire.[44]

Every empire is gained by war, which always involves harm for the gods of the conquered as well as for the conquered themselves.[45]

Drawing on the sceptical thinking of Carneades, Philus says, 'If the Romans decided to be just and return other people's property, they would at once revert to poverty and live in huts'.[46] Philus's witty comment on empire here immediately brings to mind Pericles admitting to his fellow Athenians, as evoked in Thucydides' *History* (2.63), that it may have been wrong for Athens to have taken possession of its empire in the first place, because it had become a tyranny, but if the Athenians wish to continue as a great society, they must not let their empire go. Philus rebukes the Romans for their imperial arrogance, in wishing to 'rule over as many subjects as possible, enjoy pleasures, and revel in power, supremacy, and dominion'.[47]

In these critical reflections, Philus also reprises the ethical questioning of empire in Herodotus's *Histories* (1.204–14 and 3.21), in the powerful speeches to the invading Persians by the Queen of the Massagetae and the King of Ethiopia. 'Justice', Philus insists, in the anti-ethnocentric and cosmopolitan spirit of Herodotus and Thucydides' histories, 'teaches us to spare all men, take thought for the interests of mankind, give everyone his due, and not lay hands on the things belonging to the gods, the state, or somebody else'.[48] We might recall here that central to Lemkin's thought are notions of world culture and the oneness of the world, valuing the variety and diversity of human cultures.[49] Philus suggests, then, that the history of Rome, 'whose empire now controls the world', is not a narrative of justice for humanity, but of its reverse, a story of what has been gained in terms of particular Roman interests: 'Wealth, positions of power, possessions, offices, military commands, and dominion over individuals or nations'.[50] And as Philus has just noted, there is no natural or divine right by which any one nation such as that of Rome lays hands on things 'belonging to the gods'.[51] In Philus's view, the Roman Empire is not divinely ordained.

In these counterpointings in Book Three, it is clear that what is universally natural and just for Laelius represents in Philus's view local and arbitrary acts of self-interest, the self-interest of empire and those who are advantaged by it; a self-interest always put forward, and indeed believed in, as just according to natural law, imbued with honourable intentions, defensive in orientation, never aggressive towards other nations and peoples, never covetous and self-seeking.

## CONCLUSION: 'THE DREAM OF SCIPIO'

I will close this discussion of the polyphony of Cicero's great *Republic* with a brief glance at its final scene, 'The Dream of Scipio', a most interesting short narrative. In Book One, Scipio had stated with great certainty that the human species is 'not made up of solitary individuals or lonely wanderers', but is inspired by an innate desire to form communities.[52] In Book Two, Scipio had complained of coastal cities that they encourage a dangerous wandering of body and mind, which he associated with Carthage but also Greece as a mark of weakness and inferiority.[53] Yet in Book Six, in 'The Dream of Scipio', in a state of solitude, Scipio's mind does indeed wander. We can regard 'The Dream of Scipio' in Bakhtin's terms in *Problems of Dostoevsky's Poetics* as a miniature menippea, a fantastical journey. The story partakes of the menippean opportunity of observation from unusual heights, as Philus had talked of in relation to someone looking down at the world from a chariot. The menippea also, as Bahktin notes, permitted exploration of unusual moral and psychic states, revealed in unrestrained daydreaming or strange dreams; in such dreams, a person loses his or her finalized quality and ceases to mean only one thing; one ceases to coincide with oneself; there can be a dialogic relationship to one's own self, with the possibility of split personality.[54]

In 'The Dream of Scipio', a dialogue of the dead occurs in a dream, so Scipio reports to his friends, that he once had in Africa. Scipio says he had come to Africa as military tribune of the fourth legion, two years before he destroyed Carthage. He pays his respects to a local ruler, King Masinissa, a close friend of his own illustrious military family, in particular Scipio's (adoptive) grandfather, Africanus. After he goes to bed, Scipio falls into a deeper sleep than usual, and while he is asleep, the souls of his dead grandfather and his father Paulus appear to him in his dream. They engage Scipio in a startling conversation, a conversation we can describe as carnivalesque, overturning his usual modes of perceiving and valuing his life and Roman imperial society more generally. The souls of his grandfather and father are in heaven. They take Scipio on a journey where he is able to look down on the earth from 'a high place which was clear and shining in the radiance of starlight'.[55]

From this heavenly vantage point Scipio can comprehend the whole universe, and the effect is to disturb his self-image that he is central to and a victor in history, part of a glorious empire that, as is frequently repeated by the interlocutors in *The Republic*, covers and controls the world. Wandering on high in his dream, Scipio has a nightmarish realization: 'Now the earth itself seemed so small to me that I felt ashamed of our empire, whose extent was no more than a dot on its surface' (I'm repeating here my second epigraph). Not only is the earth small, but the Roman empire is only a dot on the earth. Consider, Africanus tells Scipio, that the world is encircled by two habitable belts; the one on the south could never be part of the Roman empire, because from the point of view of the northern belt its people walk upside down; as for the northern belt, the Roman empire is only a tiny area. The 'glory' which you, Scipio, Africanus says, are so eager to extend, and the 'fame' you seek, has never gone beyond the far side of the Caucasus or swum across the Ganges, nor is it present in the remaining areas of the east and west, north and south. Fame and glory never in any case endure anywhere on earth, Africanus tells his grandson: 'a person's reputation' does not last for ever, and 'vanishes as posterity forgets'.[56]

In this part dream, part nightmare, becoming like a solitary individual or lonely wanderer enables Scipio to open his thinking to new perspectives that question the hubris of empire he so conventionally accepts and extols. His own hubris and the value of his life as a conqueror are brought into question. In his dialogue with his dead grandfather and father, seeing his world from another place, Scipio becomes an outsider, a stranger, to his own previous life, implying the possibility of transformation and metamorphosis. 'The Dream of Scipio' perhaps anticipates the baroque *memento mori* of early modern European cultural history, where consideration of the nearness of death, and of the judgement of the soul that will ensue, prompts thought about the illusions of worldly pursuits, here empire and its supersessionist delusion of everlasting worldwide greatness and glory as if they should constitute life's purpose.

Cicero's *Republic* ends, then, in dazzling ambivalences and intriguing questioning of a remarkable menippean and contrapuntal kind.

# 5  VICTIMOLOGY
AND GENOCIDE:
THE BIBLE'S EXODUS,
VIRGIL'S *AENEID*

And I [God] am come down to deliver them out of the hand of the Egyptians, and to bring them up out of that land unto a good land and a large, unto a land flowing with milk and honey; unto the place of the Canaanites, and the Hittites, and the Amorites, and the Perizzites, and the Hivites, and the Jebusites.

(God to Moses, Exodus 3: 8)

He [Aeneas] will wage a great war in Italy and crush its fierce tribes. He will build walls for his people and establish their way of life.

(Jupiter to Venus in Virgil, *Aeneid*, Book One)[1]

At last she [Dido] replied on a blaze of passion: 'You are a traitor. ... He [Aeneas] did not sigh when he saw me weep. He did not even turn to look at me. Was he overcome and brought to tears? Had he any pity for the woman who loves him? ... He was thrown helpless on my shores and I took him in and like a fool settled him as a partner in my kingdom. He had lost his fleet and I found it and brought his companions back from the dead. ... And now we hear about the augur Apollo ... and to crown all the messenger of the gods is bringing terrifying commands

[ 113 ]

down through the winds from Jupiter himself. … I do not hold you or bandy words with you. Away you go. Keep on searching for your Italy with the winds to help you. Look for your kingdom over the waves. But my hope is that if the just gods have any power, you will drain a bitter cup among the ocean rocks, calling the name of Dido again and again, and I shall follow you not in the flesh but in the black fires of death and when its cold hand takes the breath from my body, my shade shall be with you wherever you may be. You will receive the punishment you deserve, and the news of it will reach me deep among the dead.

(Dido to Aeneas, *Aeneid*, Book Four)[2]

… the whole agony of exile.

(*Aeneid*, Book Five)[3]

Why is it right for Trojans to raise the black-smoking torches of war against Latins, to put other men's lands under their yoke, to carry off plunder, to pick and choose who are to be their fathers-in-law, to tear brides from their mothers' laps and to hold out the olive branch of peace with their weapons fixed on the high sterns of their ships?

(Juno to Jupiter, *Aeneid*, Book Ten)[4]

… the genocidal advocacies of the Pentateuch.

(Robert P. Carroll, *Wolf in the Sheepfold*)[5]

Throughout this book I argue that Greco-Roman polytheism and Jewish and Christian monotheism shared concepts and notions that are important in world history for their relationship to violence. Notions of divinely sanctioned genocide and victimology, conquest and colonization, along with supersessionist discourse, can be perceived crossing the monotheism–polytheism divide. In the ancient world of the Mediterranean and Middle East, the Greco-Roman polytheistic and Jewish and Christian monotheistic peoples did not necessarily have to know each other for them to interact and converge; convergence could be at the level of ideas, though the different histories did increasingly intersect as the Roman Empire spread, with the Empire finally becoming Christian.

My aim in this chapter is to complicate the polytheism–monotheism divide itself. I will be suggesting that in the ancient world what we now take to be a kind of absolute opposition between polytheism and monotheism, as hostile philosophical and cosmological systems, could be blurred, inchoate, incomplete and confused. A monotheistic father god could see himself (the supreme god always being presented as male) as one amongst other gods and divine figures, for all he might desire was absolute power over a particular people; a polytheistic god, especially one designated as all-powerful, could conduct himself very much as we usually conceive a monotheistic father god. In addition, the historical claim that a crucial distinction between them is that in monotheism God is hidden and invisible, while polytheism stresses the visuality of its deities, can also be questioned. Wasn't the Egyptian supreme deity Ra hidden, invisible, inscrutable? Wasn't the character we call God in the biblical stories very often visible?

To pursue these questions I will bring into conversation, for their narrative and ethical similarities, the biblical story of Exodus and Virgil's *Aeneid*, two of world history's most powerful and lastingly influential victimological narratives. By victimological narrative, I mean, as outlined in the introduction to this book, the belief that earlier bondage, persecution and suffering justifies later violence, conquest and destruction. In their operation, reception and eventual imbrication in Western history, these texts represent an ethical disaster, with highly destructive consequences for humanity as a whole, especially for indigenous peoples and peoples already in a land coveted by others as chosen and promised.

Lemkin thought that instances of the formerly persecuted becoming persecutors themselves, victims in the past becoming oppressors in the future, were a recurring feature in the history of genocide. Such exchanges between persecuted and persecutors, victims and perpetrators, help shape the narrative of Exodus and of other aspects of the Pentateuch and Old Testament concerning the ending of exile in a homeland, as well as the *Aeneid*. In this chapter I will be considering Richard Waswo's remarkable *The Founding Legend of Western Civilization* (1997), which contends that the *Aeneid* was and remains, some two millennia after its writing, of central importance to Western notions of colonization and expansion into other people's territories, with associated valuing of agriculture, culture-bearing, law and cities, and an overriding distinction between civilization, represented in the city, and barbarity, signified by forest and wilderness.[6] While I find Waswo's argument persuasive, I will be suggesting that Exodus is equally powerful, and equally pernicious, as a founding legend of the West.

## VICTIMOLOGY AND GENOCIDAL VIOLENCE: EXODUS AND THE *AENEID*

The narrative similarities of these two great legendary stories are startling. Both Exodus and the *Aeneid* tell the harrowing tale of peoples whose long historical existence in a certain place has been destroyed, for the Israelites in Egypt by Pharaoh, for the Trojans in Troy by the Greeks led by Agamemnon and Ulysses, the latter a figure of hatred in Virgil's long epic poem. In Exodus, the Israelites, led by Moses as saviour and father of his people, guided by a monotheistic God with whom he enjoys frequent intimate talks, leave Egypt (with some difficulty) and wander in the desert for many years of exile, hardship and suffering. At last they approach the land of Canaan, which God has promised will be their new home: a land which, with God's advice, encouragement and assistance, they will genocidally conquer after fierce warfare against the peoples already there, its indigenous inhabitants. In the *Aeneid*, as Troy falls to the Greeks, Aeneas the Trojan warrior, also a saviour and father of his people, leads a group of survivors out of the burning city. The Trojans will wander across the desert-like Mediterranean sea for many years of exile, hardship and suffering, until they can approach the land of Italy, which Jupiter, the near-monotheistic Olympian father god, has promised to them as their new home; a land which, with the advice, encouragement and assistance of Jupiter and fellow gods Venus (Aeneas's mother) and the prophet god Apollo, they will genocidally conquer after fierce warfare against the indigenous peoples already living there.

In the early part of these narratives, the Israelites and Trojans start out as victims of persecution and destruction, as people of great suffering; in the middle part of the narrative, they continue to suffer in their wanderings as lost and homeless people; in the final section, their wanderings and misery end as they become victors and conquerors themselves. What is the ethical relation of that earlier suffering to that which in these narratives the Israelites and Trojans eventually do, the terrible violence they commit, in other places and upon other peoples? It is this question that in recent times has energized discussion of Exodus and the *Aeneid* in critical and cultural theory concerned with questions of settler colonialism. From the late twentieth century, both texts, and their historical consequences, have been sharply – if usually separately – interrogated on ethical grounds. I'll try now to bring that questioning within the one discussion.

In *The Founding Legend of Western Civilization*, Waswo does acknowledge similarities between the Old Testament and the *Aeneid* as foundational creation stories, the one sacred, the other secular, but he does not pursue the comparison in his book.[7] With my own interest in the importance of a postsecular perspective, I will do so here, with the proviso that I cannot see why we should regard the *Aeneid* as any less a religious text than is Exodus, or later books like Joshua and Judges which evoke the invasion of the promised land, as God and Moses in Exodus had recommended.[8]

## EXODUS (AND JOSHUA AND JUDGES)

The contemporary critique of Exodus in terms of postcolonial and exilic diaspora theory was inaugurated by a striking and now classic postsecular essay by Edward Said, 'Michael Walzer's

*Exodus and Revolution*: A Canaanite Reading' (1986). Said suggests that the dangerous seductiveness of the Exodus story, promising liberation to the suffering and oppressed, should be resisted. The narrative of Exodus, Said points out, considered as a whole, has an inspiring vision of freedom for one people that is yet premised on defeat and even extermination for another, the Canaanites, those who already inhabit the Promised Land, a land which by divine injunction is to be conquered and occupied. Said sees the displaced and dispossessed Palestinians as the present-day Canaanites of the Middle East, part of a world history where Exodus has unfortunately proven all too exemplary, inspiring Puritans in New England to slay Native Americans or South African Boers to lay claim to and move in on huge areas of African lands.[9]

In an essay of great acuity and wisdom, 'The Lie of the Land: The Text beyond Canaan' (1989), Harry Berger Jnr, discussing Genesis and Exodus, contrasts what he refers to as 'possessive nomadism' to mobile pastoral nomadism, to customary wanderers who wish to keep wandering. In these terms, the Israelites, by taking possession of the Promised Land, the land of Canaan, lost their diasporic freedom to wander and to think as wanderers. Descending on Canaan, the Israelites placed themselves in bondage to possessive nomadism, the species of nomadic group who invade and take over a settled agricultural society. The inevitable corollary of such a conception of the nomadic is a notion of exile as separation from a land claimed to be one's own, exile as loss that has to be remedied. In conquering the land of Canaan, however, Berger points out, the Israelites went from fugitives to 'captors and victors themselves', and in doing so they incorporated features of social, state and religious organization of the land they had fled from, imperial Egypt, in the new society they developed. In Canaan, the Israelites instituted a kingdom that was bureaucratic, hierarchical and authoritarian, with its instituted judgeship, notions of monarchy, settled state and rule-bound priesthood; in Berger's felicitous phrasing, the Israelites, in the apparently new society, legitimated restoration 'of the very world from which Exodus relates the exodus'.

Yet Berger feels that Exodus is not a closed text; it remains open and contradictory, as does the textuality of the Old Testament in general, in the ways it both represents ideas and desires yet subjects them to 'continuous critique', and so keeps alive customary wandering as a mode of thought. In such textuality, tensions between tent as against house, nomadism as against agriculture, wilderness as against possessing Canaan, wandering and exile as against settlement, diaspora as against ingathering in a state, remain unresolved. Old Testament textuality, Berger feels, becomes, in its self-criticality, a kind of travelling ark of interpretation and reinterpretation, permitting in the dispersal of diaspora the possible development of an 'ideal of autonomous internalized ethical art'.[10]

Berger's notion here of exile enabling adventures of ideas and ethical arts of self-fashioning, in one way looks back to Spinoza's judgement on Moses and Exodus in *Tractatus Theologico-Politicus*, that the flight from Egypt delivered the Hebrews into another kind of 'bondage', where Moses 'commanded' them to love God and keep his Law. In Spinoza's view, Moses infantilized the Hebrews, teaching them how to act and behave in the same way as parents teach children who have not reached the age of reason; Moses sought to promote obedience, not to impart knowledge, and hence denied them true freedom, the freedom to reason for themselves and accept God in their own individual ways, from their own independent mind and spirit.[11] In another way, Berger's argument is clearly close to Said's own conception of exile and diaspora as conflicted, as both pain and loss yet also opening onto the possibilities for the individual thinker of unhoused speculation, the creativity of new and unexpected perspectives.[12]

In *The Curse of Cain: The Violent Legacy of Monotheism* (1997), Regina M. Schwartz comments on the influence of the Exodus story in authorizing a biblical version of the victimological narrative: that earlier victimhood warrants later violence and justifies present exclusionary or discriminatory policies. Old Testament narratives like Exodus, Schwartz argues, have been and continue to be vastly influential not only in the history of Christianity, but in secularized forms in modern European history in the phenomenon of collective identities like nationalism. Schwartz sees Zionism and the modern nation state of Israel as part of this history.[13] Like Berger, Schwartz also wishes to stress that the narratives of Exodus and the Old Testament more generally (we could also think of the book of Job) are nonetheless richly heterogeneous, complex and contradictory, always offering grounds for counter-movement, doubt and critique, both supporting and unseating authorized codes like conquest of a promised land.[14] Berger and Schwartz's approach resonates with Robert Carroll's argument in *Wolf in the Sheepfold*, that the sheer wildness, opacity and unruliness of biblical stories, metaphors and images will always exceed and confound every attempt in Western history, not least in Christian theology, the object of his spirited critique, to systematize the Bible into coherent or essentialized or absolute meanings.[15]

Such writing by Said and Schwartz proved to be profoundly influential in stimulating postsecular critiques of the power of narratives like Exodus in settler-colonial situations and histories around the world, in Palestine-Israel, the United States and Australia. In her well-known essay 'Antinomies of Exile: Said at the Frontiers of National Narrations', Ella Shohat suggests that the United States is so receptive to Zionism, rather than to the plight of the Palestinians, because Americans like to stress their similarity with Israelis in relation to British colonialism, the British pharaoh, which each rejected and fought against. Americans admire the image of the *sabra* pioneer, the new Israeli-born Jewish man, just as they admire in themselves the true American as Adam charged with a civilizing mission in a New Canaan, the Promised Land of the New World, in a virgin state until the American Adam's redemptive arrival. Both New Jewish Man and New American Man see themselves as blessed with the divine prerogative of naming the elements and features of the new world they encounter. And in each case the presence and societies of the indigenous inhabitants, the Palestinians and

Sephardi and Oriental Jews in Israel and the Native Americans in North America, are ignored or held to be of no account.[16]

In another well-known essay, 'Expulsion, Exodus and Exile in White Australian Historical Mythology' (1999), Ann Curthoys notes that in its engagement with victimology white Australian history reveals the uneasy workings of both Genesis and Exodus. In the popular mythology of the settler colony – an ongoing history – there is a persistent strand of discourse where white Australians are perceived as having been expelled from the British Eden conceived as the mother land, a primal wound in the white Australian psyche, of rejection by the mother. Popular mythology also, however, draws on a myth of exodus from the British pharaoh and settlement in a promised land far from the British pharaoh's shores, enabling a new society and national narrative and sensibility to be created. Curthoys argues that white Australians see themselves in originary ways as victims: victims as convicts and, as pioneering settlers in a harsh land, of drought and fire and flood; victims too of misuse by powerful nations like Britain or the United States. Regarding themselves as victims, aware always of their own suffering and hardship and defeats, they cannot, Curthoys suggests, view themselves as victimizers, as responsible for the suffering and hardship and tragedies they inflict on others, those they displace and dispossess and persecute.[17]

In *The Bible and Zionism* (2007), Nur Masalha analyses the manifold ways that Exodus has been used as a creation story by Zionism since the late nineteenth century, and has become crucial as the mythological underpinning for the modern settler colonial state of Israel. Masalha supports Said's path-breaking postcolonial reading of Exodus, and also refers to a Saidian critique of Exodus's narrative from an indigenous viewpoint by the North American author Robert Allen Warrior, who writes that those who seek to see in Exodus a kind of liberation theology overlook what happened to the Canaanites: 'Especially ignored', Warrior points out, 'are those parts of the story that describe Yahweh's command to mercilessly annihilate the indigenous population.'[18]

Masalha also highlights the contribution to these debates of the late Michael Prior, whose writings, influenced by Said's turning a Canaanite lens on Exodus, analyse the ways in which the Bible has been deployed to justify Western settler colonialism in Latin America, South Africa and Palestine. Prior critiques conventional Christian theological support for Zionism and its unwillingness to question the biblical narratives that Zionism has called on to justify its historical project, especially Exodus, Deuteronomy and Joshua, that mandate genocide against the indigenous peoples of Canaan. In terms of contemporary international law, Prior noted, the practices recommended in these narratives, of ethnic cleansing and extermination of peoples cast as enemies, would now be considered war crimes and crimes against humanity.[19]

It's as well to quickly remind ourselves how genocidal, in Lemkin's terms, the Pentateuch and other early books of the Old Testament like Joshua and Judges egregiously are. Famously, Moses died before he reached the promised land, but in the book of Joshua we find that Joshua, Moses' disciple and successor, successfully carries out the long-planned invasion. Joshua and the Israelite army cross the Jordan to launch their military conquest of the promised land, where on the east and west live the Canaanites, in the mountains live the Amorites, the Hittites, the Perizzites and Jebusites, and also in the land reside the Hivites (Joshua 11: 3). The kings of these peoples meet and decide to resist. God tells the Israelites not to be afraid, because he will assist them to fall on these kings' armies and slay them across the whole land, which duly occurs, the Israelites smiting them until none remains, indeed, 'utterly destroying them'. Joshua also burns the cities of these kings (Joshua 11: 5–17). It's difficult not to recall here the mythology, epic and drama of the Greeks conquering Troy, looting its treasures, killing all the men and capturing and selling into slavery the women and children. We learn in the book of Joshua that the Israelites smote every man with the edge of the sword 'until they had destroyed them, neither left they any to breathe'. However, 'the spoil of these cities, and the cattle' the Israelites reserved for themselves (Joshua 11: 14), though it is not clear here what the Israelites, if they had killed all the men and looted treasures and cattle, did with the enemy women and children, unless they also were killed. Nonetheless, in other places in Joshua, when cities were taken, everyone and everything that breathed was put to the sword (Joshua 10: 28–40). In sum, we learn, 'Joshua smote all the country of the hills, and of the south, and of the vale, and of the springs, and all their kings: he left none remaining, but utterly destroyed all that breathed, as the Lord God of Israel commanded' (Joshua 10: 40).

After destruction comes replacement. 'So', we are told in the final verse of Chapter 11, 'Joshua took the whole land, according to all that the Lord said unto Moses; and Joshua gave it for an inheritance unto Israel according to their divisions by their tribes' (Joshua 11: 23). Lemkin's definition in *Axis Rule in Occupied Europe*, then, where an abiding feature of genocide is the destruction of a society and its replacement by an incoming group, clearly applies to the book of Joshua. The Israelites with God assisting enact genocide on the peoples who already inhabit the land of Canaan, destroying their societies and then dividing the land up amongst themselves, at the same time taking possession of their cities, vineyards and olive groves (as God reminds the Israelites in Joshua 24: 13). The Israelites under the command of Joshua invade the land of Canaan because they have been commanded to do so by Moses in Exodus, and Moses in turn has been commanded by God. At the end of the book of Joshua, Joshua adds another reason why the Israelites should remain obedient. He tells the Israelites that for their own sake and safety they should obey God, because God had aided them in their endeavours in Canaan just as he had helped them in Egypt (Joshua 24: 7), and because he is clearly 'a jealous God' who will not forgive their 'transgressions nor … sins' (Joshua 24: 19).

The book of Joshua suggests a fundamental question: who or what is God? In general, the Old Testament stories create God as a character who speaks or whose views are reported by other characters like Moses and Joshua, and who on more than one occasion shows himself in some form. Near the beginning of Exodus, for example, and rather comically, God appears before Moses as a burning bush ('God called unto him out of the midst of the bush, and said, Moses, Moses' – Exodus 3: 4). Indeed, it has long been noticed, from Spinoza in the seventeenth century to Daniel Boyarin and Robert Carroll in the twentieth, that God is fond of making an appearance. In *Tractatus Theologico-Politicus*, Spinoza refers to Exodus 24, where the Israelites' chief men behold God on Mount Sinai (another incident amuses Spinoza, when God appears to Moses but, playfully and rather lewdly, only shows his back parts – Exodus 33: 23).[20] Boyarin also draws attention to sightings of God in Exodus at vital moments in the narrative, in the crossing of the Red Sea and the giving of the Torah.[21]

As Robert Carroll astutely notes, each story of the Old Testament constructs the character of God as part of a specific narrative infused with troubling or puzzling metaphors and images, where the different representations of the deity do not add up to a single, consistent description. In this sense, Carroll reflects, God is a figure of fiction, sometimes arbitrary, savage and cruel, who at times deceives and lies even to prophets, who creates evil as well as good, who can slaughter thousands of people, who even, early in Exodus, for reasons that are not explained, tries to slay Moses ('And it came to pass by the way in the inn, that the Lord met him, and sought to kill him'), who is only saved by the quick thinking of Zipporah, Moses' Midianite wife (Exodus 4: 24–26).[22] Furthermore, Carroll observes, images relating to the alleged hiddenness of God, a notion so important to theology, indeed a fiction of theology, are only a small part of the Old Testament, and much more common are occasions when God is, energetically and visibly, present in various stories, events and encounters.[23] We can conclude that the historical claim that polytheism and monotheism divide over the issue of visibility or hiddenness cannot be sustained. We will return to this issue in our next chapter commenting on German religion in Tacitus' *Germania*.

In the book of Joshua, we can contemplate in Lemkinian spirit the motivation of the character called God to commit genocide.

God insists to Joshua that the Israelites should remember his active interventions on their behalf on their journey towards and during their invasion of Canaan. God says he destroyed peoples like the Amorites because they were in the way of the Israelites ('I gave them into your hand, that ye might possess their land; and I destroyed them from before you' – Joshua 24: 8). Near the end of the Book of Joshua, God admits that he had provoked the wars with the kings who ruled in Canaan, he had chosen 'to harden their hearts, that they should come against Israel in battle', so that Joshua could then 'destroy them' (Joshua 11: 20). (It is worth interpolating here that the contemporary Israeli military have for many years continuously deployed a similar strategy to the one God confides to Joshua; the military provoke the Palestinians into violent resistance; the Israelis then claim to the Western world that they are victims of Palestinian aggression, enabling them to turn far greater violence on the long-suffering people of Palestine.) God's motivation, it would appear, is that he wishes that he and he alone, not other strange gods, should be followed and obeyed by the Israelites. He knows the Israelites have followed other gods in the past and might be tempted to do so again, but now he wants them to 'put away the gods which your fathers served on the other side of the flood, and in Egypt' (Joshua 24: 14). Otherwise, as Joshua warns, God will 'turn and do you hurt, and consume you' (Joshua 24: 20). The Book of Joshua invites us to ponder the moral character of a deity whose only interest seems to be in himself and his own desires and ambitions, for whom and for which the peoples he destroys or helps destroy are of no interest, except that their destruction will help him secure the loyalty of a people he feels he needs to obey him and only him.[24]

In the Book of Joshua, God does not condemn the Israelites for having been polytheistic in the past. He only says he wants them to select and be loyal to him as their god, and to help them in their decision he will use his superpowers – which he had already deployed to best Pharaoh, as he showed to spectacular effect in Exodus[25] – to gift them other peoples' countries, lands, cities, groves and fields (Joshua 24: 11—16).

In the Book of Joshua, God is created as one of the Old Testament's greatest, and therefore one of history's most influential, genocidists.

In terms of Lemkin's outline, in the Book of Joshua, God, Joshua and the Israelites are guilty of genocide on all counts.

In terms of victimology, where before the Israelites had been victims, now they are perpetrators; where before they had cruelly suffered, now they make others cruelly suffer.

In his illuminating notes to the Book of Joshua in the edition of *The Bible* he co-edited, Carroll points out how influential this 'savage' narrative was in later times, not least in early modern England. The annihilation of those perceived as enemies in Joshua and other biblical books was taken to heart by the seventeenth-century English Puritans. Contemporary Protestant discourse equated Catholics with heathen Canaanites. When, in 1649, Oliver Cromwell invaded Ireland, he slaughtered those Irish Catholics who refused to surrender their cities, as in the massacres of Drogheda and Wexford; with the book of Joshua as their divinely prescribed military handbook, Cromwell's men in Ireland behaved like the ancient Israelites in Canaan.[26] In *God, Gulliver, and Genocide*, Claude Rawson also writes that Cromwell saw the conquest of Canaan celebrated in the Book of Joshua as the prototype of his subjugation of the Irish; Cromwell told his troops embarking at Bristol that they were Israelites about to extirpate the idolatrous Canaanites.[27]

I'll close this part of my argument with some brief reflections on the Book of Judges. In his Bible notes, Carroll points out that whereas the book of Joshua gives the impression that Joshua and his army successfully annihilated the Canaanite kings and took over their cities and lands, Judges gives a different picture. Here the Canaanites were not driven out of some of the cities, and in other areas the Israelites were unable to drive them out of the valley; the Canaanites survived in various areas to live alongside the Israelites.[28] In the first chapter of the Book of Judges, we learn that after the death of Joshua, the brothers Judah and Simeon slew many Canaanites and Perizzites (Judges

1: 5) and, as the Greeks had done to Troy, they destroyed Jerusalem: 'Now the children of Judah had fought against Jerusalem, and had taken it, and smitten it with the edge of the sword, and set the city on fire' (Judges 1: 8). Yet, as Carroll comments, conquest was not complete. Thus the Lord assisted Judah to drive out the inhabitants of the mountains, but he 'could not drive out the inhabitants of the valley, because they had chariots of iron' (Judges 1: 19). When the Israelites had become 'strong' in the new land, 'they put the Canaanites to tribute, and did not utterly drive them out', with the surviving Asherites and Amorites also becoming 'tributaries' (Judges 1: 28–35). Rather than being exterminated, as in the Book of Joshua, the Canaanites in Judges were subjugated and reduced to being 'tributaries', perhaps in a state close to slavery.

Recall Lemkin's definition of genocide in Chapter 9 of *Axis Rule in Occupied Europe*, where he makes a distinction between two kinds of destruction and replacement as processes: after destruction of the national pattern of the oppressed group, the imposition of the national pattern of the oppressor 'may be made upon the oppressed population which is allowed to remain, or upon the territory alone, after the removal of the population and the colonization of the area by the oppressor's own nationals'.[29] Such could describe the difference Carroll notes between the books of Joshua and Judges. Genocide as a process of removal of the population and colonization of the area by the oppressor's own nationals would fit the Book of Joshua. Genocide as the imposition on the surviving inhabitants of the land of the oppressor's national pattern would fit the Book of Judges.

Contemporary Zionist Israel, in the late twentieth and early twenty-first centuries, justifying itself in terms of biblical stories, represents an uneasy and unstable blending of both kinds of genocidal processes as described by Lemkin, which is why contemporary scholars have reached for a variety of terms by which to evoke modern Israel as genocidal or on the way to being genocidal. Baruch Kimmerling referred to 'politicide' to evoke the destruction of the national political life of the Palestinians. I have invoked Lemkin's definition in Chapter 9 of *Axis Rule* linking genocide with colonization to refer to Israel as a genocidal settler colony, reducing and replacing the Palestinian population where it can. Ilan Pappé has called on terms like ethnic cleansing, urbanicide and 'memoricide' to describe continuing Israeli attempts to destroy Palestinian society and identity.[30]

In his brilliant chapter 'The Memoricide of the Nakba' in *The Ethnic Cleansing of Palestine*, Pappé evokes the appalling ways that the Zionists from 1948 have deployed biblical sources, in a systematic scholarly, political and military project, to de-Arabize the terrain of conquered Palestine, its names, geography, ecology and history. The Israelis, Pappé writes, seek always to establish a 'metaphorical palimpsest': 'the erasure of the history of one people in order to write that of another people's over it'.[31] We might think here of Deuteronomy, where God instructs the Israelites to carry out precisely such erasure on the landscape of Canaan, to de-Canaanize it:

> Ye shall utterly destroy all the places, wherein the nations which ye shall possess served their gods, upon the high mountains, and upon the hills, and under every green tree:
> And ye shall overthrow the altars, and break their pillars, and burn their groves with fire; and ye shall hew down the graven images of their gods, and destroy the names of them out of that place.
> (Deuteronomy 12: 2–3)[32]

Do such processes of divinely promoted and assisted genocide and colonization, of destruction, ethnic cleansing, politicide, urbanicide, memoricide, replacement, feature in the events and episodes of Virgil's masterpiece?

And what should we think of Jupiter, Yahweh's equivalent divine power in the *Aeneid*? In *Wolf in the Sheepfold*, Carroll says that Yahweh in the Old Testament stories is created very much like other deities in ancient literature, sitting on his throne between the host of heaven (other divine beings). In this sense, Carroll feels,

Yahweh is very similar to other supreme gods in the ancient Near East, its religious cultures tending to have one high god who controls all the other gods, like Zeus in Homer.[33]

## THE *AENEID*

In *The Founding Legend of Western Civilization*, Waswo's analysis of the *Aeneid*, from what we might say is a 'Canaanite' optic, is similar to the Said-inspired postcolonial critique of Exodus and related biblical stories. Waswo evokes the wandering Trojans, looking for a home promised to them by Jupiter, very much in Berger's terms concerning different kinds of nomads. Wandering forlornly for seven years across and about the Mediterranean, the Trojans are not customary wanderers who wish to keep wandering in place, time and thought; rather, the Trojans are beholden to a notion of possessive nomadism, the mindset of a nomadic group who invade and take over a settled agricultural society. And just as the Israelites go from being a people fleeing loss and experiencing suffering to being captors and victors themselves, from victims to perpetrators, so the Trojans in the *Aeneid*, Waswo points out, go from being a people fleeing a burning Troy to a people who invade and conquer Italy and assume power over its local inhabitants, thence founding Rome and setting the scene for the greatest empire the ancient world had yet seen.

In the spirit of Berger and Regina Schwartz talking about Exodus and Old Testament textuality, Waswo asks us to consider the *Aeneid* as a great poem that offers grounds for being critical of the 'linear teleology' that drives the epic relentlessly along. We must distinguish, in Waswo's view, between the consciousness of Aeneas, the poem's hero, and the events, representations, images and motifs of the poem as a whole. 'In sum', says Waswo, 'it would be hard to overestimate either the intelligence or the complexity and ambivalence of Virgil's founding epic.' In particular, Waswo argues, the poem in its entirety as a text demonstrates the 'cost' of what Aeneas achieves in his invasion of Italy. Aeneas and the Trojans face Latins, along with Etruscans and Rutulians, who already possess what the Trojans value, civilization based on agriculture and cities. The Trojans assume, nevertheless, that these peoples and societies haven't got as much of such civilization as the cultivated Trojans, for the Trojans never lose their assumption that they are superior, they are history's paradigmatic culture-bringers. Aeneas and the Trojans will bring civilization as they understand it to the Italians, and as Waswo acidly notes, what we register is that in the process the rude Italians may get civilized, or become more civilized, at the hands of the Trojans, but also, 'most of them get dead'.[34]

Waswo suggests that the predominant way the *Aeneid* has been received in Western culture does not, however, recognize the poem's complexity and self-questioning. On the contrary, from Roman antiquity to modernity, the *Aeneid* has been perceived as an honourable justification for invasion, colonization and destruction of indigenous societies. What developed, he feels, is a Western 'myth' of the *Aeneid*, even to the fantastical extent of accepting it for 2,000 years after its writing as actual history.[35]

In his preface, Waswo outlines the constituent elements of the myth that is diffused about the poem. The *Aeneid* is taken as defining what culture is and who possesses it. Culture signifies cultivation, which is linked both to notions of high culture, as in religion and art, and to the act of tilling the soil. Civilization signifies a settled agricultural community that sows, harvests, builds cities and institutes law. The reverse of civilization is savagery, from the Latin *silvestris*, of the woods, and the designation of savagery can be applied to all other relations that human beings may have with the earth, as in hunting, gathering and nomadic pastoralism. Civilization also, however, makes journeys, is in constant motion. Civilization always comes from elsewhere. Here the journey of Aeneas and the Trojans, as escapees from the destroyed city of Troy who proceed to settlement and empire-building in another place, to which they bring culture, learning and law, is exemplary. The Trojans then become the ancestors of choice for medieval Europeans from Britain to Bohemia, from

Sicily to Iceland. In their successive journeys and settlings, from the Trojans as heroes in the *Aeneid* to medieval and later times, Trojan-like culture-bringers 'assimilate or destroy the indigenous people and ways of life they find there'. Even when, Waswo reflects, it ceased to be regarded as actual history, the definitions and categories associated with the accepted myth of the *Aeneid* were absorbed into the fabric of Western discourse. In particular, the myth's emplotment of admirable conquest and settlement becomes a universal Western narrative that prescribes, up to the very present, what is civilized and what uncivilized for all culture, and hence what is progress for humanity.[36]

In the myth associated with the *Aeneid*, Waswo maintains, because the Trojans founded Rome and become Romans, all those who subsequently deployed the myth as justification for what they did in its name could claim not only the Trojans but the ancient Romans, they who had established a great empire, as their spiritual ancestors; they could claim not only Aeneas as a founding father figure, but Rome's first emperor, Augustus, portrayed in the *Aeneid* as Aeneas's lineal descendant. Furthermore, Waswo points out, having effected a settlement and taken possession of somewhere, as Columbus did when he was held to *discover* America, the culture-bringers also inaugurate history itself in the new place or new situation; all indigenous histories, including the aboriginal languages, before the culture-bringers come and found the new, are infantilized, are regarded as of little contemporary interest. Here again the story of the coming of Trojan Rome is regarded as exemplary, ignoring or minimizing its costs and consequences for those who were there before Rome. As Waswo graphically writes, the foundation of Rome inevitably entailed the unfounding of somebody else: 'The walls and towers of Rome rise over and upon the blood and bones of non-Romans.' And here Waswo, like so many others who ponder the history of the West and its alleged deserved triumph as a civilization, is moved to call on Walter Benjamin's aphorism – or should we say epitaph? – in 'Theses on the Philosophy of History', that there is no document of civilization which is not at the same time a document of barbarism.[37]

## NARRATIVE AND COUNTER-NARRATIVE: THE COSTS
## OF CONQUEST, COLONIZATION, EMPIRE

Waswo's analysis is very illuminating indeed. What I would like to do now is extend his argument by pursuing a comparison of the *Aeneid* with Exodus and other Old Testament narratives, in terms of my interest in Jupiter's similarities with the character of God in stories like the books of Exodus and Joshua, and my more general interest in notions of victimology, genocide, supersessionism and ethical deterioration. In *The Founding Legend of Western Civilization*, Waswo stresses not only the costs involved in the Western myth of the *Aeneid* for those, especially the indigenous of the world, who are killed, removed, displaced, subjugated and assimilated by 'Trojans' who are idealized as, or idealize themselves as, rightful conquerors and culture-bringers; he also points out the costs of conquest and notions of culture-bringing for the conquerors and colonizers themselves, in terms of ethical deficiencies and limitations. Here, his book suggests, in the complex and ambivalent structure inhering in the *Aeneid*, there is a tension between on the one hand a triumphalist narrative of Trojan success leading to the founding of Rome as city and empire, and on the other hand a counter-narrative, of the costs and consequences for both conquered and conquerors of that success.[38]

For example, as Waswo says, a notorious feature of the *Aeneid* is the 'passivity of its hero' and 'the general apparent lack of any human agency'. Aeneas, usually described as dutiful and pious, father of his people, the embodiment of its culture and civilization, throughout the poem hopes and trusts that he is carrying out a teleological plan already thought out for him by Jupiter. Aeneas, Waswo observes, never initiates any course of sustained action. He might worry about what is happening, or what he should do next, or mistake where to go, or react to what others say and do. But if he strays too far away from Jupiter's preordained project of conquering Italy and creating Rome, when for instance he falls in love with Queen Dido in Carthage and looks like he will stay there with her in marriage and partnership, Jupiter will intervene to remind him of his eventual goal and steer him onwards towards it. Aeneas's frequent perplexity and anxiety is related directly to his lack of knowledge of what Jupiter might want him to do at any stage of his journey, but he never questions the rightness and correctness of what, once he learns what Jupiter wants, he should do. It is Jupiter who, Waswo notes, despite the contrary efforts especially of his wife and sister Juno to secure a different outcome, controls, from beginning to end, the overall journey and its goal.[39]

Let's now compare Aeneas with Moses in relation to human and divine agency in terms of Spinoza's judgement that Moses in Exodus infantilizes his followers, making sure they submit to God's commands. In so doing, Moses himself experiences a severe ethical limitation: he refuses what Berger refers to as an ideal of autonomous internalized ethical art. Perhaps here is one meaning of the strange incident I mentioned before that occurs early in Exodus, when God attacks Moses even before he has returned to Egypt on God's suggestion to rescue the Israelites from bondage.

> And it came to pass by the way in the inn, that the Lord met him, and sought to kill him.
>
> Then Zipporah took a sharp stone, and cut off the foreskin of her son, and cast *it* at his feet, and said, Surely a bloody husband *art* thou to me.
>
> So he let him go: then she said, A bloody husband *thou art*, because of the circumcision.
>
> (Exodus 4: 24–26)

As bafflingly opaque and obscure as this episode is, it could suggest that the character we know as God in Exodus is warning Moses, to the point of violent death, never to be independent, never to cultivate an autonomous internal ethical art. Moses should carry out God's commands when he learns what they are, he should never subject them to profound interrogation and challenge, neither in terms of developing in himself and the Israelites a sensibility of questioning and self-questioning, nor in terms of the costs to other nations of what God enjoins the Israelites to do when they eventually invade the promised land. Should they invade the lands of others? Here, surely, Moses and Aeneas share a disturbing lack of criticality and self-criticality.

There is, however, an interesting difference in terms of gender signified in the incident of God attacking Moses in the inn. Throughout the encounter, Moses remains curiously passive. But Zipporah does not remain passive before God, she immediately acts, heroically and resolutely, to save Moses. Zipporah's action underlines her belief in the strength of their relationship, and how much women can act powerfully in history; she reminds us of the formidable women of classical Greek tragedy, of Clytemnestra or Andromache. In Book Four of the *Aeneid*, Jupiter, irritated that Aeneas is 'dallying' with Dido, tells his messenger Mercury to go 'speak to the Trojan leader who now lingers in Tyrian Carthage without a thought for the cities granted to him by the Fates'.[40]

Alighting in Carthage, Mercury quickly reminds Aeneas that his 'destiny' is to obey the commands of Jupiter, 'the ruler of the gods himself, by whose divine will the heavens and the earth revolve'. Just as the God of Exodus and Joshua had reminded the Israelites that they were to take over the land of Canaan for their inheritance, Mercury reminds Aeneas that his son and heir Ascanius will one day inherit 'the land of Rome and the kingdom of Italy'. As soon as he hears what Mercury has to say, Aeneas jumps to attention, longing 'to be away and leave behind him this land he had found so sweet'. When Dido tells him that she feels 'utterly betrayed and desolate', Aeneas struggles 'to fight down the anguish of his heart', but acquires the necessary determination when he recalls Jupiter's warnings. He informs Dido that he has no choice: 'Do not go on causing distress to yourself and to me by these complaints. It is not by my own will that I search for Italy.' The cost of that search to himself, then, will not only be the love and passion he shares with Dido but also his own capacity for *Bildung*, his ability and desire to cultivate an autonomous internal ethical art, his freedom to think and be different from what the father god has decreed is his fate.[41]

Part of Dido's anger at Aeneas, as we can see from our epigraph, is her realization that Aeneas has no will of his own, that he has made himself an instrument of a destiny and purpose designed for him by Jupiter and Apollo, and that he won't resist these gods, he won't stand up for his love and his relationship with Dido even as he sees how distraught and despairing she had become at the news of his departure, which he had tried to conceal from her.[42]

The story of Dido is a key part of the counter-narrative of the *Aeneid*, her pathos and tragedy an eternal commentary on the human costs of Aeneas's ethical passivity.[43] (We might think here of Rebecca in Walter Scott's *Ivanhoe*, created like Dido as oriental, her near-death as a witch in late twelfth-century England a sad commentary on medieval Christian exclusions, persecutions and brutality.)[44]

## WOMEN AND MEN

In the *Aeneid*, women are hindrances and obstacles, as Dido unhappily proved to be. Women are to be left behind or abandoned or lost sight of. In Book Two, 'The Fall of Troy', as Troy burned at the hands of the Greeks, Aeneas loses sight of his wife Creusa and never sees her again, though she appears before him as a ghost to reassure him that the 'King of High Olympus' has decreed that she not go to Italy where the Trojans' 'long exile' will be ended: 'There prosperity is waiting for you, and a kingdom and a royal bride.'[45] Creusa: gone! Women also become possessed by irrational madness, as occurs with Dido in Book Four when she is overwhelmed by grief. In her desire for revenge against Aeneas, Dido even sows the seeds of the future destruction of Carthage by the Romans. Dido prays to her fellow Tyrians that 'you must pursue with hatred the whole line' of Aeneas's descendants in time to come: 'Make that your offering to my shade. Let there be no love between our peoples and no treaties.'[46] In Book Five, 'Funeral Games', when the Trojan fleet stops over at a friendly shore, the women, while the men participate in various games and contests, realize they are tired of travel across endless seas; they long to stay where they are and build a city to live in. Their feelings of exhaustion and weariness are worked on by Juno's messenger Iris into a kind of madness, the women setting fire to Aeneas's ships so that the Trojan journey may end. Fortunately, on Aeneas's appeal, Jupiter sends down a 'deluge of torrential rain' which saves most of the fleet. Aeneas then decides to leave the women behind, along with the old men and anyone else worn down by their long exile. Only a 'small band' of 'warriors', 'their hearts ... high for war', would now press on to fulfil 'the command of Jupiter'.[47]

In the *Aeneid*'s counter-narrative, it is women even in what appears to be their irrational madness who are strong, the men weak because without will or ideas of their own. Like Zipporah in Exodus, women in the *Aeneid* can choose to be indifferent to divine plans, to the father god, can resist, can insist on other courses or values, can be independent unlike pious, dutiful, obedient men such as Aeneas. I'm reminded of an observation by Gandhi: 'To call women the weaker sex is a libel; it is man's injustice to woman ... If by strength is meant moral power then woman is immeasurably man's superior.'[48] As Waswo's book argues, and as the victimological narrative shared by both Israelites in Exodus and the Old Testament and Trojans in the *Aeneid* appears to warrant, those who have suffered persecution and exile, and believe the father god is arranging their destiny, and are sure they are superior culture-bringers, feel they have the right to go anywhere without asking permission of a land or island's inhabitants. As soon as they arrive on a shore, they assume rights of plunder or settlement, without checking to see if it is inhabited or not.

It is resisting women or female figures, like the Harpies or Juno, who in the *Aeneid* spell out the costs and consequences of conquest and colonization. In Book Three, 'The Wanderings', Aeneas relates how his ships are thrown off course in a storm; they drift blindly in the waves for three starless nights, until they happen upon the Strophades, islands in the Ionian sea. The Trojans are unaware that the islands are inhabited by Harpies, whom Aeneas regards as 'the vilest of monsters', 'birds with the faces of girls, with filth oozing from their bellies, with hooked claws for hands and faces pale with a hunger that is never satisfied'. On entering a harbour, the Trojans see on every side rich herds of cattle and flocks of goats unguarded on the grass; they draw their swords and rush upon them, 'calling on the gods and on Jupiter himself to share our plunder'. As they sit about feasting on this 'rich fare', they are suddenly attacked by the Harpies. Aeneas immediately orders his 'men to arm themselves to make war against this fearsome tribe'. In reply, Celaeno, one of the Harpies, challenges the right of the Trojans to land anywhere and plunder:

> Is it war you offer us now, sons of Laomedon, for the slaughter of our bullocks and the felling of our oxen? Is it your plan to make war against the innocent Harpies and drive us from the kingdom of our ancestors?[49]

Celaeno's question is the cry of the invaded through history, a cry we have already witnessed in the King of the Ethiops and Queen of the Massagetae in Herodotus, and made by the women of Troy in Euripides' tragedies.

It is another powerful female figure, this time Juno herself, Queen of Heaven, who, as we can see from our epigraph, provides the counter-narrative of the *Aeneid* with sharp questioning of the presumed ethical right of the Trojans to conquer and colonize Italy. In Book Ten, in defiance of Jupiter's support for the Trojan invasion, Juno wonders why it is that he does not support the indigenous leader Turnus instead of the invader Aeneas. Why is it wrong, she asks, 'for Turnus to take his stand in the land of his fathers'?[50]

Juno is not heeded by Jupiter, who continues to support Aeneas's invasion and forbids her from any further interference.

It is not a woman of power, authority and equality in relationship that Aeneas, guided by Jupiter, ends up with in Italy. When he secures the hand of the Italian king's daughter Lavinia in marriage, the weak Lavinia is but an instrument of the advancement of his conquest and final terms of settlement with the subjugated peoples of Italy. She has no say in the matter, Aeneas does not love her, and they enter a loveless marriage together. Lavinia, however, had been loved by Turnus ('Turnus was distraught with love' – Book Twelve)[51] – who is savagely killed by Aeneas at the end of the poem.[52]

## ORIENTALISM AND EUROPEAN IDENTITY

Juno, nonetheless, is listened to by Jupiter on another matter, the question of what kind of people the Trojans, once successful in their conquest of Italy, should be in terms of ethnos: should they remain an oriental people, from Troy/Asia, or become a European people? Recalling Agamemnon's contempt in Aeschylus' great tragedy for Troy as oriental and effeminate in its liking for beautiful materials, Aeneas, in his journey westwards, is frequently perceived as oriental. In Book Four, in Carthage, Mercury notices that Aeneas's sword is 'studded with yellow stars of jasper, and glowing with Tyrian purple there hung from his shoulders a rich cloak given him by Dido into which she had woven a fine cross-thread of gold'. In Book Nine, in Italy, Ascanius is mocked along with the other Trojan warriors as an effeminate Phrygian: 'you like your clothes dyed with yellow saffron and the bright juice of the purple fish. ... You have sleeves to your tunics and ribbons to keep your bonnets on. You are Phrygian women, not Phrygian men!' In Book Twelve, Turnus also accuses Aeneas of being an 'effeminate Phrygian'.[53]

In Book Twelve, the final book of the *Aeneid*, Juno suggests to Jupiter that he should not command the defeated Latins of Italy 'to change their ancient name in their own land, to become Trojans. ... They are men. Do not make them change their voice or native dress.' Juno's urging that the 'stock of Rome be made mighty by the manly courage of Italy' is readily agreed to by Jupiter, who says he will make the Trojans and the peoples they've conquered 'all Latins, speaking one tongue'. Juno is arguing against a genocidal aspect of assimilation, that the conquered peoples of a land should lose their culture and identity. Yet the effect of Juno's intervention is a repudiation of aesthetic and cultural aspects of the Orient from which the Trojans had come, in terms of dress, style and language. The Trojans will be de-orientalized and de-Asianized, to become Romans and Europeans. To be European is to be manly, not effeminate, and perhaps another implication of Aeneas's eventual marriage with Lavinia is that European women should be like Lavinia, insipid and accepting, not strong, powerful and passionate like the oriental Carthaginian Dido.

The cost of such repudiation of the Orient is a loss of conversations and mutual interactions with the Orient. As the Trojans become Romans, the European and Western ethnos is remodelled into a single exclusive identity.


## CONCLUSION

Neither of the father gods, Jupiter or God, brooks any disagreement with their plans and commands, which are set firmly against the indigenous peoples and nations of Italy or of Canaan, or by extension of anywhere else in the world. The narratives of Exodus and *Aeneid* suggest, reassuringly for those who wish to engage in such activities, that divine sanction is given to conquest, colonization and genocide. In terms of Waswo's important insight in *The Founding Legend of Western Civilization*, the rights of invading culture-bringers are privileged over the rights of the indigenous of any land, who should not resist their coming.

If the moral character of both father gods is dubious and dangerous for humanity, so too is the moral character of Aeneas and Moses. Aeneas and Moses are unchanging or fixed characters as defined by Mikhail Bakhtin in his famous essay 'Forms of Time and Chronotope in the Novel' in *The Dialogic Imagination*; their qualities as heroes in a narrative are tested in situations of danger and tribulation, through which their initial virtues are proved and affirmed, but they do not open themselves to transformation and metamorphosis.[54] If Jupiter commands Aeneas, and the God of Exodus commands Moses, neither Aeneas nor Moses can exercise any ethical choice when it comes to conquest and colonizing, even when they know what the destructive consequences for other peoples and nations will be. Moses knows, since God has told him early in Exodus, that the lands of a considerable number of societies, those of the Canaanites, Hittites, Amorites, Perizzites, Hivites and Jebusites, along with their milk and honey, will be violently taken away from them (Exodus 3: 8). Moses does not question the justice of such a genocidal procedure, he does not say to God, such an action with such consequences would be wrong.

Similarly, early in Book Six, 'The Underworld', when Aeneas consults the Sibyl of Cumae concerning the future of the Trojans, she replies that the Trojans, 'the sons of Dardanus', will come into their kingdom in Italy ('put that fear out of your mind'), but, she says, 'it is a coming they will wish they had never known. I see wars, deadly wars, I see the Thybris foaming with torrents of blood.'[55] When in the underworld Aeneas meets his father, Anchises, he learns from him of the 'glory that was to come' for the Trojans and Rome and its 'mighty empire', glory that would be won by war against and slaughter of many peoples, from the Nile to the Caspian Sea, including the wars that Aeneas himself would have to fight in Italy in order to establish Rome. Given such prophecy and knowledge, Aeneas could, but does not, question the rightness of the wars to come, the justice of war, conquest, colonization and empire.[56]

In Raphaël Lemkin's terms, the Trojans enact genocide on the peoples and nations of Italy. Such genocide, however, is not carried out on the model of what occurs in the Book of Joshua, where the Canaanites and other peoples are exterminated. Rather, it is similar to what occurs in the Book of Judges, where the Canaanites and Perizzites and the other nations are not utterly destroyed or driven out, but are subjugated and become tributaries.

In this sense, the Trojan invasion of Italy in the *Aeneid* recalls that part of Lemkin's definition of genocide in *Axis Rule*, where, after destruction of the national pattern of the oppressed group, the national pattern of the oppressor is imposed upon the oppressed population which is allowed to remain.[57]

Two final reflections. As Waswo remarks, the extreme violence and fury of Aeneas's killing of the indigenous leader Turnus, the event that brings the *Aeneid* to a close, clearly reprises the savagery of Achilles' killing of Hector in the *Iliad*.[58] Aeneas and the Trojans, in terms of their moral consciousness as created in the *Aeneid*, have learnt nothing from the Greek destruction of Troy: despite their sufferings, they took away no fundamental sense that it is morally wrong to invade, destroy, reduce, burn, subjugate, enslave another city, another people, another land. What Aeneas and his band of Trojan male warriors ('their hearts … high for war' – Book Five), took away as a lesson of history from the Greek destruction of Troy was that they were victims who were now condemned to years of wandering and homelessness. But they did not conclude that they themselves, if they had a future opportunity, should not inflict destruction on other peoples in other lands, especially if they could claim that they had a distant ancestral connection with a land, the Trojans frequently reminding themselves that they were descended from Dardanus who had once come from Italy and had founded Troy.[59] In terms of supersessionism, throughout the *Aeneid* the Trojans express their dislike and contempt for the Greeks, their desire that they supplant them in history, often to the point of anti-Greek racism, characterizing 'the ways of a whole people' (Book Two) in terms of treachery, cruelty, artfulness, scheming, cunning and cowardice.[60] Yet by poem's end, in the culmination of the counter-narrative in Aeneas's killing of Turnus, the Trojan invaders and colonizers are the new Greeks of their world, the successors of Agamemnon and Ulysses as ruthless, brutal conquerors.

Similarly, in the biblical stories, the Israelites, having experienced oppression and persecution in Egypt, did not resolve that they should abjure violence, oppression and persecution in relation to other peoples, as in the land of Canaan. Similarly with the contemporary Zionists. The Zionists, who created the modern state of Israel in 1948 and who since that time have dominated Jewish organizations and community thinking across the globe, did not take away from the Holocaust a historical lesson that different peoples should live in amity, share a polity and learn from each other, be cosmopolitan and international. Nor did they become interested in non-violence, as in Gandhi or, in Jewish tradition, Josephus.[61] They did not look back to Moorish Spain, to the living together in the one land of Jews, Muslims and Christians, as an inspiring example of what a society could ideally be. To the contrary, the Zionists have kept on working towards achieving a European nationalist and settler-colonial ideal that they had conceived in the 1890s: they have kept on working towards genocide of the Palestinians, to subjugate, reduce, displace, expel and kill them whenever and wherever within Palestine-Israel they can, in order to replace them with their own colonial settlements and exclusive society. They refuse to the indigenous of Palestine, the Palestinians and Sephardim and Oriental Jews, equality, dignity, sharing, interaction, mutual respect. The Zionists, since the 1890s, have seen themselves as European culture-bringers, before whom the rights of the indigenous peoples of Palestine are of no account. Every day the Zionists commit genocide against the Palestinians in Lemkin's terms of displacement and replacement, and every day the Western world looks on approvingly, only occasionally murmuring if the Zionists move towards genocide based on Joshua rather than Judges. The West does so, to adapt Waswo's terms in *The Founding Legend of Western Civilization*, because the West accepts that 'Trojans' and 'Israelites', culture-bringers and rightful colonizers, as in the *Aeneid* and Exodus, have every right to go anywhere, while the indigenous of any land have no or minimal rights.

My last point concerns first contact, and returns us to puzzling aspects of the overall history of Western conquest, colonization and empire, engaging with the important question of intent.[62]

How much did the Trojan entry into Italy in the *Aeneid* involve conscious deception of the indigenous inhabitants? In

Book Seven, 'War in Latium', Aeneas orders a hundred men to go to the local king, Latinus, bearing olive branches and 'carrying gifts and asking for peace for the Trojans'. Meanwhile, belying such apparently peaceful intentions, Aeneas immediately busies himself at his 'first settlement on the shore with a stockade and rampart as though it were a camp'. Latinus 'kindly' offers his visitors 'guest-friendship'. Ilioneus, spokesman for the Trojans, tells him of their sufferings after the fall of Troy and their sailing over desolate seas since that 'cataclysm'; in their homelessness, all the Trojans ask, he pleads, is 'for a little piece of land for our fathers' gods, for harmless refuge on the beach, for the air and sea which are there for all men'. He also brings some 'small relics' from Aeneas, gifts to the king rescued from the flames of Troy, a gold cup, a sceptre, a sacred headdress. Yet Ilioneus also introduces a larger purpose, and hints at a threat of force, telling the king that the Trojans are seeking out his country by 'the commands of divine destiny', 'the destiny of Aeneas and his right arm ... strong in war and the weapons of war'. He advises the king to submerge his interests in the destiny of Aeneas and the Trojans, for that way the king will win 'great fame'.[63] In his image of the 'air and sea which are there for all men', there is a hint of the doctrine of natural law that had been both put forward as natural and right but also sharply questioned as indefensible and unjust in Cicero's *Republic*: that people have a natural right to go anywhere, it is the human condition itself.

In such conversation with the indigenous inhabitants of Italy, are the Trojans being truthful and honourable? Do they really mean it when they say they would rest content with a little piece of land and harmless refuge on a beach? Or are they, in passing before their interlocutors the image of Aeneas's military prowess, 'strong in war and the weapons of war', intimating, threatening and promising force and war in the service of a wider aim, which they regard as divinely sanctioned and prophesied, to take possession of the whole land they have arrived at and subjugate the peoples therein? Do the Trojans themselves know what they mean? Have they arrived as supplicants or invaders, courteous curious visitors or with conquest in their hearts? We know from elsewhere in the *Aeneid* that the Trojans admire warrior ideals and anticipations of glory and glorious death. (In Book Six in the underworld, Anchises' visions of the Trojan future in Italy kindled in Aeneas's mind 'a love for the glory that was to come ... the wars he would in due course have to fight'; in Book Nine, Nisus and Euryalus earn a glorious death by their military deeds.)[64] Are the Trojans, ur-colonizers as it were, uncertain and confused, and so do they create uncertainty in and confuse those they talk to in the land to which they have come?[65]

Such questions will have resonance in our following chapters, and indeed have keen resonance for the whole history of European colonization from early modern times onwards.

# 6 ROMAN SETTLER IMPERIALISM IN BRITAIN: NARRATIVE AND COUNTER-NARRATIVE IN TACITUS'S *AGRICOLA* AND *GERMANIA*

On them [the Romans] I impose no limits of time or place. I have given them an empire that will know no end ... the people of Rome, the rulers of the world, the race that wears the toga. So it has been decreed.

> (Jupiter to Venus, *Aeneid*, Book One)[1]

Pillagers of the world, they [the Romans] exhausted the land by their indiscriminate plunder, and now they ransack the sea. A rich enemy excites their cupidity; a poor one, their lust for power. East and West alike have failed to satisfy them. ... To robbery, butchery, and rapine, they give the lying name of 'government'; they create a desolation and call it peace.

> (The Caledonian leader Calgacus in Tacitus,
> the *Agricola*, Chapter 30)[2]

In this chapter we explore the *Agricola* and *Germania*, the works by which Tacitus launched his career as a historian, written early in the Common Era (both appearing in 98 CE), as the Roman empire attempted to secure its ongoing imperial domination in Britain and Germany. To move from Exodus and the *Aeneid*, in order to analyse the *Agricola*, and to a lesser extent the *Germania*, is to move from poetry to historiography. Yet if the texts of Exodus and the *Aeneid* are conflicted, are crossed by tensions between a narrative that affirms certain values and a counter-narrative that interpolates doubts, so too are these historical texts, which reveal, in Mikhail Bakhtin's terms, quite an abundance of polyphony.

In Bakhtin's view, genres have their own memory. In *Problems of Dostoevsky's Poetics*, Bakhtin writes that a genre is always the same and yet not the same, always old and new simultaneously. A genre lives in the present, but always remembers its past, its beginnings, even its archaic elements. At every new stage in the development of literature and in every work of a given genre, genre is reborn and renewed.[3] The *Agricola* and *Germania* move between a number of genres: biography, eulogy, ethnography, military history, family history; and these genres in turn are inflected by the literary-philosophical mode of the menippea, with its sharp edges and reflective ethos. The menippea does not resolve textual tensions.[4] In these terms, the *Agricola* and *Germania* are intriguingly grainy, not smoothly finished, texts.

In contrast to Herodotus and Thucydides in relation to imperial Athens, Tacitus was throughout his life at the centre of Roman society and culture, as orator, senator, consul, provincial governor, however difficult he might find life under unjust and cruel emperors. He became the son-in-law of Julius Agricola (40–93 CE), governor of Britain 77–84 CE, and he himself would become governor of the prized Roman province of Asia. I will, however, observe the critical convention of distinguishing between the author and historical figure Tacitus, and 'Tacitus' as troubled and uncertain narrator of a text with its own independent life and force and long generic history. I am mindful here of Bakhtin's observation, in the essay 'Forms of Time and Chronotope in the Novel' in

*The Dialogic Imagination*, that in literature at the time of Tacitus and Plutarch in the Hellenistic and Roman era, the image of the public unity and wholeness of the individual was beginning to break up, accompanied by a differentiation between biography and autobiography.[5] Tacitus inherits aesthetically and discursively powerful modes and models of historical writing, including rhetorical strategies concerning the set speeches of various protagonists in historical situations for or against a particular action or design. Indeed, we might also say that rhetoric has its own memory. By such rhetorical strategies, in an interplay of affirmative narrative and critical counter-narrative, his historical writing participates in those traditions of questioning fundamental values of one's world evident in Cicero's *Republic* and Virgil's *Aeneid* as much as in their great predecessor texts in the classical Greek world, Herodotus's *Histories* and Thucydides' *History of the Peloponnesian War*.

There are fissures within the narrative voice, especially of the *Agricola*, between a monologic, centripetal desire to stress a single positive meaning for empire, and a dialogic, centrifugal release of other perspectives, unsettling, dissenting, anxious. Biography as eulogy meets autobiography as doubt and detachment. Biography as admiring family history of an imperial colonizer becomes entangled with intimations of disintegrating family life for those experiencing imperial and colonial rule, including the kidnapping of children (*Agricola*, 15). In terms of ethnography, the sympathies of the narrator become divided and confused; there is no univocal rendering of a triumph of values of the victors in history. As military history, it is made clear how the values of the invading army conflict with the very different values of those attempting armed resistance.

The play of narrative and counter-narrative constitutes these texts as menippean, the testing of an idea, embodied in the image of a wise man who seeks the truth of this idea in extraordinary situations, in unknown and fantastic lands.[6] In the *Agricola* and *Germania*, that idea is the notion and possibility of honourable colonization. The wise man, or apparently wise man, who seeks to embody this idea is Agricola, the Roman governor of Britain, Tacitus's own father-in-law and putative hero of his narration, come to reside at the edge of the known world.

In the *Agricola* and *Germania* as menippean texts we witness tensions between the discourse of honourable imperial and colonial rule, and critical reflections, both from indigenous figures experiencing the Roman imperium and the narrator himself, which test and interrogate that discourse. These tensions also work themselves out as conflicts between inherited historical ideals, between the cosmopolitanism, anti-ethnocentrism and internationalism of Herodotus and Thucydides' histories, and rival claims to the centrality of Rome, divinely assisted in its imperial glory.


## AFFIRMATIVE NARRATIVE

Tacitus's *Agricola* and *Germania* would prove profoundly influential in later European colonizings and empires, conceived as a history of sensibility and consciousness. The idea of honourable colonization became an extremely important discourse in European and Western history, enabling colonization, with the best and most sensitive and highest of motives, to occur and keep occurring; motives that apparently transcend the particular consequences for those being invaded, colonized and dispossessed.[7] In the figure of Agricola, Tacitus' text, as biography and eulogy, appears to celebrate successful imperial power, wise administration and Roman glory. In Agricola as a created character, we can witness the actions and thinking of the honourable colonizer.

Agricola, passing his boyhood and youth in the 'cultivation of all the liberal arts', appreciated 'Greek refinement', though he also came to realize that contemporary Roman society differed in its attitudes to knowledge from classical Greece. Tacitus as narrator recalls that Agricola would say that 'in his early youth he was tempted to drink deeper of philosophy than was allowable for a Roman and a future senator' (4). In a Rome that would periodically banish its philosophers, Agricola knew that he would never succeed in an active life if he did not dampen his enthusiasm for philosophy (2, 4). In Rome and the empire, political and military success were entwined, and it was a military path that Agricola pursued. When young, the *Agricola* tells us, Agricola served his 'military apprenticeship' in Britain, and his spirit became 'possessed by a passion for military glory' (5).

When, later in life, Agricola took control of Roman rule in Britain, he liked to infuse his soldiers with a similar passion. In one campaign, Agricola goes north to combat and attempt to subdue the Caledonians. In his pre-battle speech, he reminds his soldiers that he and they are conquering Britain 'in the name of imperial Rome's divinely guided greatness' (33). As it turns out, Agricola decisively wins the battle, the Caledonians flee and 'pursuit' of them goes on 'till night fell and our soldiers were tired of killing'; 'some 10,000' of 'the enemy' are killed (37). With this victory Agricola secured a large degree of Roman domination of Britain, a domination he nevertheless wished could be complete. Agricola, Tacitus records, was often heard to say that he would like to conquer Ireland, for if the Britons were completely surrounded by Roman armies so that 'liberty' became unthinkable, the Roman hold on Britain would become much easier to maintain (24).

The affirmative narrative is staunchly committed to the overwhelming importance of Rome in and to the world and to certain Roman ideals. The narrator admires martial virtues and military glory, however suspicious emperors were of those who achieved fame by such means (5). When Vespasian (father of Domitian) had restored stable government to Roman Britain, there came to the island, Tacitus as narrator enthuses, a 'succession of great generals and splendid armies' (17). By his successful campaigns in Britain, Agricola was extolled as a brilliant governor, though Agricola himself wisely decided, the narrator adds, not to 'use his success to glorify himself', even choosing to say that his action in subduing one tribe was not a 'campaign of conquest' but merely one of keeping a defeated tribe under control (18). At the end of his biography as eulogy, Tacitus acclaims the 'glorious life' of Agricola (45), a glory based mainly on imperial military success.

The narrator tends to judge a people or society by its possession or not of military virtues. The Gauls are commented on harshly for brave displays in challenging danger yet 'cowardice in shirking it when it comes close' (11). The Romans will achieve 'glory' even if they die in battle, for, as Agricola says to his soldiers before the battle with the Caledonians, such 'honourable death' is better than a 'disgraceful attempt to save our lives' (33). Above all, the narrator believes in the 'glory of Rome' and its empire, a glory and empire that, as Agricola assures his troops in Britain, is 'divinely guided' towards 'greatness' (23, 33).

The narrator believes that peace is disabling for a society, remarking of the Britons in the *Agricola* that they show more spirit than the Gauls because they, the Britons, 'have not yet been enervated by protracted peace' (11). It is a view that, rather in the spirit of Pericles in addressing the Athenian assembly, lauds warfare and anticipation and enjoyment of war as worthy ideals of an active energetic society. Romans are also to be admired for their historical consciousness, their knowledge of and capacity to reflect on their own history. By contrast, 'barbarians' like the Britons are barbarians in a pejorative sense (not simply foreigners) because they lack historical consciousness, Tacitus observing of the Britons that they knew nothing of where they had come from, whether they were 'natives or immigrants' (11). The 10,000 Caledonians killed by Agricola's troops appear to inspire no pity in Tacitus as narrator, no *Iliad*-like foregrounding of the misery of war. Instead, he records with sadness the death of a Roman soldier Aulus Atticus who had perished through youthful impetuosity, carried deep into the ranks of the enemy by his mettlesome horse (37).

Many of these themes and motifs are shared between the *Agricola* and the *Germania*, though there is more ethnography in the *Germania* than in the *Agricola*, with its biographical portrait. The narrator of the *Germania* admires many qualities of the Germans, for example, their generous hospitality, including to strangers, and the strength of relationships between men and women. In battle, squadrons and divisions are composed of men of one family or clan; close by them in the fighting are their 'nearest and dearest, so that they can hear the shrieks of their women-folk and the wailing of their children'. The women and children are the witnesses that each man reverences the most and whose praise he most desires; it is to their mothers and wives that they go to have their wounds treated; the women also carry supplies of food to the combatants and encourage them in the battle. The *Germania* praises the monogamous German marriage code, where on marrying the new wife is encouraged to be the partner of her husband's 'toils and perils', sharing his sufferings and adventures in both peace and war; the wife realizes that she is not 'excluded from aspirations to manly virtues or exempt from the hazards of warfare' (*Germania* 18, 21).

The *Germania* says it is on record that German armies wavering and on the point of collapse have been rallied by the women, 'pleading heroically with their men, thrusting forward their bared bosoms, and making them realize the imminent prospect of enslavement', a fate, the narrator comments, that the 'Germans fear more desperately for their women than for themselves'. The Germans believe that there resides in women an element of 'holiness and a gift of prophecy', and they take heed of their advice. One German group, the Suebi, sacrifice to Isis, a form of worship, the narrator notes, that must have come from abroad (*Germania* 7, 8, 9).

The *Germania* admires the Germans because they possess a spirit of 'freedom', more than other peoples the Romans faced, not only in Spain and Gaul but also the Carthaginians, as well as the whole of 'the East'; the 'freedom' enjoyed by the Germans enables them to be 'more energetic' in military actions than Eastern peoples under 'despotism' (37). Nevertheless, however much the *Germania* admires certain aspects of the Germans, which remind the narrator of earlier simpler virtues of the Roman republic, the narrator has no doubt that Rome has a historic right to conquer Germany. It has this right because the Romans are a chosen people, chosen to be great by 'the gods' who support their spread of empire by means of 'military discipline'; an empire chosen by 'destiny' (30, 33).

There are aspects of German society that the text doesn't admire. The *Germania* convicts the Germans of being 'barbarians' because of their lack of historical consciousness; their unreflectiveness in terms of mind and intellectual capability. Referring to the Aestii, who collect amber to serve 'Roman luxury', Tacitus comments on their lack of curiosity about amber's origins: 'Like true barbarians, they have never asked or discovered what it is or how it is produced' (45). The *Germania* is also critical of the Germans for their method of worshipping the god Mercury: they 'include human victims in the sacrifices offered to him'. Such human sacrifice is contrasted with worship of Hercules and Mars, who are appeased by 'offerings of animals, in accordance with ordinary civilized custom' (9). However, in other terms, the *Germania* admires the religious consciousness of the Germans, who do not think it in keeping with the 'divine majesty to confine gods within walls or to portray them in the likeness of any human countenance'. Rather, the Germans, whose holy places are in woods and groves, apply the names of deities 'to that hidden presence which is seen only by the eye of reverence' (9). I might recall here my discussion in the previous chapter that the monotheism/polytheism divide is not necessarily defined by the claim that in polytheism there is always visuality, while in monotheism the deity is hidden.

## COUNTER-NARRATIVE

If the narrative affirms, the counter-narrative disturbs. This happens in two ways: through the divided consciousness of the narrator, and through the powerful anti-imperial speeches by Britons that protest at Roman colonizing and critically reflect on Agricola as colonizer and empire builder. Bakhtin noted in *Prob-*

*lems of Dostoevsky's Poetics* that in the menippea there was often an interest in split personality, and such can be wondered of the narrator of the *Agricola* and *Germania*.[8]

Referring to the recurrent Roman attempts to pacify Britain's 'barbarians' (*Agricola*, 11), the counter-narrator explains why Britain was 'worth conquering', for its 'gold, silver, and other metals' (12). However, the Britons, as colonization continued, while they were 'broken in to obedience' were not as yet habituated to 'slavery' (13), and revolts break out, as in the time of the governor Suetonius Paulinus.

When, this more detached and reflective narrator tells us, Agricola arrives as governor in Britain, he establishes a sound administration, encourages the building of temples, public squares and good houses, and educates the sons of the British chiefs in the liberal arts. There occurs a kind of cultural conquest by, as Jupiter puts it in the *Aeneid* in our epigraph, the people that wear the toga. The counter-narrator's evocation is not at all free of critical scrutiny of Agricola and Roman colonization:

> The result was that instead of loathing the Latin language they became eager to speak it effectively. In the same way, our national dress came into favour and the toga was everywhere to be seen. And so the population was gradually led into the demoralizing temptations of arcades, baths, and sumptuous banquets. The unsuspecting Britons spoke of such novelties as 'civilization', when in fact they were only a feature of their enslavement.
>
> (*Agricola*, 21)

In Lemkin's terms, what is invoked here as the irony of assimilation is genocide of the distinctive culture and life world of the indigenous. I'm reminded of a quote from India's 1930 Declaration of Independence, concerning British education in India: 'Culturally, the system of education has torn us from our moorings and our training has made us hug the very chains that bind us.'[9]

Despite such attempts at assimilation and complete domination, unrest continues, and Agricola has to launch campaigns against remaining British resistance, as in the northern campaign against the Caledonians. Here, as in Thucydides' *History*, the *Agricola* provides opposing speeches for the leaders of the two sides about to be locked in battle. Agricola's exhortations to his troops we have already noted as part of the text's affirmative narrative. The *Agricola* also sets before us the comments of Calgacus, the Caledonian leader who laments what is happening to his people at the hands of the Roman invaders. Calgacus says that 'there are no more nations beyond us; nothing is there but waves and rocks', a distance that had protected his people until the Romans came: 'We, the most distant dwellers upon earth, the last of the free, have been shielded till today by our very remoteness and by the obscurity in which it has shrouded our name' (30). Calgacus is 'a man of outstanding valour and nobility', who might well remind us of the Syracusan leader Hermocrates during the Athenian invasion of Sicily (Thucydides 6.76–77).

This, says the counter-narrator, is the 'substance of what he is reported to have said' in denouncing the Romans, hoping his revolt will begin the restoration of 'liberty for the whole of Britain'. We have already read part of this extraordinary condemnation in our second epigraph:

Nature has ordained that every man should love his children and his other relatives above all else. These are now being torn from us by [Roman] conscription to slave in other lands. Our wives and sisters, even if they are not raped by enemy soldiers, are seduced by men who are supposed to be our friends and guests. Our goods and money are consumed by taxation; our land is stripped of its harvest to fill their granaries; our hands and limbs are crippled by building roads through forests and swamps under the lash of our oppressors. ... We Britons are sold into slavery anew every day. ... We, the cheap new acquisitions ... are marked out for destruction.

(*Agricola*, 31)

Calgacus' denunciation of Rome and its empire reprises a history of similar powerful anti-imperial speeches, from the Queen of the Massagetae and King of the Ethiops in Herodotus's *Histories*, Hermocrates and the Melians in Thucydides' *History*, Philus in Cicero's *Republic*, Celaeno the Harpy and Juno in the *Aeneid*. In the *Agricola*, the Britons protest at the slavery that they are being asked to submit to: 'We gain nothing by submission except heavier burdens for willing shoulders. ... Our bondage is ... ruinous. ... Nothing is any longer safe from their greed. ... [The Romans] seize our homes, kidnap our children, and conscript our men' (15).

The counter-narrative of the *Agricola* critically reflects on the various meanings of slavery, for both colonizers and colonized. For the Britons, slavery, as these powerful speeches of protest make plain, means submission to Roman rule and loss of their liberty, independence and distinctive culture; recall that, as Tacitus records, Agricola was often heard to say that he would like to conquer Ireland, for if the Britons were completely surrounded by Roman armies 'liberty' would become unthinkable (24). Clearly, for Agricola, liberty was reserved for the imperial colonizers; in such a view, encouraging a desire for liberty in the colonized would only fan their desire for freedom and independence, a threat to imperial control and domination. Liberty for the circle of colonizers, but denial of liberty to those being colonized, would become a very long tradition indeed in the history of Western colonization.[10]

Aspects of what it means to be a slave or slave-like, however, can also encompass the victors, the imperial and colonizing Romans themselves. The *Agricola* begins its narrative by denouncing the rule of the previous emperor Domitian (81–96 CE), who for 15 long years had nearly destroyed what Tacitus admires as the 'Rome of old', republican Rome which had explored and enjoyed 'the utmost limits of freedom' in terms of political liberty to debate and discuss and exchange ideas in conversation.[11] In Domitian's time, however, there were informers everywhere, and Romans were reduced to 'subservience', indeed, to the 'depths of slavery' (2–3). Romans could also be corrupted by their colonial possessions, or at least tempted to be corrupt. When younger, Agricola had been elected quaestor in the wealthy Roman province of Asia under the proconsul Salvius Titianus, who was, says Tacitus, an 'abject slave to greed' (6); the prudent Agricola, however, chose not to emulate his superior.

If the Romans are the chosen people of the gods, the counter-narrator also ponders that Rome's divinely ordained destiny to be a great empire is actively assisted by discord among the foes it encounters. The *Germania* refers to a battle between a German group, the Bructeri, and a coalition of neighbouring tribes, which was believed to have been observed by the Romans:

> We were even permitted to witness the battle. More than 60,000 were killed, not by Roman swords or javelins, but – more splendid still – as a spectacle before our delighted eyes. Long, I pray, may foreign nations persist, if not in loving us, at least in hating one another; for destiny is driving our empire upon its appointed path, and fortune can bestow on us no better gift than discord among our foes.
>
> (*Germania*, 33)

The *Germania* entertains the playful thought that the battle may have been a 'special favour accorded to us by the gods' (33). Yet perhaps, amidst the triumphalism of the moment, a slight but significant doubt about the effectiveness and duration of Rome's divine support may be implied here. The Roman hold on the world might be more fragile than appears, for it may only be weakness and division amongst its enemies that maintains imperial power. Not too far away might be the thought that those the gods select as a chosen people may be, as it were, unchosen. We might recall that Josephus in *The Jewish War* had judged that God had unchosen the Jews because of their folly in the revolt of Jerusalem against the Romans, and that the Romans were now his chosen people; but that state, too, Josephus reflected, may not last; chosenness could be transferred to yet another nation or people.[12]

## CONCLUSION: A DIVIDED LEGACY

The *Agricola* and *Germania* as troubled, edgy, nervous menippea could not but leave a fissured legacy for the future of European ideas of colonizing and empire, especially in the Renaissance where so much of classical thought energized intellectual life, including in ideas about how to promote and justify the establishing of colonies in Ireland or outside Europe.

On the one hand, these texts affirm the supersessionist notion of the Romans as a chosen people, assuring the conquerors' nation and empire of a divine status, a rightness in history. Also in supersessionist mode, the texts assume that the Romans are superior to barbarians in their possession of historical consciousness (*Germania*, 45): a notion of a hierarchy of humanity that would prove constitutive of future European racial thinking. It is a notion, for example, important in Kantian philosophy and articulated with enthusiasm by nineteenth-century historians like Ranke and Burckhardt.[13] The belief in a hierarchy of humanity supported and assisted centuries of worldwide colonization, empires, genocide and the Holocaust.

On the other hand, there are moving speeches of those like Calgacus who wished to resist colonization so that the Britons will not lose their freedom. We also witness the counter-narrator's reflections that the Britons in adopting Roman culture were losing their own culture, and his anxiety that the Romans might experience through colonization and empire an ethical deterioration; they might be enslaved by 'Asiatic' indulgence (*Agricola*, 6) in possessing lands whose wealth tempts the colonizers to greed and lassitude.

Nevertheless, the framework of thinking in the counter-narrative has its limits, its boundaries. The counter-narrator at no stage in the *Agricola* permits himself to venture that Roman colonization should cease and the Romans should leave Britain and go home and so restore to the Britons their freedom, independence and their own culture. Not colonizing at all, or withdrawing from colonizing when its destructive effects became clear, appeared not to be thinkable. The ultimate ethical test for those who participate in colonization would be that if one sees that colonization is going terribly wrong for the colonized, as the speeches of those facing colonization like Calgacus in the *Agricola* testify, then what would be truly honourable would be to say: 'We have to leave, we have to stop being colonizers.' The counter-narrator signally failed this test of honour. There is here, in aspects of the counter-narrative, a kind of bad faith.[14]

There are other troubling aspects of these texts. At one point the narrator in the *Germania* refers to a non-German people, the Sarmatians, as of a 'repulsive appearance' (*Germania*, 46), suggesting a discourse of racial judgement and contempt, based on physical appearance and aesthetic judgement, that looks forward to Enlightenment and post-Enlightenment European racial thinking and actions.[15] Unlike the Germans, who have 'settled homes', the Sarmatians 'live in wagons or on horseback' (46). We might think here of the distinction Waswo makes in *The Founding Legend of Western Civilization* between the settled as signifying the civilized, the unsettled as indicating those who are barbarous in history. The distinction between the Germans as a settled people residing in houses, their soil good for 'cereal crops' (5), and the Sarmatians as living in wagons or on horseback, might have helped influence a long tradition in Western thought distinguishing between supposedly settled peoples in history and hunter-gatherer or wandering pastoral peoples, to be regarded with disdain; we might recall Hugh Brody's argument in his *The Other Side of Eden* concerning the world-shaping hostility of agricultural society to hunter gatherers.[16]

The invocation by Tacitus in the *Agricola* of the threat of 'Asiatic' corruption by wealth and luxury continues an Orientalist aspect of the *Aeneid*, when Jupiter agrees with Juno that the Trojans should in effect repudiate their Oriental past as coming from an Asian culture. Both the *Aeneid* and the *Agricola* in this respect prepare the way for and anticipate what would become a strand of Western historical consciousness, a long-standing contempt for Asia; as we noted in our analysis of the *Aeneid*, this became a way of defining Europe, as if a self-contained entity, against Asia.

In more general terms, we can conclude our chapters on key texts of the Greek classical and the Greco-Roman world with the thought that such a multiply inflected legacy was influential in the centuries of European colonization after 1492, and continues to be so. Divided and conflicting ideas, ideals, representations, images and modes of sensibility and consciousness have for millennia been entwined and entangled.

# 7 THE HONOURABLE COLONIZER

> Thou [Gog of the land of Magog] shall fall upon the mountains of Israel, thou, and all thy bands, and the people that *is* with thee [from 'Persia, Ethiopia, and Libya']: I will give thee unto the ravenous birds of every sort, and *to* the beasts of the field to be devoured. ... And I will send a fire on Magog.
>
> (God on Gog, Ezekiel, 39: 4–6)

In this chapter I investigate notions of colonization, conquest and empire in early modern Europe, in terms of the guiding concepts of this book: genocide, supersessionism, victimology, chosen people, promised land and culture-bringers. I will focus on the manifold, heterogeneous and contradictory ways European colonizers, from early modern times onwards, justified their colonizing projects, including in terms of the law of nations, or international law, the claimed purity of their intentions, biblical justifications, and myth and fantasy. Waswo's notion in *The Founding Legend of Western Civilization* of wandering Trojan-like colonizers as self-admiring culture-bringers, and his interpretation of early modern European understandings of natural law, will be invaluable for these analyses, and for the critique of Shakespeare's *The Tempest* I essay here. The notion of the colonizer as culture-bringer is allied with, close to, the notion of honourable colonization, the overall focus of this chapter and a major concern of this book.

I begin these explorations through a critical reading of Andrew Fitzmaurice's striking and informative *Humanism and*

*America: An Intellectual History of English Colonization 1500–1625* (2003). For my reading I will draw on the playful, irreverent Nietzschean spirit of historiography so admired by Foucault, in his essay 'Nietzsche, Genealogy, History', that we should occasionally laugh at history.[1] As I will suggest, Fitzmaurice, while he usually writes with sympathy and praise for the learning, high ideals and exemplary intentions of the Renaissance English humanist promoters of colonization who are the subject of his book, is himself drawn to occasional moments of comic wonder at his material. I would like to conduct with *Humanism and America* a lively dialogue, and in doing so pursue more general questions concerning motivations for colonization, conquest and empire. My directing question is, how did the English Renaissance humanist promoters help establish the conceptual foundations for the genocidal destruction of the indigenous peoples of North America?

## PROMOTERS AND ADVENTURERS

In *Humanism and America* Fitzmaurice sets himself a revisionary historiographical task.[2] He wishes to dispel what he sees as a reductive, anachronistic view amongst theorists of colonialism and empire that British ideas of colonization in the sixteenth and seventeenth centuries were continuous with later British possessive expansionism. He also wants to challenge a common perception that when the early modern promoters of colonies in Ireland and North America revealed a pervasive 'ambivalence over profit', this was merely a 'cynical cloak' to cover their avariciousness.[3] Such a view, he comments, is far too simple, and discounts the motivating power of ideas in history, in particular ideas inherited from Greco-Roman moral and political philosophy, as in Cicero, and historical writing, as in Tacitus.

Since I also believe in the power of ideas in history, I am very sympathetic to Fitzmaurice's project. His approach, however, draws on that of the well-known intellectual historian

Quentin Skinner, and so adopts Skinner's essentializing 'neo-roman' approach to the history of ideas. As revealed in his programmatic *Liberty before Liberalism* (1998), a study of the 'coherence' of the 'neo-roman theory of free citizens and free states' in mid-seventeenth-century England, Skinner narrowly conceives of intellectual history as the study of political ideas.[4] *Liberty before Liberalism* also reveals that Skinner's intellectual history project is uninterested in the ideas of the colonized. For example, in relation to the American Revolution against British rule in the eighteenth century, his focus is only on relations between metropolitan Britain and the white colonial group in America. Skinner admires the 'exceptional courage' of Richard Price (in his *Two Tracts on Civil Liberty* of 1778) in protesting to the British government that the American colonies were in a state of dependence that amounted to 'enslavement'. Startlingly, however, the enslavement of African Americans, and the genocidal destruction of the foundations of life of the Native American colonized, are simply not present in Skinner's tender concern for the English/American colonists.[5] Such disregard of the views and feelings of the colonized would surely have surprised the Tacitus of the *Agricola* and *Germania*. Skinner's legacy and influence for those who choose to follow his prescriptive approach into the study of colonialism, though promising, as he says in *Liberty before Liberalism*, broader traditions and frameworks of thought, would appear to be very restrictive, very problematic, indeed.

A dubious Eurocentric methodological inheritance, then, hangs over Fitzmaurice's book. *Humanism and America* is certainly an illuminating contribution to the history of ideas that informed early modern and modern European colonization. In what follows I hope I make it clear that I very much admire *Humanism and America*, from which I learned a great deal. I will also, however, be gently deconstructing it; I will be drawing out from it biographical sketches, and the implications of different kinds of history, in order to test the limits of its as it were Skinnerian 'intellectual history'. My argument will be that the very rationalism of this mode of intellectual history leads to certain worrying kinds of naivety and narrowness when applied to the history of colonization and empire.[6]

*Humanism and America* contends that thinking about colonizing in the period 1500–1625 emerged from Renaissance humanism, with its complex inheritance of high neo-roman ideals stressing republican virtue, a selfless morality and notions of wise governance, where thought is always combined with action (*vita contemplativa* entwined with *vita activa*). Renaissance humanism also revealed a cyclical view of history, unlike a later notion of inevitable progress as in the nineteenth century.[7] Such humanism included protest at colonization where it was pursued only for profit, rather than for glory. It viewed colonization as wrong when it denied justice to those being colonized, and where it might involve a deterioration of morality in the metropolitan society or amongst the colonizers themselves, especially when profit was pursued in a Machiavellian spirit concerning means and ends. The humanists did not exclusively represent the indigenous Americans as 'backward and savage', for while they frequently commented upon what they saw as the 'simplicity of the native culture' and the 'obnoxious nature of some its practices', they could also admire the Native Americans' possession of 'classical virtues', in terms of government, manners, athleticism, oratory and martial valour.[8]

Fitzmaurice draws attention to arguments from Roman moralists like Sallust, Cicero and Tacitus who suggested that the virtue of the Roman republic was always in danger of being undone by the corrupting influence of Rome's foreign possessions, an ethical threat conceived both in Roman antiquity and in the English Renaissance as 'Asiatic'.[9] Cicero, Fitzmaurice notes, recognized that while the strongest ties are with those closest to us, there should also be an ideal of unlimited fellowship among humanity. Cicero – here perhaps echoing Pericles' Funeral Oration in Thucydides' *History* (2.40) where he reflected on Athens' empire, though Fitzmaurice doesn't make this comparison – lamented that there was a time when the Roman empire had been maintained through acts of kind service, a time when wars were ended with mercy, such that then Rome was more a protectorate of allies than an empire ruling by injustice.[10]

Tacitus, Fitzmaurice tells us, enjoyed great popularity in Europe in the sixteenth and seventeenth centuries, when English colonial activity in America began in force; in Elizabethan and Jacobean England he was held to be foremost among Roman historians. Fitzmaurice observes that the English promoters – or adventurers as he also often calls them – frequently participated in colonizing projects in both Ireland and North America. They were, he stresses, especially wary of being perceived in the way Calgacus, the British leader, had in Tacitus's *Agricola* described and judged the Romans in Britain, the Roman empire a mere name for those given to plunder, butchery and theft. As Fitzmaurice puts it, the English promoters of colonies had 'little stomach' to be accused of identifying colonizing or empire with, as Calgacus had graphically phrased it, robbery, slaughter and plunder.[11]

In the terms of my book, the promoters saw themselves as honourable men, honourable colonizers.

Fitzmaurice repeatedly tells us that the English promoters of colonies, inspired by the Roman moralists, placed ideals above profit, though like the Romans they certainly saw profit as a proper element of colonizing, particularly when it was for the benefit not of the colonizers themselves but altruistically of the colony and the empire as a whole. It is in this spirit that Fitzmaurice decries historians who have in his view suggested that the early modern English colonizers were interested only in profit. On the contrary, Fitzmaurice argues, if we look at their pamphlets, sermons and poems we see that their 'humanist imagination' was enthused by what he refers to as the 'highest ideals of the Ciceronian conception of the active life'. The *vita activa* involved the leading of a virtuous life working for the common weal not private wealth; it pursued honour and glory, and admired martial virtues, including preparedness to risk one's life in distant endeavours.[12]

How could the English promoters of colonies pursue colonization and yet *not* be indicted as violent, destructive and enslaving colonizers in the way Calgacus had indicted the Romans in

Britain? How could they envisage colonizing without colonizing? How could they be colonizers without being colonizers? How could they be honourable colonizers?

Fitzmaurice's answer, his book-length answer, is disturbingly ingenuous and disablingly rationalist. He appears to assume that the neo-roman ideals and thinking of the early modern English promoters of colonies, trained in the neo-classical learning of Renaissance humanism, must be wholly admirable, or nearly so. Furthermore, in Fitzmaurice's view, the English promoters of colonies deserved praise for their utopianism. The promoters were, Fitzmaurice says, drawn to New World colonies as a chance to realize dreams of ideal commonwealths of the kind extolled in More's *Utopia*.[13] Here once more Fitzmaurice is writing in the tradition of Skinner, who in *Liberty Before Liberalism* warmly defends utopianism: 'I have never understood why the charge of utopianism is necessarily thought to be an objection to a theory of politics.'[14]

We might contemplate, however, how much utopianism has proved an inspirational force in the history of European colonization from early modern times to modernity, associated with the attempted realization of certain ideals at the expense of the colonized and indigenous. Such colonizing utopianism reached its apogee in the history of Nazism. Wendy Lower in her *Nazi Empire-Building and the Holocaust in Ukraine* tells us that in the interwar period the colonialist fantasies of Nazi Party ideologues, based on admiration for what the British had done in India, and to be enacted with catastrophic consequences in Ukraine during the Second World War, combined utopianism about the possibilities of *lebensraum* with racism, *völkisch* nationalism and anti-Semitism. Hitler had a vision of Ukraine as Germany's New Indian Empire.[15]

Such ingenuousness on Fitzmaurice's part is, I think, an effect of writing within the Skinnerian mode of intellectual history when it assumes that the history of ideas can be divorced from wider histories that might, for example, explore the devastating consequences of colonization. Fitzmaurice explicitly argues in relation to English colonization of the New World that we must be careful 'not to argue from consequences'.[16] Perhaps not, but the knowledge of devastating consequences should at least make us wary, and in any case, as this chapter will argue, the motivations of the promoters were more questionable than Ftizmaurice allows.

How questionable, how often absurd, such motivations could be is revealed by Fitzmaurice himself, for example, in his analysis of 'legal humanism', which he says furnished a number of arguments held by the English promoters in the sixteenth and seventeenth centuries to constitute a legal right to colonize in North America. Legal humanism, Fitzmaurice points out, provided an entirely separate basis for European colonizing from other legal concepts like natural law, the law of nations, the notion of *res nullius*, rights to trade, rights of strangers and friendship, and just war. The English promoters, says Fitzmaurice, were distinctive as colonizers in devoting far greater space in their texts to historical claims, claims which stressed legal rights to territory conferred by discovery and precedent. There was urgency in such thinking, Fitzmaurice explains, for the Spanish had in effect claimed the whole of the Americas for Spain by right of discovery of the New World by Columbus.[17]

The English promoters elaborated in their writings a rival set of historical claims, repeated from one writer to another, one text to the next. Fitzmaurice attempts to keep a straight historian's face in informing us that the English promoters decided to repudiate the Spanish claims by bringing forth their own Columbus figure. They countered with what Fitzmaurice himself designates as 'the fantastic story' of a legendary voyage by the Welsh prince Madoc in 1170. John Dee, one of the promoters, argued in the 1570s that Madoc had crossed the Atlantic and established a colony. Furthermore, Dee wrote, the explorers John Cabot and Sebastian Cabot were the first to discover the mainland of North America. Dee's claims about Madoc and John Cabot (the Venetian sea-captain who crossed the Atlantic in 1497 with a patent from Henry VII) and Sebastian Cabot (who crossed to the New World in 1508–9) were then repeated and enlarged upon by other and succeeding promoters. George Peckham, for example, lent credence to a story that Montezuma had once told his people that their forefathers had in ancient times come from a far away country; they had sent back a king to this country, who had then sent Madoc to Mexico as their ruler. Peckham also was sure that the Amerindian languages were indebted to Welsh, for the word *penguin* seemed to be common to both.[18]

At this point Fitzmaurice laments that the philological skills deployed in the development of legal humanism had 'degenerated into unintentional burlesque'. Indeed. Such stories of exaggeration heaped upon exaggeration struck me as decidedly Falstaffian in their rhetorical technique, if I may invoke another Renaissance cultural context, of carnivalesque theatricality. They also reminded me of the entirely legendary stories of the *Aeneid*, where a justification for the Trojans saying they had a right to be in Italy was that a distant ancestor, Dardanus, had come from there. But, says Fitzmaurice, rallying, we should note that the promoters themselves were 'serious' in deploying the Madoc 'myth', because in quoting one another they could assemble an appeal to historical precedent that secured the legal humanist basis for colonization. The promoters could now assert that these discoveries by Madoc and the Cabots, borne out by chronicles, patents and maps, preceded every other European nation in the discovery of North America. Such could now be proffered by the promoters to be an ancient English right and claim. Yet, in a slight note of scepticism and discomfort, Fitzmaurice admits that the consensus on 'historical myth', built up by mutual reference in print to each other's writings that constituted their legal case, was wholly self-referential and owed much to what he describes as the humanist gift for advertising and self-promotion. Through such self-reference and self-promotion, Fitzmaurice dryly notes, colonization could become the legitimization of itself.[19]

I'm reminded here of Larissa Behrendt, contemplating European law in the context of the colonization of Australia, remarking that international law is a literature that is constitutively infused with metaphors, tropes, narratives, myth and fantasy.[20]

## FOUNDING LEGENDS

I'm reminded too of Waswo's *The Founding Legend of Western Civilization*, concerning the enduring power in European colonizing around the world of the legend of Aeneas in Virgil's *Aeneid*. As we saw in our chapter on Exodus and the *Aeneid*, Waswo argues that in the Western myth that developed around Virgil's epic, the Trojans who escape the destroyed city of Troy, regarding themselves as history's ideal culture-bearers, feel they have a right to end their wanderings in colonizing and conquering elsewhere. Their abiding notion of culture distinguishes themselves, the agricultural 'civilized', they who cultivate the soil, build cities, establish law, from those who are 'savages' because of their hunting and gathering or nomadic pastoralism. The myth of Trojan descent was, Waswo observes, eagerly adopted as a founding story in medieval Europe by peoples from elsewhere who wished to dispossess and replace, or dominate and assimilate, the indigenous or prior inhabitants of a land. Waswo refers to its popularizing in the twelfth century by Geoffrey of Monmouth, in a reworking of the legend where the incoming Britons are referred to as Trojans and build a city on the Thames known as New Troy, later to be renamed London. They first have to overcome the indigenous giants of the island, saving only one, Gogmagog, for a walk-on part in their foundational narrative; we will return to this aspect of the story in a moment. Another aspect of the story as Geoffrey of Monmouth tells it is that the Trojan leader, named Brut, divides Britain among his three sons. Waswo points out that this story of the three sons would be 'alleged in legal negotiations by two late medieval English kings', Edward I and Henry IV, 'to justify England's claim to feudal sovereignty over the Scots'. A fantastical legend, Waswo comments, would help shape the history of European international law.[21]

In Chapter 15, 'Myth in Law', of his book, Waswo argues that international law was developed as a special branch of law that could negotiate conflicts among the major European powers, conflicts intensified by competing claims over territory and trading privileges in the New World, and also over vexed questions concerning the respective rights of the colonizers and colonized. In this chapter, Waswo discusses a lineage of early modern European theorists of international law from the Salamanca school of theologians to later legal thinkers like Hugo Grotius and Samuel Pufendorf, forming a tradition that is usually held to be highly critical of European colonization in the Americas. Waswo, however, questions this conventional view, suggesting that such theorists do indeed offer a justification for colonization, a justification that would become enormously influential in later European thought, and highly productive of colonization and the way it was conducted. Waswo points, for example, to the Salamanca school theorist Francisco de Victoria (an alternative name for Francisco de Vitoria, as he is more commonly known), who in the sixteenth century rejected 'almost all contemporary justifications for the Spanish takeover of America but one'. Victoria set about refuting all usual arguments that justify the Spanish conquest: neither their gross sins nor their heretical unbelief bars the Americans from ownership or sovereignty; they possess reason, as is evident in features of their society such as their orderly arrangements in politics, marriage, magistracy and systems of exchange. Furthermore, in Victoria's view, since neither Christian prince nor the Pope can claim temporal lordship of the globe, then the Americans cannot be attacked and dispossessed for refusing their demands, even if these demands are based on truth. The Americans cannot be colonized and dispossessed because they are unbelievers.[22]

How, then, does Victoria justify colonization, by what principle? Waswo contends that Victoria invokes the universalism enshrined in Roman notions of natural law; notions we encountered in Chapter 4 while discussing Scipio's defence of natural law in Cicero's *Republic*. In Victoria's view, natural law is more universal than Christianity. Victoria homes in on the claim in natural law that humanity has a natural right of sociability and fellowship; in these terms, all people have the right to travel, visit, settle, trade and mine in the territory of others, so long as they do no harm. Waswo suggests that Victoria's support for a universal natural law of friendship permitting travel anywhere and requiring hospitality from those one visits, is influenced by the mythical events of the *Aeneid*. He cites a crucial passage in Book One concerning the arrival of the Trojans at Carthage. The old Trojan Ilioneus complains to Queen Dido that their ships, buffeted and scattered by a storm, had washed up on the Carthaginian shore; instead of receiving hospitality as was the right of travellers and strangers, however, the Trojan sailors had been treated harshly and refused entry by Dido's coast guards.[23] We could also recall here what Ilioneus says much later in Book Seven, after the Trojans first land in Italy and Aeneas sends members of his group to talk to the Italian king Latinus. We 'ask', says Ilioneus to Latinus in phrases that remind us of the claims to universality of Roman natural law theory, 'for a little piece of land for our fathers' gods, for harmless refuge on the beach, for the air and sea which are there for all men'.[24]

Now, Waswo argues, Victoria has his justification for both colonization and just war. There is a universal right to travel, visit, settle, trade and mine, and if any of these are refused, even though asked for nicely as Waswo wittily puts it (and in Book Seven, we note, Ilioneus did ask King Latinus nicely for a tiny plot of land), then here is a reason for just war; after all, the visitor is only defending what is a worldwide natural right. Victoria's one principle, Waswo sadly reflects, was infinitely extendable, leading to the assumption of a right to settle territories and carry on trade, culminating in the dispossession of the indigenous of the New World on a huge scale, the extermination of whole cultures, and appalling atrocities and cruelties. In the remainder of this illuminating chapter, Waswo points out how the natural law principle of friendship and hospitality, permitting territorial expansion of Europe around the world, was reprised and developed in later European thinking in figures like Grotius and Pufendorf.[25]

We could add here that Victoria's principle of friendship as Waswo outlines it, of universal sociability and fellowship, extends also to the later Enlightenment, in Kant's complex musings in his 1795 essay 'Perpetual Peace: A Philosophical Sketch'. In his 'Third Definitive Article of a Perpetual Peace: Cosmopolitan Right shall be Limited to Conditions of Universal Hospitality', Kant writes that hospitality:

means the right of a stranger not to be treated with hostility when he arrives on someone else's territory. He can indeed be turned away, if this can be done without causing his death, but he must not be treated with hostility, so long as he behaves in a peaceable manner in the place he happens to be in. ... All men are entitled to present themselves in the society of others by virtue of their right to communal possession of the earth's surface.[26]

It is a principle that is also clearly related to notions of honourable colonization evident in the early modern English thinking about colonization that Fitzmaurice analyses.

In *Humanism and America*, Fitzmaurice alerts his readers to the importance of the theological and philosophical arguments of the sixteenth-century Thomists at the University of Salamanca, who included Francisco de Victoria and those they influenced like Bartolomé de Las Casas. Fitzmaurice records that the English promoters believed that it was legal to take the land away from the indigenous peoples of North America because, unlike the peoples encountered by the Spanish, they had not exploited the natural resources of the land and so had no rights of property; they had never established ownership.[27] Fitzmaurice notes, however, that while the Salamanca school authors were interested in abstract philosophical questions, the English promoters devoted themselves to 'practical ends'. Once the promoters had satisfied themselves that their aims were legal, just and 'honourable', they moved directly to their 'concern', Fitzmaurice tells us, 'with how to establish colonies', to the 'honour and advantage of the adventure'.[28]

## INTERNATIONAL LAW, EARLY MODERN ENGLISH STYLE

Fitzmaurice points out that the promoters were 'cynical' in the opportunistic ways they mixed and matched contradictory arguments from international law to justify their planned activities, though, somewhat obscurely, he defends their cynicism as a 'mechanism through which political argument responds to its context'.[29] In any case, they could be observed employing a 'whole battery of frequently conflicting arguments' associated with the justification of 'agricultural colonies and conquest'. For example, John Donne, in a sermon before the Virginia Company (published in 1622) stressed that under the law of nations if a land is not being improved by cultivation, that is, it is in a state of *res nullius*, then it can be possessed by those who announce a desire to improve it. But Donne also suggested another argument besides *res nullius* and indeed contradicting it, this time that if the indigenous of a land produce an abundance because, it now turns out, they do cultivate the land and yet they don't share this abundance with others, then under the law of nations force is justified in remedying this situation.[30]

For the promoters, colonization could be justified in a remarkable number of ways, reminding me of Hermocrates of Syracuse in Thucydides' *History* observing the readiness of the leaders of the Athenian empire to offer different reasons for depriving the Ionians of their independence, 'bringing forward ... any plausible excuse to fit each particular case' (Thucydides, 6.76). There was, for example, Fitzmaurice writes, making us immediately think of Waswo's discussion of Victoria, the promoters' expansive understanding of the natural law position on 'rights of trade and friendship', highly generous to themselves, requiring that the indigenous should not prevent the entry onto their land of people who want to form communities of friendship. Under the law of nations protecting strangers, the indigenous should give safe harbour to such peaceable strangers, who might then wish to trade as is their right. The indigenous should not prevent such trade, which includes the right of colonizers to trade for the indigenous inhabitants' land. It is also part of the law of nations that the settlers can take possession of any land they judge the indigenous inhabitants can spare, including land for planting.[31]

Furthermore, while the promoters and adventurers do not believe in force, violence and conquest, they do believe in force, violence and conquest. They were, Fitzmaurice points out, frequently drawn to the Roman law doctrine of the right of conquest, which met the 'humanist appetite for glory'.[32] The Roman law doctrine of just war could also be invoked, for if the indigenous peoples employ violence against the colonizers, they are justified in resisting force with force; they can draw their swords to defend themselves.[33]

The doctrine of just war in colonial situations would appear to work on the trope of victimology and narrative reversal whose salience and longevity in settler-colonial situations Ann Curthoys has commented on; when the colonized resist colonization, the colonizers can now see themselves as the victims in the colonial situation.[34] As we saw in Chapter 4, the universal claims of just war were disputed in Cicero's *Republic* by Philus, in an exemplary dissection. There is also in Book Three of the *Aeneid* the interesting episode involving the Harpies, when the Trojans enter the harbour on their island without seeking permission, proceed to feast on the Harpies' cattle and goats, yet are surprised when the Harpies suddenly swoop down on them in anger. Aeneas immediately orders 'his men to arm themselves to make war against this fearsome tribe'. We are left to contemplate the Harpy Celaeno's condemnation of Aeneas and his warriors. 'Is it your plan to make war against the innocent Harpies and drive us from the kingdom of our ancestors?'[35]

## BIOGRAPHY AND MORALITY

Fitzmaurice's admiration for the English promoters of colonies – even the 'burlesque' of the Madoc stories is, in his view, 'unintentional' – seriously frays at the edges when he turns to biographical sketches of some of the key figures. Here biography perhaps unwittingly extends this kind of intellectual history into turbulent and discomforting areas of social history, where the adventurers might reveal themselves to be the reverse of admirable; they could be pirates, thieves, killers and cannibals.[36] Fitzmaurice tells us of an early expedition in 1536 led by a Richard Hore; on board one of his ships, the *Trinity*, were many gentlemen; while the *Trinity* succeeded in crossing the Atlantic it became stranded on the coast of Labrador, the gentlemen on board suffering such extreme privation that they began to eat one another, or perhaps the crew. Fortunately, a well-provisioned French ship came into the same bay, and the English somehow – Fitzmaurice does not divulge the presumably violent details – overcame the French ship and sailed off in it. As Fitzmaurice comments, there was 'no material here for a humanistic celebration of glorious deeds', for praise of honourable actions.[37]

Fitzmaurice's portrait of the prominent humanist adventurer Humphrey Gilbert also threatens to undermine his admiration for the neo-roman promoters of colonies. Gilbert was, says Fitzmaurice, the first to formulate colonizing designs for both Ireland and America. Gilbert had, we learn, a passion for the *studia humanitatis*, was respected by his contemporaries for his learning, and wished from 1570 to establish a new university in London devoted to a humanist curriculum. He became interested in colonization, which he saw as a field of application for humanism, and he was drawn into the project to colonize Ireland by Sir Henry Sidney, appointed in 1565 Lord Deputy of Ireland; a project not considered warmly or favourably by the Irish themselves. In the four years Gilbert spent in Ireland, from 1566 to 1570, he was, Fitzmaurice remarks, 'effective and brutal in quashing resistance', for which he was knighted. He announced plans to voyage to new lands, though Fitzmaurice notes that such plans to establish colonies overseas may have been 'intended also in part to hide' from the Spanish ambassador an interest in 'privateering'.[38] When in 1578 Gilbert was granted the first letters patent by the English crown to establish a colony in the New World, he was given the power:

> To discover ... such remote and heathen and barbarous landes ... not actually possessed of any Christian prince ... And the same to have hould occupie and enjoye ... all the soyle of such landes.

As it turned out, the expeditionary force of eleven ships and 500 men, including his half-brother Walter Raleigh, never crossed the Atlantic, being more interested in piracy against French and Spanish ships.

In 1583, however, Gilbert did set out on a colonizing expedition with five ships and made for Newfoundland; when he landed in the harbour of St John's he claimed possession of the land within 200 leagues. In a storm soon after the *Squirrel*, in which Gilbert was travelling, disappeared and he was not seen again.[39] Rather fortunately for those facing colonization at his hands, one might think.

It's of interest to glimpse Gilbert in the accounts and evaluations of other historians, especially in their observations of Gilbert as an important, not to say infamous, figure in the sixteenth-century Elizabethan conquest and colonization of Ireland. The mentions of Gilbert in these accounts sometimes refer to incidents also discussed by Fitzmaurice. Colm Lennon tells us that, faced with rebellion in Munster, Sir Henry Sidney appointed Gilbert as colonel and governor of the province in September 1569. Empowered to govern by martial law, Gilbert took to his task of quelling the revolt with 'ruthless efficiency': 'Within six weeks he had taken twenty-three castles and slaughtered all occupants, men, women and children'; indeed, Lennon comments, his 'savage methods', including the killing of non-belligerents and the arranging of a 'corridor of severed heads' to induce abject surrender, not only won Gilbert notoriety but introduced a new dimension into Irish warfare.[40] In *A Military History of Ireland*, Gilbert is noticed as distinguishing himself amongst Elizabethan military commanders by his recourse, on a 'limited scale', during the first Desmond rebellion, to 'total war by means of scorched earth and territorial clearance'.[41]

Patricia Palmer, in her work on English Renaissance literature and imperial expansion, sees Gilbert as a figure who should be rightly mocked and scorned.[42] Palmer regards Gilbert as an Elizabethan linguistic nationalist, his military and intellectual endeavours revealing a unity of purpose. In Ireland, Gilbert was heard to say that he thought his dog's ears were too good to listen to the Irish speech of the Munster rebels, however noble by descent they were. A year after quelling the rebellion with 'calculated savagery' – leaving behind his own *legenda negra* in songs and rhymes – Gilbert wrote *Queene Elizabethes Achademy*. Here he advocated the establishment of a London variant of Oxford, where there would be a stress on teaching in English not Latin, and where civil and military subjects were to be combined; there would be training in navigation, mapping, artillery, marching and skirmishing. When he arrived in the harbour named by the English as St John's, in Newfoundland in 1583, Gilbert, before a motley assembly of European fishermen, formally took possession of the territory for Queen Elizabeth and her church by making a speech. Palmer notes that there is 'no mention of native witnesses to the performance', the only interpreting being done between the Europeans there. In Palmer's view, Gilbert's declaration, reminiscent of the proclamations of ownership delivered in Spanish to the bewildered indigenous occupants of New Spain, evinced an 'arrogant absurdity', and 'would be risible were its implications not so far-reaching'.[43]

Clearly, these references to and interpretations of Gilbert create a far more disturbing portrait of the adventurer than Fitzmaurice, perhaps blinded by his affection for the neo-roman humanists, permits himself.


## THE RIGHT TO COLONIZE

In my view, the English humanist adventurers were highly contradictory in what they wrote and did because they were thinking and acting in terms of highly contradictory frameworks. They did not wish to harm or dispossess the Americans in any way because they desired to present themselves, and to regard themselves, as sensitive and honourable colonizers; but they also believed in martial virtues and military glory, and how were such to be gained except in warfare? They believed in just war theory, where they would arrive peacefully in a place and only take up arms when forced to defend themselves against attacks by the colonized. Yet they knew or must have known from previous colonizing, by the Spanish to the south in the Americas, or their own experience in Ireland, or their reading of Tacitus, their favoured Roman historian, that those experiencing colonization were very likely to become violent when faced with those they considered illegitimate intruders on their lands and feared as usurpers of their world, their cosmos, their livelihoods and their lives.

The right to colonize could also be sought in religion. Indeed, the promoters' fealty to God and Christianity, an inspiration which suggests not a cyclical but a teleological and supersessionist view of history, is reminiscent of the right of conquest divinely supported by God in Exodus and Jupiter in the *Aeneid*. For the promoters, this was an ideal of progress in and across the world for those who possess the Christian spirit and feel authorized to act by God and Christian rulers.

Religion, as Fitzmaurice on occasion observes, complemented the promoters' neo-roman humanism, in particular a sense of serving the glory of God. The egregious Gilbert, we've seen, was given in 1578 the power by the English crown to possess any 'remote and heathen and barbarous landes' not actually 'possessed of any Christian prince'. Some promoters like Samuel Purchas also felt that God himself had commissioned them to plant and create plantations, which would then reflect glory on God. It was also important to attempt to convert the indigenous infidels of new lands to Christianity.[44] International law, then, was crossed and entwined with a Christian desire to be culture-bringers. The promoters offered to indigenous peoples 'spiritual goods', Christianity for their souls; such goods could be traded for land.[45]

The right of conquest could include a specifically Christian component. One promoter, Robert Gray, pondered the problem of what should the English do when they were 'unwronged or unprovoked' by indigenous people. By what right or warrant can we, he asked, 'enter into the land of these Savages, and plant ourselves in their places'? Gray's anxiety is soothed by arguments from religion that justify colonization in these unfortunate circumstances. It was, Gray wrote, lawful for a Christian king to make war 'upon barbarous and savage people' in order to reclaim them for a life of 'humanitie, pietie, and honestie'.

Gray says more, and more fantastically, when he invokes the warrant of the Old Testament. The English promoters, Fitzmaurice quotes him saying, can heed Joshua's advice to his people, which is to 'destroy God's enemies', who were 'Perrizzites and Giants', but may be any 'abominable Idolators'.[46] In Gray, it very much appears, ideas of colonization drawn from neo-roman humanism, international law, Christianity and the Old Testament, however contradictory they may be, mix, conjoin and support each other.

Let's follow up Gray's reference to the Perizzites, whom we noticed in Chapter 5. In Genesis, God says to Abraham he will make a covenant with him and his descendants so that they can possess 'land from the river of Egypt unto the great river, the river Euphrates', a vast stretch of territory that would include the lands not only of the Perizzites but also of the Kenites, Kenizzites, Kadmonites, Hittites, Rephaims, Amorites, Canaanites, Girgashites and Jebusites (Genesis 15: 18–21). In Genesis 17, God says that if Abraham circumcises, this would guarantee the covenant and its consequences. God will then 'give unto thee, and to thy seed after thee, the land wherein thou art a stranger, all the land of Canaan, for an everlasting possession; and I will be their God' (Genesis 17:8).[47] Recall also that in succeeding Old Testament stories, in Exodus, Joshua and Judges, as the Israelites embark on what is finally a colonizing and genocidal journey to the promised land of Canaan, God frequently reassures them that he will personally remove, or assist them to remove, any peoples who are an obstacle to their possession of Canaan, peoples who include of course the Perizzites (Joshua 11:3, 5–17). With God's help, the Israelites can also take their land. All such peoples are now to be superseded in history.

What of Gray's lurid vision of giants, when he advises the English promoters to heed Joshua's advice to his people, to 'destroy God's enemies' such as 'Perrizzites and Giants'? Gray's linking of Perizzites and giants suggests a biblical source, and resonates with contemporary scholarship. In an essay on Gog and Magog, who figure in Ezekiel as giant and land of giants (as in our epigraph), Victor I. Scherb writes of their long history from biblical story, where God wipes out these apparently appalling monsters living to the north of the Israelites – whom, we might add, God provokes into war, as he had provoked into war the Canaanites and Perizzites and other nations, in Joshua – to the ways they figure as characters in medieval and early modern English cultural and political history.[48]

Along the way, from biblical antiquity to early modernity, the stories accumulate and diversify, with Gog and Magog becoming the names of giants, their names sometimes conjoined as well, as Goemagog or Gogmagog. Scherb tells us that by late classical times, biblical commentators and romance writers had linked Gog and Magog to the story of Alexander the Great, who with God's help encloses these monstrous beings in the Caucasus mountains, behind iron gates (commonly known as the Caspian Gates). In this romance tradition, Alexander is horrified at their barbaric customs, which include cannibalism as in eating their dead. English romance writers added incest, free love, lawlessness and bestiality to their satanic sins, as well as the eating of pregnant women, and they could be variously identified with Celts, Goths, Scythians, Huns, Arabians, Turks, Magyars, Parthians and Mongols. In medieval literature, as in English versions of *Mandeville's Travels*, the Jews are indicted as primal outsiders, with Gog and Magog identified with the Ten Tribes of Israel, posing an apocalyptic threat because if they were to escape from their mountain prison, they would organize the world's Jews to destroy Christianity.[49]

In his *Historia* Geoffrey of Monmouth weaves, Scherb argues, Gog and Magog into a narrative of successful colonization. In England there lived an indigenous race of giants. Fortunately, they were defeated and mostly slain by the incoming Britons, who regarded themselves as descendants of the Trojans. One giant, however, Goemagog, is kept alive and finds himself pitted in a wrestling match against Corineus, champion of the Trojans/ Britons. Finally, Corineus manages to hurl Goemagog off a cliff into the sea.[50] (There is perhaps a trace in this story of the Olympians defeating the Titans in Greek mythological history.) The defeat of Goemagog reveals to the satisfaction of the Trojans/Britons that they are a chosen people who, in so gloriously vanquishing the indigenous inhabitants of the island, will now move forward in history. However, Scherb recounts, Goemagog, or Gogmagog as he would become known, also emerges in later cultural history as the chronicler for the medieval English of their historical origins, relating how he was overcome by the champion of the Britons/Trojans, was converted to Christianity, and is now accepted as an English giant. In early modern English culture, Scherb observes, these various traditions of Gog and Magog, biblical, romance and historical, are invoked for story telling. Sometimes now Magog is a giant who, riding a camel, is associated with the Saracens and other exotic eastern peoples; again, however, on being converted and taking a new name, he testifies to the power of Christianity. By the sixteenth century, civic authorities regularly appropriate Gogmagog and his conqueror Corineus for ceremonies, greeting visiting royalty as pageant giants who bespeak Britain's claim to an ancient and noble genealogy traceable back to Troy; they are now particularly associated with London, capital city of a new international empire.[51]

Shino Konishi has pointed out that a belief in giants – giantology – was long-standing in Western representations of indigenous peoples such as Australian Aboriginals. When in the late eighteenth and early nineteenth-century French explorers like Nicolas Baudin visited Australia on scientific voyages, they nevertheless seriously entertained the view that New Holland harboured giants. As Konishi comments, it is clear that the Enlightenment never severed reason from fantasy.[52] Nor, we might add, had the early modern English humanist promoters of colonization in North America.

If, in this long tradition of representation, Gogmagog signified the indigenous of England who are rightfully conquered by
the incoming Trojans/Britons, those same Trojans/Britons now,
Gray's suggestion is, had the right to conquer and destroy any
indigenous giants and monstrous beings they found in North
America.

## HONOURABLE COLONIZATION IN *THE TEMPEST*

Let's look now at the Shakespeare play famous for its
exploration of questions of colonization. We can view *The
Tempest* in Bakhtin's terms as polyphonic in its different
perspectives, and menippean both in its fantasticality and its
refusal of any certain position by which to judge ideals and
actions. As in the character of Agricola created by Tacitus, the
philosophical idea that *The Tempest* explores as a menippea is
that of honourable colonization, an idea embodied in a wise
man, or man who designates himself as wise, Prospero the magician, exile and would-be ruler of an island, with a new subject,
Caliban, its previous sole occupant. *The Tempest* develops in its
own distinctive ways the tradition of evocation of genocide,
colonization and conquest, and questioning of genocide, colonization and conquest, that I have been exploring in Herodotus
and Thucydides' histories, Greek tragedy in Aeschylus and
Euripides, biblical stories like Exodus, Joshua and Judges,
Cicero's *Republic*, Virgil's *Aeneid* and Tacitus's *Agricola* and
*Germania*. Caliban reprises those figures, not least the British
leader Calgacus in the *Agricola*, who in this tradition have
passionately protested against the conquest and colonization
visited upon them by conquerors from elsewhere.

Briefly, I'll analyse aspects of the play in relation to concepts
I have been developing so far in this book and that bear on the idea
of honourable colonization: victimology, genocide and Waswo's
notion of colonizers as culture-bearers, at least in their own self-
admiring image. Let's think first in terms of victimology, where

those who escape violence and possible death in one place wander in misery and then claim another land or island, while feeling that their previous sufferings justify any violence and sufferings they might inflict on others in another place; we have discussed the narratives of Exodus and the *Aeneid* in these terms. Prospero decides to give up governing as Duke of Milan for a while to pursue a life of contemplation; he is then usurped by his perfidious brother Antonio, who arranges for Prospero and his then little daughter Miranda to be put on a ruined 'barque'. They are left to die on the open sea. Fortunately as it turns out Prospero has with him some books he prizes 'above my dukedom' (1.2: 140–51, 161–8); he has knowledge to bring somewhere, if he can reach a place of safety. Prospero and Miranda wander in the wilderness of the sea, arriving at last at an island, which they find to be inhabited by someone else, Caliban, who regards himself as its rightful owner.

Prospero, however, feels no need to ask Caliban for permission to be on his island. Rather, he immediately assumes possession and rights of settlement. In Waswo's terms in *The Founding Legend of Western Civilization*, Prospero, coming from elsewhere like the Trojans, intensely aware of his own agony as a displaced ruler, sees himself as a culture-bearer who has a right to be on the island because he comes as a voyager requiring refuge and hospitality. He is an honourable visitor, friendly and helpful to Caliban. He and Miranda try to teach the local inhabitant elements of their superior culture, reminding us of Tacitus's *Agricola* where the Romans wish to absorb the Britons into Roman culture; such assimilation is judged as a form of enslavement by the *Agricola*'s sceptical narrator.

Caliban, however, reminding us of Calgacus decrying the loss of liberty and independence of the Britons at the hands of the Roman invaders, protests, pointing out that Prospero has dispossessed him of his world, his way of life that he enjoys and that he feels constitutes his distinctive existence, that had been rightfully given to him by his mother Sycorax. Let's quote the famous passage, Caliban's eternal cry of the indigenous and dispossessed:

This island's mine by Sycorax my mother,
Which thou tak'st from me. When thou cam'st first,
Thou strok'st me and made much of me; wouldst give me
Water with berries in't, and teach me how
To name the bigger light and how the less,
That burn by day and night; and then I loved thee,
And showed thee all the qualities o'th' isle,
The fresh springs, brine pits, barren place and fertile –
Cursed be I that did so! All the charms
Of Sycorax, toads, beetles, bats light on you!
For I am all the subjects that you have,
Which first was mine own king, and here you sty me
In this hard rock, whiles you do keep from me
The rest o'th' island.

(1.2: 331–44)

It is a speech that perhaps has something of the tragic grandeur of Shylock's protest at his belittlement and humiliation in *The Merchant of Venice*.

Caliban resists his dispossession not only in bitter angry words but also in action, violently so, attempting to violate Miranda (no longer a child). In terms of natural law, Caliban is no longer providing hospitality to the strangers who have come to his shore, and so the stranger, the visitor, the new settler, has the right to reply with force. Prospero now visits upon Caliban just punishment. In terms of Lemkin's definition of genocide in *Axis Rule in Occupied Europe*, of genocide as destruction of the foundations of life of an oppressed society, subjugation of its local population and replacement by the new pattern of the oppressor, Prospero destroys Caliban's world and replaces it with his own, reducing the once proud and independent Caliban to slavery. Prospero exploits Caliban's labour, which he knows he cannot do without, in the agricultural project that Prospero hopes to realize on the island, attempting to replace the savage, that is to say, non-agricultural mode of existence Caliban has enjoyed before the awful magician's arrival. In the masque performed in Act 4 there is a hymn to an ordered and idyllic agricultural abundance, Iris addressing Ceres as 'most bounteous lady' and wishing for 'rich leas / Of wheat, rye, barley, vetches, oats, and peas; / Thy turfy mountains, where live nibbling sheep ...' (4.1: 60–2).

Prospero needs Caliban's labour; the master needs his slave. In terms of medieval and early modern legends, we can think here of the Trojans coming to a land or island and conquering indigenous giants like Gog and Gogmagog while keeping one alive, to be made useful to the conquerors. The 'Trojan' Prospero, having conquered the monstrous figure of Caliban, whom he scornfully describes as 'not honoured with / A human shape' (1.2: 283–4), puts him to use as a kind of domestic and agricultural labourer. We could also think here of genocide theory. In his report, 'On Genocide', that he presented to Bertrand Russell's International War Crimes Tribunal in 1967, Sartre contends that, unlike in the American war in Vietnam, in the French colonization of Algeria the genocidal desire to destroy and replace the indigenous society was inhibited by the economic necessity to use Algerian labour.[53]

Let's also think now of the categories, discussed especially in my analysis of Euripides' Trojan plays, by which Lemkin wished to analyse historical genocides.[54] In Lemkin's outline, he refers under the heading 'Conditions leading to genocide' to the category of 'economic exploitation (e.g. slavery)', and such is painfully clear for Caliban; Prospero, too, is angered that he as master is dependent on the labour of a slave and cannot rid himself of him (1.2: 310–15). Another category under this heading is 'evolution of genocidal values in genocidist group (contempt for the alien, etc)', and here we think of the change from friendliness in Prospero as honourable colonizer, consequent upon Caliban's resisting colonizing and his attempt to rape Miranda, to the violent language of insult and goading that Prospero continually rains down upon Caliban.

When a still uncowed Caliban refuses to show himself when called, Prospero regales him: 'Thou poisonous slave, got by the devil himself / Upon thy wicked dam, come forth!' (1.2: 319–20). Under the heading 'Methods and techniques of genocide – Physical', Lemkin refers to 'mutilation', and here we can think of the cruelties and tortures that Prospero makes Caliban suffer: cramps, side-stitches, being pinched and stung all over his body (1.2: 325–30). Under 'Methods and techniques of genocide – Cultural', Lemkin refers to 'demoralization', and here we can think of the fear of Prospero that Caliban experiences and which keeps him subjugated (1.2: 365–73); we can also think of the ignominious drunkenness that Caliban increasingly falls into as the play goes on. Under the heading 'The Genocidists', there is also a category of 'demoralization', and here we might contemplate Prospero's ethical deterioration as a genocidist colonizer: his resort to a language of insult with not only Caliban but his other slave Ariel; his querulousness and authoritarianism, even with Miranda; his use of torture and the pleasure he takes in Caliban's pain; his manipulativeness, as when he uses his daughter for his own ends in relation to Ferdinand. Under the heading of 'Responses of victim group', both active and passive, Lemkin refers to differing features that we can see characterizing Caliban's responses to his situation of oppression and enslavement: 'submission' through 'terror', yet also 'resistance' both to 'assimilation' and 'subordination', though by play's end Caliban appears to be completely demoralized. He has descended from a near-tragic figure revealed in his great speech to a minor fool, similar perhaps to the way, as Erich Auerbach pointed out in an essay in *Mimesis*, Shylock descends as a character delivering a great anti-racist speech to, by the end of *The Merchant of Venice*, a low figure of farce.[55]

## CONCLUSION

The humanist imagination, we can observe, was disordered, incoherent, chaotic and fantastical.

I'll close with some reflections on international law. In the affirmative narrative of Tacitus's *Agricola* and *Germania*, as we noted in the previous chapter, the Romans are to be considered a chosen people of the gods who have the right to supersede other and lesser peoples (though such people as the Britons and Germans could be admired in some ways when they remind the Romans of their better and older selves). The Romans are now the heirs of history, rightful conquerors of lands near and far. In these terms, the early modern English promoters of colonization were also clearly supersessionists. They, as Christian Europeans and more particularly as Christian English, versed in the Old Testament as well as the learning and thinking of the pagan Romans, in possession of honourable ideals, were now a chosen people of history, with the right to discover and claim the rest of the world, though they had to overcome the ever present danger that other Christian European powers might have got to a place before them and established, what to fellow Europeans at least, was a plausible legal claim by discovery and precedent (that is, repetition of the claim of discovery).

The law of nations, or international law, as it developed in early modern English humanism, was a historical fantasia of justifications, stories, legends and myths. International law was a repertoire by which to sanction colonization and empire with the highest of motives and ideals. What was designated international law were principles, often contradictory, agreed to by the powerful and influential of European states. International law has been, and in some respects still is, conceived and continuously refined not to protect the colonized from conquest or colonization or empire or war but rather to regulate conquest and colonization and war amongst the powerful nations at any one time.[56]

Early modern English notions and myths of international law could be laughed at in the spirit of Nietzsche and Foucault were it not for the genocidal consequences of colonization and empire.

# 8 WAS THE ENLIGHTENMENT THE ORIGIN OF THE HOLOCAUST?[1]

> It seemed less desirable to give a merely narrative account of the growth and vicissitudes of the philosophy of the Enlightenment than to set forth, as it were, the dramatic action of its thinking.
>
> (Cassirer, *The Philosophy of the Enlightenment*, Preface)[2]

> Religion did not merely retain a powerful presence throughout eighteenth-century Europe, it was central to the Enlightenment project itself.
>
> (Grell and Porter, *Toleration in Enlightenment Europe*, Introduction)[3]

In the second half of the twentieth century and in the new millennium the Enlightenment has been indicted for initiating, providing and lending its authority to the conceptual underpinnings of the Holocaust. The influential frame-story here is *Modernity and the Holocaust* (1989), with Zygmunt Bauman in the preface telling us that he once thought the horror and inhumanity of the Holocaust was a momentary madness that grew like a cancerous growth on the body of civilization and modernity. Bauman hopes his book will contribute to Western self-awareness and self-questioning, that it was modernity itself, in its ordinary practices of passionless impersonal rationality, bureaucratic efficiency and social engineering, that enabled and was manifested in the Holocaust; a point he feels that had already been made by Hannah Arendt in her 1963 *Eichmann in Jerusalem* but which still needs insisting on and drawing out.[4]

In implicating the Enlightenment in the Western 'civilizing process' of which modernity and the Holocaust are outcomes and expressions,[5] Bauman draws on George L. Mosse's *Toward the Final Solution: A History of European Racism* (1978), which argues that eighteenth-century Europe was the 'cradle of modern racism'. The 'major cultural trends' of the eighteenth century 'vitally affected the foundations of racist thought', in particular an entwining of science and aesthetics. Scientific endeavour, with its interest in observation, measurement and comparison, was 'directed towards a classification of the human races according to their place in nature and the effect of the environment'. The comparative physical measurements made in the new sciences like anthropology, phrenology and physiognomy relied on a resemblance to ancient beauty and proportion; such fusion of classificatory science with ideals of 'Greek beauty', embodying 'order and harmony', determined the 'value of man'; henceforth racial judgements were to be based on a particular kind of outward appearance. Such 'continuous transition from science to aesthetics' became a 'cardinal feature of modern racism'.[6]

Bauman contributed the opening essay 'The Duty to Remember – But What?' to the collection edited by James Kaye and Bo Stråth, *Enlightenment and Genocide, Contradictions of Modernity* (2000), where he restates the conclusions of *Modernity and the Holocaust*. We should cease seeing the Holocaust as a 'bizarre and aberrant event' and rather view it as had in their separate ways Adorno and Arendt: 'It was my intention to pick up where Adorno or Arendt had left a blatantly unfinished task: to exhortate fellow social thinkers to consider the relation between the event of the Holocaust and the structure and logic of modern life', with its exaltation of abstraction, (mis)treating people as categories and impersonality; genocide in modernity, in the Holocaust in the near past as in Rwanda in the near present, is the 'ultimate triumph of all-defining, all-classifying modern bureaucracy'.[7]

In *Enlightenment and Genocide, Contradictions of Modernity* Bauman's contribution is immediately followed by way of contrast with Robert Wokler's essay, 'The Enlightenment Project on the Eve of the Holocaust'. Wokler says as a scholar of the eighteenth century he will defend the Enlightenment in this discussion, as he has done elsewhere, against its assorted critics, modernist, postmodernist, feminist.[8] Wokler sees Bauman's harsh judgement on modernity as a continuation of Adorno and Horkheimer's pessimistic view in *Dialectic of Enlightenment* (1944), that through its enactment of the Holocaust civilization rendered itself perfectly barbarous, not by abandoning its principles but in fulfilling them.[9] Rather than Adorno and Horkheimer, Wokler suggests that scholarship could well return to Ernst Cassirer's project in his life work, especially in *Die Philosophie der Aufklärung*, written in the winter and spring of 1932 and the last book he produced in Germany: to portray the pervasive cosmopolitanism of European thought, that German thinkers were influential in the European Enlightenment as a whole, and that the real spirit of Germany was not nationalist and militarist but humanist, tolerant, pluralist, and cosmopolitan, in the tradition of Leibniz, Goethe and Lessing.[10] In Wokler's view, the pathos of Cassirer journeying into exile with the coming to power of Hitler was not that Nazi Germany and the Holocaust fulfilled the foundational modes of thought of the Enlightenment. Rather, what characterized Nazi Germany was its nationalism, which was a culmination of the conception of the nation-state brought into play in modern European history by the French Revolution. As revealed in the course of the Revolution from 1789, and particularly in the Terror of 1793–94, the modern nation-state required that those who fall under its authority be above all united, that they form one people, morally bound together by a common identity. For Wokler, the unitary principle of the post-French Revolution modern nation-state leads to violence, including totalitarian violence.[11]

In Wokler's view, then, it is the French Revolution and the modern nation-state which 'betrayed' the Enlightenment's notions of common humanity and attachment to universal rights.[12] For henceforth only persons comprising nations which formed states could have rights, so that modernity has been marked by the abuse of human rights by nation-states which alone have the authority to determine the scope of those rights and their validity. Wokler suggests that the Enlightenment by contrast admirably embodied the principles of civilization in its ideals and discursive practices of toleration of religious minorities, dislike of bigotry, and opposition to persecution of heretics. The Enlightenment Project was, Wokler suggests, an active 'campaign' for the creation of a party of humanity (here Wokler calls on Hume), an international society of the republic of letters, practised in the eighteenth century's literary salons, journals and academies. And many Enlightenment figures were themselves forced into exile, to become, as Wokler puts it, an intellectual diaspora, part of an 'outcast culture' which fermented more richly abroad than in their home societies. Given such dimensions, Wokler feels, the 'Enlightenment did not just exclude the possibility of the Holocaust but in fact combated ethnic cleansing in all its pre-modern forms'. The Enlightenment Project, Wokler urges, can be conceived as 'civilization's confrontation with barbarism' and proactive opposition to 'genocide' in its every manifestation.[13]

In their introductory essay to the volume, editors James Kaye and Bo Stråth point to the conflict of optimistic and pessimistic views between Wokler and Bauman. Yet it quickly becomes clear that Bauman is the hero of their narrative, that Wokler's protests are in their view unconvincing, and Bauman's negative dialectic of the Enlightenment and modernity has for them the status of unchallengeable truth.[14] Appealing to Bauman as authority, they constate as axioms of history that the 'very foundations' of the Enlightenment knew 'little or no doubt'. The Enlightenment's enshrining of reason went hand in hand with abstraction: a 'veritable obsession to categorise and classify emerged', which promoted the 'instrumental dimension in the concepts of reason and rationality'. The Enlightenment's 'driving force' was the 'quest for absolute knowledge' and 'total/final rationality' to the 'end of changing *i.e.* improving the world'. Enlightenment involved the idea that modernity was perpetually unfinished, it was always restlessly envisaging 'utopian ideas of some end goal'. As a 'messianic and millenarial project', Enlightenment is hence 'fundamentally linked' both to modernity and genocide.[15]

The editors do concede that one criticism of Bauman's seeing the Holocaust as the expression of a general modernity is the question of why the Holocaust came to be engineered in Germany in particular, why not elsewhere; they also agree with Wokler that the French Revolutionary conception of the nation-state must be brought into the discussion.[16] Kaye and Stråth could, however, have also pointed out that while Bauman appeals to Hannah Arendt's famous analysis of the banality of evil in relation to Eichmann and the industrial killing of the Holocaust, Arendt in her multi-faceted thinking was not necessarily opposed to the Enlightenment and the 'long eighteenth century': there is, for example, her appreciative portrait of Lessing in *Men in Dark Times* (1970), her admiration for Berlin's cosmopolitan salon culture of the 1790s, her interest in Jeffersonian democracy in America.[17] Furthermore, Arendt gave a number of reasons for the historical development of National Socialism, including in *The Origins of Totalitarianism* that imperialism from 1884 to 1914 was a formative influence: 'Some of the fundamental aspects of this time appear so close to totalitarian phenomena of the twentieth century that it may be justifiable to consider the whole period a preparatory stage for coming catastrophes'.[18]

It is not hard to appreciate Wokler's own pessimism that Enlightenment scholars are on the defensive, feeling that they are not being heard in the face of a general contemporary anti-*Aufklärung* orthodoxy, disheartened that their appreciation of the Enlightenment based on intimate knowledge and familiarity with the 'long eighteenth century' is being disregarded.[19]

Contrary to Bauman's harsh judgement and linear historiography, I will evoke my own enchantment especially with theologico-philosophical writing in the late seventeenth and early to middle eighteenth century, from Spinoza to John Toland to Hume.[20]

I wish to give edge to my enchantment by deploying a post-secularist approach.[21] Arguments about monotheism, polytheism, world religions and the continuing importance of interpretations of biblical narratives bear directly on how we conceive the Enlightenment. I wish to join those historians of ideas like Grell, Porter, McCalman, Champion and Berti, who dispute a historiography of the Enlightenment as a desire to create a secular world of reason and science.[22] Postsecularist historiography draws attention to the salience of religion in the Enlightenment in both its Radical and Moderate branches, that in thinkers from Spinoza to Isaac Newton to John Toland to Joseph Priestley there was a continuum of interests in their writing and speculation, from astronomy and mathematics and chemistry to arguments over the Trinity, biblical dating and prophecy, philosemitism, millenarian visions, politics and civil society and the public sphere, the problem of the multitude, the place of philosophy, the freedom of intellectuals.

I will be further agreeing with, and trying to extend, a suggestion of Wokler concerning a possible convergence between the writing and thinking of Enlightenment figures, and postmodernist appreciation of variety, difference, alterity, plurality, specificity, uniqueness, toleration, anti-colonialism, anti-Eurocentrism.[23] I will argue that postmodern theorists do not simply join in the modernist condemnation of the Enlightenment (as in Adorno and Horkheimer) but are in their attitudes and musings highly ambivalent and contradictory and often reveal – as in Deleuze and Lyotard – significant affinities with aspects of the Enlightenment.

Throughout I will be pondering the question, Was there ever a single unified 'Enlightenment Project'?

In my conclusion I will return to the haunting question: is there imbrication of the Enlightenment with barbarism, with violence?

## SPINOZA

Do philosophy and theologico-philosophical speculation, major defining genres of the Enlightenment, bear out the Bauman–Mosse thesis? For many years now historians in the field of Enlightenment studies have defined 'the long eighteenth century' as beginning in the latter part of the seventeenth century. In these terms, how does the Bauman–Mosse thesis and more general anti-Enlightenment condemnation fare when the thought of Spinoza and Spinozism is considered? In particular, did the Enlightenment – here the Radical Enlightenment – work by a discourse of certainty that knew not doubt? Was it obsessed by categorizing and classifying? Did it aim for final, exhaustive knowledge as its ideal and practice? Was it supremely instrumental in its notions of reason? Was it directed by the messianic and utopian?

Intellectual historians have pointed out aspects of Spinoza akin to mysticism, enjoyment of enigma, and practices of writing that undermine certainty. Deleuze – recall Wokler's urging of affinities between postmodernism and Enlightenment – points to a kind of split or doubled textuality in the *Ethics*, the flow of definitions, propositions and demonstrations in contrast to the passionate scholia.[24] Yirmiyahu Yovel suggests the influence of his Portuguese Marrano family and diasporic history on Spinoza's consciousness and philosophy, creating the great early Enlightenment figure as harbinger of the sensibility of modernity – and, we might add, postmodernity as well. The implications of Yovel's argument are that Spinoza and Spinozism were radically anti-utopian: the intellectual emerges from this cultural history as a connoisseur of ambiguity, ambivalence and paradox, enjoying an ironic self-consciousness that preserves a detachment from any community that might claim his/her identity or belonging; both inside and outside a society at the same time; careful, cautious, wary of the tyrannical majority (the multitude) stirred into mob violence by persecutory theologians, priests, preachers and pastors; yet adventurous in thought and writing and belonging only to an international, cosmopolitan republic of letters.[25]

The feminist postmodern philosopher Genevieve Lloyd, taking as her point of departure Yovel's portrait of Spinoza as Marrano and outsider, evokes in Spinoza fascinating ideas about mind, body, death and eternity.[26] Lloyd says that a startling aspect of Spinoza's thought in the *Ethics* (published posthumously in 1677) is his anti-Cartesian argument that the mind is the 'idea' of the body. The mind is the idea of an individual body, and therefore, Lloyd points out, there is no way it can totally transcend its limited position in the whole to understand all things adequately. Further, since mind and body are entwined, the mind ceases to exist when the body ceases to exist; the mind, like the body, will after death have no duration, no immortality. Yet, in the final, difficult, highly speculative Part Five of the *Ethics*, Lloyd says we must ponder the quite different implications of Spinoza's proposition XXIII, that *the human mind cannot be absolutely destroyed with the body, but there remains something of it which is eternal.* Lloyd points out that Spinoza posits a highest form of knowledge, the intellectual love of God where God and Nature are interchangeable; such a form of knowledge is open only to the wise, those who are self-reflexive about knowledge, it is not open to the multitude. This highest form of knowledge is not accessible by means of reason alone, but in reason working with intuition, imagination, emotion (love) and recognition of 'fiction' and even of 'feigning'.[27]

How can this be? Spinoza, says Lloyd, believes that the eternity of the mind emerges from considering the intellectual love of God only when it is related to the mind. The mind might have a form of being that somehow remains beyond the existence of the body, and the mind's understanding of itself as eternal is its highest achievement, the state of blessedness. Yet here the mind, in understanding itself as eternal, has to resort to a fiction, a feigning: in the highest form of knowledge the mind begins to know its own eternity, that we are in God and are conceived through God. But if the mind is already eternal, then there can be no question of beginning. The idea of a beginning of consciousness of one's mind as eternal is then a fiction, a necessary fiction to aid understanding of one's mind as eternal; but one's mind has always been eternal. The mind needs such a fiction of a beginning in order to relate to history, to being in a certain time and place. In this way, the mind shifts between two ways of understanding itself in relation to the substance of which the universe is composed. In one way the mind understands itself as eternal, in another it knows itself as durational, as involved with time and place. Nevertheless, Lloyd feels, Spinoza was very aware that the state of blessedness is difficult to reach, for no mind is always wise and wisdom is in any case always precarious.[28]

In *Collective Imaginings: Spinoza, Past and Present*, Moira Gatens and Genevieve Lloyd evoke a Spinoza whom they feel is of great contemporary relevance in conceptualizing notions of freedom, responsibility and difference. Gatens and Lloyd suggest that Spinoza's philosophy, reprising yet also transforming concerns of ancient philosophy especially in the Stoics and Epicurians, does not attempt to transcend difference or assimilate differences into a universalized sameness. Rather, Spinoza conceived of bodies and minds as involving both affinities and antagonisms, harmonies and conflicts. For Spinoza, because the universe consists of one substance (God or Nature), it has no final causes or telos, no natural end or aims, hence permitting the flourishing of difference, diversity and experimentation. Such monism is to be understood as a multiplicity of irreducibly distinct individual modes. And because, famously and mysteriously, Spinoza treats the mind as the 'idea' of the body, human minds consequently reflect human bodies in their persistence and flourishing and their equally complex vulnerability to antagonistic powers. The body, imagination and affect do not in themselves represent limits to reason and knowledge, and through reflecting on them we come to develop our powers of reason and increase our knowledge. In particular, Spinoza highlights the imagination, which plays a positive role in even the highest forms of intellectual life.[29]

In *Neuropolitics: Thinking, Culture, Speed* (2002), William E. Connolly likewise suggests that Spinoza's thinking is opposed to 'narrow intellectualism', that Spinoza sees not only the mind's but the body's powers as mysterious and unpredictable. Connolly quotes from Part Three proposition II of the *Ethics* here: *Nobody has yet determined the limits of the body's capabilities.* Spinoza at this point is arguing that the mind cannot control or dominate the body: 'the body can by the sole laws of its nature do many things which the mind wonders at.'[30]

In *Radical Enlightenment: Philosophy and the Making of Modernity 1650–1750*, a remarkable work of transnational history, Jonathan I. Israel suggests that the Enlightenment was multiply-stranded, between and within the Moderate and the Radical, and that such multiplicity and tension and conflict between the various strands meant that the European intellectual arena grew ever 'more complex, fragmented, and uncertain'; there came everywhere to prevail 'confusion, hesitation, and a rapid fragmentation of ideas'; there was bafflement, 'dilemma' and 'enigma'. In the drama of the Enlightenment, Israel accords Spinoza a central role.[31] Israel argues that Spinoza and Spinozism became the formative influences that created the Radical Enlightenment in its relations with the Moderate Enlightenment and in shaping the key ideas and urbane cosmopolitan culture of Enlightenment philosophy throughout Europe.[32]

Spinoza, Israel writes, was influential in all spheres of new thinking in the 'long eighteenth century', the political, the ethical, the erotic, the cosmological. Spinoza was the first major thinker in modern times to embrace democratic republicanism as the highest and most fully rational form of political organization. In works like *Tractatus Theologico-Politicus* (1670) and the *Ethics* Spinoza was a leader in the Enlightenment struggle for toleration, toleration as the enjoyment of individual freedom in thought and speech as well as freedom to publish and to distribute what one has published. Spinoza believed in political freedom in a positive active sense, rather than as being defined negatively as absence of obstacles. Yet Spinoza did not believe in overthrowing a monarch or ruler even when a regime's tyranny was apparent to all; he was anti-revolutionary, he disliked political violence and was intensely wary of mass conformity, believing the common people usually venerate whatever form of power there is that rules them. Since Spinoza held that there was no transcendental God who would guarantee or could ordain any form of morality as absolute, his thought suggested the relativity of good and evil, that they were modes of thinking, and that depending on circumstances the same thing can be considered good, bad or neutral.[33]

Spinoza himself, Israel points out, used terms like 'unmanly' to indicate those who did not seek the guidance of reason, and he considered women naturally intellectually weak. But, says Israel, Spinoza's views on the nature of the universe had widespread implications for issues of sexuality, eroticism and the place of women in society, for the more radical the philosophical standpoint as in Spinoza and Spinozism, the more emphatic the levelling and egalitarian tendencies which in turn generated impulses towards not only female emancipation but emancipation of the human libido itself. There were also implications for freedom of conversation between men and women, in a kind of new Epicureanism. In such a libertarian culture or Radical Enlightenment public sphere, which thrived in the fluid social relationships afforded by the tea and coffee shops that began to proliferate in Holland, London and Hamburg from the 1660s and 1670s, what mattered was not membership of a particular family or noble group, but a new kind of meritocracy of mind and attitude, given to philosophical knowledge, irreverent writing and refined pleasure-seeking.[34]

In my own *1492: The Poetics of Diaspora*, I point out that in *Tractatus Theologico-Politicus* Spinoza does not believe in the hubris of reason, that it can master or control the world. We should not imagine Nature is so limited that 'man' is its chief part. In discussing the biblical stories, Spinoza asks: 'Could we live our lives wisely if we were to accept as true nothing that could conceivably be called into doubt on any principle of scepticism? Are not most of our actions in any case fraught with uncertainty and hazard?'[35] In a letter to Blyenbergh, Spinoza stressed the value of uncertainty, of not knowing: 'For my own part, as I confess plainly … I do not understand the Scriptures.'[36] It is the necessity of uncertainty and the hazards of interpretation, in a spirit of wryness and the cultivation of doubt about the limitations of knowledge, that Spinoza stressed in his works and in correspondence with his contemporaries. He acknowledged the value of recognizing unknowability.

## TOLAND

It was my fascination with Spinoza which led me to become interested in John Toland, perhaps the most well-known and controversial 'English' freethinking theologian of the early 'long eighteenth century' – born in 1670 near Londonderry, educated in Glasgow, Leiden and Oxford, advocating cosmopolitanism for intellectuals meeting in coffee shops and salons while always under the political pressure of patrons like Shaftesbury and Harley, dying in poverty in 1722.[37]

Toland is usually referred to as a kind of English Spinozist. I will argue that their intellectual relationship is not at all simple; their ideas meet and miss in a complex choreography in terms of biography, situation and philosophy.

Jan Assmann in *Moses the Egyptian* tells us that so infamous a figure was Spinoza in European intellectual and theological life after *Tractatus Theologico-Politicus* that he could often only be referred to by his admirers by a code-name, 'Egypt'. Assmann feels that in England Toland was a Spinozan in the sense that he followed Spinoza's dramatic philosophical claim that God is Nature and Nature is God; since there is no anthropomorphic or transcendental God, there did not need to be a Mosaic Distinction between one true religion following the one true god and false religions following a false god or gods; such was the ground of pantheism, the pantheism that Toland would champion in the eighteenth century.[38]

Yet there is I think a play of similarity and difference between Toland and Spinoza. In terms of affinity, Toland as a young man published in 1696 his *Christianity Not Mysterious*, in which like Spinoza before him he finds, deploying a sustained detailed forensic textual critique, that the notion of miracles is contrary to 'natural reason' and always misused to their own advantage by power-seeking priesthoods and orthodox divines.[39] Not long after he visited his native Ireland, there to find a hostile reception: the book was burnt by the common hangman, and Toland escaped arrest for blasphemy by returning to England. He was now an outsider – as Spinoza had been in relation to the Dutch Sephardim – to his own community of origin. Toland would henceforth become, in Georg Simmel's terms, a stranger amongst the nations, someone who comes today and stays tomorrow,[40] in various societies and courts in England and Europe, living in exile from his native Ireland and the Catholicism he was born into. Toland shared with Spinoza an approach to religion that is sociological and historical. Toland's writing and thinking is also Spinozan – and 'marrano' – in suggesting that philosophers must necessarily be Janus-faced, distinguishing between public utterance and private thought. Such, Toland would argue, had been the practice of philosophers in pre-Christian times and in non-Christian philosophies and religions.

In *Clidophorus* (1720) Toland, like Spinoza before him, contemplates how intellectuals can act in the world. How can they escape threat, harm and persecution? Toland suggests that the ancient pagan philosophers effected a careful distinction between an external doctrine, which was open and public and accommodated to popular prejudice and religious practices established by law, and a philosophy that was hidden and secret, safe from the attentions of 'ambitious Priests, supported by ... the Mob', an internal realm of ideas discussed by the capable and discreet few, who addressed truth and the nature of things. In the spirit of Egyptology, the conviction that ancient Egypt is the source of the wisdom of the ages, Toland writes that the Egyptians, 'who were the wisest of mortals', practised such a 'two-fold doctrine', as did the Greeks, following Pythagoras, who travelled to Egypt and there 'suffer'd himself to be circumcised' so that he might be admitted to the secret sanctuaries of knowledge. In Egypt, as recorded by Plutarch, Isis was known to the vulgar as a royal ruler. But according to the philosophers Isis was 'the Nature of all things ... who held the Universe to be the principal god, or the supreme being' (a view that Toland sees as anticipating the Cabala). In this remarkable formulation, we can see why Toland could be recognized as Egyptological and pantheistic in the spirit of Spinoza. In comparatist mode Toland writes that the Egyptian double manner of teaching religion and philosophy, the exoteric and esoteric, was also in use 'among other oriental nations', especially the Ethiopians and Babylonians as well as 'antient and modern Bramins, the Syrians, Persians and the rest, principally instructed by Zoroaster'. Such a two-fold practice is prevalent amongst the 'present Chinese, Siamese and Indians'. In general for Toland, then, as for Spinoza before him, the wary life of the true philosopher consists in 'despising the Mob, detesting the Priest, and delighting in his own Liberty'. The philosopher should be very careful in relation to state power and the treachery of rulers, practising prudence, even apparent ignorance. Thales is exemplary here. When Cresus demanded of Thales what he thought of the gods, Thales obtained some days for deliberation, and then finally 'answer'd, Nothing'.[41]

In *Pantheisticon* (1751), Toland forges an exuberant witty manifesto for a modern Socratic Society composed of a Brotherhood of Pantheists, those who believe that All Things are from the Whole, and the Whole is from All Things. Pantheists deny, says Toland, that there is any 'Center of the Universe, in any Sense whatsoever'. The Brotherhood is structured on the distinction of the exoteric and esoteric, which latter always 'shuns the Multitude, as conscious of its Jealousy and Hatred'. The Pantheists meet in secret, enjoying the Socratic banquet and believing that philosophers belong to a universal city: 'The Sun is my Father, the Earth my Mother, the World's my Country, and all Men are my Relations'. In terms of such internationalist and cosmopolitan spirit, Toland writes that the Pantheists enjoy metropolitan cities like

Paris, Venice, the cities of Holland especially Amsterdam, even papal Rome, and they abound in London. The Pantheists have nothing to do with institutional knowledge, as in the British Royal Society or the French Academy. They practise in their Socratic entertainments the arts of conversation. Toland draws up a list of the ancients who taught or acted nobly, and these include not only the Greek philosophers but also Confucius.[42]

Neither Spinoza nor Toland, however, were as prudent as they thought philosophers ideally should be; both were drawn into public interventions, controversy and polemic. Leibniz related that he spoke with Spinoza about the events of 1672 when the De Witt brothers, republican political leaders, were killed and mutilated by a crowd that included respectable, middle-class burghers. Spinoza had been dissuaded by his landlord from putting up a public sign outside his lodgings denouncing barbarism, his landlord fearing his lodger would also be torn to pieces.[43] Toland had to negotiate various patrons claiming him for particular party political views and reasons of state.

Yet there are differences between Spinoza and Toland, not least in terms of gender. Toland did not share Spinoza's androcentrism, his disdain for 'womanish tears', and his employing metaphors of the witch and siren who lure men away from reason and philosophy.[44] In *Pantheisticon*, Toland reveres both the women and men among the ancient philosophers who are honourable in the history of pantheism, including the Platonic philosopher and teacher Hypatia.[45]

In 1720 Toland published an extended essay on Hypatia (*Tetradymos*, Part III), head of the flourishing Platonic academy in Alexandria early in the fifth century. Toland reproves his own gender for its 'vulgar prejudice' in slighting women like Hypatia, who was both beautiful and learned. With libertarian earthiness, Toland tells a menstruation anecdote where Hypatia, vehemently solicited in love by one of her young gentleman scholars, happened to be under an indisposition ordinary to her sex; she took a handkerchief, of which she had been making some use on that occasion, and throwing it in his face, said:

'This is what you love, young fool, and not anything that's beautiful', that is, the abstract Platonic virtues of goodness and truth. Toland writes with scorn of Cyril, the Bishop of Alexandria later monstrously made a saint, grasping for secular power and instituting with enthusiasm the schismatic practices that have characterized, says Toland, Christianity to this day. Cyril expelled the Jews of Alexandria from the city, where, says Toland, 'they had liv'd in great opulance from the time of Alexander the Great, to the no small benefit of the place'. Toland says he is accustomed to reading 'monstrous lyes of this unfortunate nation, especially that thread-bare fiction of crucifying a child'. Cyril barbarously licensed the 'multitude' to seize all the goods of the expelled Jews. In a similar act of barbarity, Cyril, who disliked Hypatia both for her wisdom and because she was a friend of and acted as an oracle for the city's governor, Orestes, had her abducted by his clergy in 415, removed to a church, stripped, killed and then taken away and burnt to ashes.[46]

Toland's story creates Hypatia as an allegorical figure, the narrative of her vibrant life and cruel death suggesting for him contemporary meanings: the desire to recover pagan knowledge ruthlessly destroyed by official Christianity; the fraught relations between an intelligentsia fighting for its own sphere of intellectual freedom in opposition to a Christianity interfering in matters of knowledge; the rights of government to insist on a civil order it controls, including in religious matters; and knowledge and gender. In the Preface to his earlier *Letters to Serena* (1704) Toland made a passionate plea that women should be able to share with men the same advantages of education, travel, company and the management of affairs; a plea that looks back to the discourse of sexual equality in Plato's *Republic* as well as anticipating similar strongly held views by Lady Mary Wortley Montagu, who in a 1753 letter to her daughter Lady Bute, on the education of her granddaughters, wrote: 'To tell truth, there is no part of the world where our sex is treated with so much contempt as in England,' where women are 'educated in the grossest ignorance, and no art omitted to stifle our natural reason'.[47]

There is a clear difference between Spinoza and Toland in evaluation of the worth and legacy of Moses and Mosaic Law. Both Spinoza and Toland were regarded as Socinians in their admiration of Jesus as man not god. Unlike Spinoza, however, Toland also frequently declared himself an admirer of the Moses of Exodus, referring to him as 'this incomparable legislator'.[48] Toland wished to reconcile Exodus and Egyptology by invoking a natural human religion that could be counterposed to the power, canonical practices and encroachments on civil society of English institutional Christianity.[49] Further, Toland's philosemitism extended to Islam as well as Judaism, whereas Spinoza appears to have been at best indifferent to Islam, certainly uninterested in its theological ideas and its possible importance in contemporary European religious history, though impressed, as he was by the Catholic Church, with its authoritarianism.[50]

## PHILOSEMITISM AND ISLAMOPHILIA

In his remarkable text *Nazarenus: Or, Jewish, Gentile, and Mahometan Christianity* (1718), Toland constructs a kind of theological detective story, discovering by chance hidden treasures as in the *Arabian Nights*. The detective narrator tells his readers that when in 1709 he was in a library in Amsterdam he was privileged to catch sight of a new gospel, a 'Mahometan Gospel', unknown to any Christians; he perceives that it was translated from the Arabic into Italian, its ink and paper delicate and fine, with notes in Arabic in the margins. He could only peruse it for a short time, but that was long enough for him to feel confident that it was based on a lost gospel of Barnabas. That the Mahometans should use for their own devotion an early Christian gospel is not, says Toland, surprising, since they acknowledge that their religion is founded in four books, the Pentateuch of Moses, the Psalms of David, the Gospel of Jesus and the Alcoran of Mahomet. The Mahometans have preserved the lost gospel of Barnabas because they are indeed a kind of

Christian sect, just as Christianity was at first esteemed a branch of Judaism. The lost gospel shows that the Mahometans have kept and continued an early form of Christianity. In particular, the Mahometans reprise in their religion 'primitive' Christianity, as with the Ebionites, also known as the Nazarenes.[51]

In the Ebionite or Nazarene system, Toland reminds us, Jesus is a man, just as Mahomet is a man, a messenger. The long-lost gospel of Barnabas in common with most of the ancient Christian sects thus disputes Paul's view that Jesus is the Son of God; and in regarding Jesus as human only, the early Christians as well as later Mahometans believe in the 'unity of the Deity', like 'our modern Unitarians' and Socinians.[52]

In opposition to Paul as well, says Toland, the Ebionites and Nazarenes were pluralistic in their religious practices, believing with Jesus that they can both be good Christians and still observe their own country's rites, that is, the Levitical law of Moses. At the same time, the Jewish Christians did not believe in imposing Levitical law on the Gentiles, for example, the rite of circumcision. For Toland, the Mahometans' practice of circumcision is following the Levitical law of Moses in the Pentateuch, in the spirit of the early Christians.[53]

Toland also defends Mahometan food laws, in particular the distinguishing between clean and unclean meat, since here again the Mahometans are following the practices of the early 'Jewish Christians' who, drawing on a passage from Genesis 9: 3–4, abstained from 'blood and things strangl'd': a practice, Toland suggests, that 'did not only continue in all places (as it still does in the Eastern churches) till Augustine's time; but, even till the eleventh century, in most parts of the Western Church'. Toland, citing Herodotus, relates such food laws to a similarity with the Egyptians, whom he elsewhere, in *Letters to Serena*, sees as indeed the source of the ancient wisdom of the Eastern nations, from North Africa through the Middle East to India, for example in notions such as the immortality of the soul.[54]

In *Nazarenus* Toland believes that the Mahometans, in looking back to the Ebionites and Nazarenes, are observing 'the true original plan of Christianity', which implies and permits a diversity of observances and ceremonies. It was not only Paul but Constantine, Toland says, who was the disastrous enemy of such plurality. By contrast, Toland observes, what is most admirable about the early Christians was their very lack of 'uniformity'.[55]

Toland believes that it was truly stupid of the Church fathers to expel the Jewish Christians simply because they wished to continue to observe older Jewish ceremonies: 'The Jews therefore were cut off for ever ... from the body of that Church which they had founded, where their Law is continually read to this day, where the Gentiles are proud to bear their proper names.' European history has been characterized by the disaster of exclusion, repression and expulsion, where the Church fathers were 'prone on the slightest occasions, sometimes for mere punctilios of Criticism or Chronology (wherein they were generally wrong) to send not onely private persons, but even whole societies, churches, and nations a packing to the Devil'.[56]

By contrast, Toland points out, the Mahometans of the Ottoman Middle East include the peoples of the four books of Pentateuch, Psalms, Gospel and Alcoran – Jews and Christians as well as Mahometans – within a multi-religious space. He suggests that 'consequently' the Mahometans 'might with as much reason and safety be tolerated at London and Amsterdam, as the Christians of every kind are so at Constantinople'. Accordingly, the 'Mahometans may be as well allow'd Moschs in these parts of Europe, if they desire it, as any other Secretaries'.[57]

When Toland suggests that modern Europe could be multi-religious and multicultural – its cityscapes graced by mosques and synagogues as well as churches – he anticipates recent thinkers like Ammiel Alcalay, Ella Shohat and Maria Rosa Menacol, who have drawn attention to a poetics of heterogeneity and *convivencia* between Muslim, Jew and Christian in the Arab and Ottoman Empires, pre-1492 Moorish Spain being, perhaps, its most spectacular example.[58]

Toland's philosemitism, embracing Islam as well as Judaism, drew on and developed a long genealogy in the 'long eighteenth century', from Stephen Nye who appears to have been the first to have introduced the term Unitarian into English literature, in his

*A Brief History of the Unitarians, called also Socinians*, published in 1691. Nye suggests that because of the corruptions of institutional Christianity in Europe, the ancient Nazarene faith that God is One has only been preserved in Turkish and other Mahometan and Pagan dominions; in Europe the true religion of the Nazarenes is, however, now being revived amongst the Unitarians and Socinians.[59] Philosemitism includes as well defences of Mahomet from the standard Christian charges made by Dr Prideaux in his 1697 *Life of Mahomet* that Mahomet was an imposter interested only in his own lust, ambition and power. Here is a remarkable literature returning the gaze and suggesting admiration for Arabia and Arabians rather than an inherited Judeo-Christian exclusive focus on the Israelites as if no other people or religion mattered in the Middle East, as in 'Mahomet no Imposter, written in Arabick by Abdulla Mahumed Omar', published in Killigrew's *Golden Medley* in 1720, a year before the publication of Montesquieu's *Persian Letters*; or the Count of Boulainvilliers' *Life of Mahomet*, translated into English in 1752, which defends Mahometan polygamy, circumcision and food laws.[60]

In such philosemitism we can see attentiveness to the possibility of cultural, philosophical and religious exchanges between Europe and Orient – to the point of questioning the very idea of 'Europe' as self-sufficient, as clearly defined and definable, as always in an opposition designated 'Europe and its others',[61] the Orientalist opposition articulated in the ancient world by characters in Aeschylus's *Agamemnon*, Euripides' *Andromache* and Virgil's *Aeneid*. Toland's Enlightenment philosemitism was an intervention into long-standing arguments and conflicts within Western thought and literature concerning differences between Europe and Orient, West and East.


## HUME, LYOTARD, DELEUZE

We come now to the irrepressible figure of Hume: Hume on polytheism and mythology, Hume on philosophy as delirium; Lyotard's affinities with Hume; Deleuze suggesting Hume's empiricism is a philosophy of difference. And Hume brings us back to Spinoza and certain Spinozan themes, of suspicion of anthropomorphic monotheism, of the notion of the mind as idea of the body, and the productive relations between reason, understanding, imagination, fiction and feeling.

Toland's *Nazarenus* and his other theologico-philosophical writings anticipate in their pluralizing and relativizing spirit Hume's explorations later in the century, in his playful, quizzical, ambivalent 1757 *The Natural History of Religion*. Hume gestures in orthodox, theological fashion that monotheism is superior to poly-theism because of its conception of God as an 'invisible spiritual intelligence', a distinction between polytheism and monotheism that, along with Robert Carroll's *Wolf in the Sheepfold*, I have been challenging in this book. Yet Hume also feels that monotheism's insistence on one sole object of devotion leads to sectarianism and hatred fuelled by sacred zeal and rancour, the most furious and implacable of all human passions (a thought as well of Spinoza, who wrote that hatred of those considered enemies of God is 'the bitter-est and most persistent of all kinds of hatred').[62] By contrast, says Hume, polytheism – which he suggests is humanity's natural original religion – exhibits, as in the Roman Empire, a spirit tolerant, sociable, international and cosmopolitan, accommodating to mytho-logical stories complex, contradictory and discordant, unburdened by any desire to find or impose inviolable scriptural canons.[63]

Hume writes – here anticipating Nietzsche – that when a deity like the monotheistic god is presented as infinitely superior to humanity, the human mind is apt to sink into abject submission, abasement, humility, mortification, penance, passive suffering, cowardice and slavish obedience. But where the gods are conceived to be only a little superior to humanity, we are more at our ease in addressing them, and may even, without profanity, aspire sometimes to rivalship and emulation: 'Hence activity, spirit, courage, magnanimity, love of liberty, and all the virtues, which aggrandize a people'.[64]

Hume relates polytheism to allegory, as in his remarks on what he refers to as the 'gross polytheism and idolatry of the vulgar', attaching divinity to visible figures and the realm of the senses. Here, he says, we will not find allegories of a refined kind. Rather, in ancient popular pagan religion, mythology and fictions, we find that the mythological stories that allegories work with are ever slipping into incoherency, as in Mars being the unlikely lover of Venus. Why is Harmony the daughter of Mars as well as Venus? Sleep we can understand as brother of Death, but why describe Sleep as enamoured of one of the Graces? Hume notes that the forms of the mythological tradition are 'wild and unaccountable'. Yet such is also, Hume thinks, a historical strength of polytheism: its stories cannot possibly be reduced to any standard and canon, or afford any determinate articles of faith, since the narratives of the gods were numberless, and though perhaps everyone believed a part of these stories, no one could believe or know the whole. All in polytheism must acknowledge that no one part stood on a better foundation than the rest, so there was no reason for preferring one to the other. The pagan religion, therefore, Hume observes, seems to vanish like a cloud whenever one approaches it. It could never be ascertained by any fixed dogmas and principles.[65]

Hume notices in polytheism what Assmann in *Moses the Egyptian* calls the principle of cosmopolitan translatability, the translation of deities from different cultures into each other.

In terms of affinities between postmodernism and the Enlightenment, Lyotard in *Just Gaming* admiringly evokes features of polytheism and mythology that reprise Hume's *Natural History of Religion*. Lyotard tells us of his delight in 'paganism', which he also identifies with 'modernity' and, in an urgent qualifying footnote, with 'postmodernity'; such are modes of thought that can exist at any time rather than being located in a specific historical period. We are in 'modernity' and 'postmodernity' whenever we lack firm 'criteria'. What is characteristic in the stories of Greek and Roman mythology as in pagan rhetoric and the thinking of the Sophists is that 'there is no stable system to guide judgments'. What we see in Greek mythology is a society of gods that is constantly forced to redraw its code; no prescription can be surely founded upon such stories. It is, says Lyotard, very much a loss, indeed it is a sign of Western ethnocentrism, that Western thought has tried to eradicate such paganism within itself and has also refused to see affinities between its own past paganism and traditional storytelling in non-Western pagan societies such as the Cashinahua, Indians from the upper Amazon. Their storytelling features poetic and rhetorical inventiveness, jokes, miming, insertion of novel episodes, so much so that when narratives get repeated they are never identical; such storytelling occurs within a world of many gods.[66]

Lyotard compares here the pagan Cashinahua with the Greek. Whereas the Christian God is a master of the word and wishes to create the world, the Greek gods are masters neither of the word nor the world. The gods 'are not all-knowing'. Whatever we know of the opinions of the gods comes from stories told about them and the stories they tell themselves. Furthermore, there can never be an original source for such stories, and there is never a first utterer. What we learn of the possible origins of stories is related 'in terms of stories that presuppose other stories that in turn presuppose the first ones'. The gods become the 'heroes of numerous, almost innumerable, narratives, all set into each other', and narratives in such a pagan world are close to games and masks: 'This bars the way to the very notion of a subject identical to itself through the peripeteia of its history.'[67]

When the gods speak to humans, as when they consult an oracle, there is always uncertainty, ruse, the possibility of deception, the allowing for chance. Whatever the oracle says is to be taken with prudence, with measure, perhaps even with humour: 'There is always the possibility of relating things differently.' The relations of humans with the gods is a space of ceaseless negotiation, between the stories the gods tell and the stories humans tell; in paganism, which is modernity and postmodernity, we are always immanent to stories in the making, there is no authoritative outside, no metalinguistic position we can take up. Further, appearance and reality don't necessarily coincide, for one does not know if the person one takes at first for a beggar is actually a god; one lives in a world of sudden possible metamorphosis, of perpetually uncertain identity.[68]

At one point in *Just Gaming* Lyotard wonderingly asks: 'Is there a real difference between a theory and a fiction?'[69] Deleuze explores just such a question in relation to Hume's theory of knowledge in his remarkable 1953 book *Empiricism and Subjectivity*, drawing threads of ideas from Hume's early work *A Treatise of Human Nature* (1739–40). Here, says Deleuze, Hume suggests empiricism is not concerned with the problem of the origin of the mind, but with the problem of the constitution of the subject. What the philosopher, the Humean subject, experiences when s/he attempts to know the world is, says Deleuze, 'madness and scepticism'.[70] Why does empiricism involve such bafflement?

In Deleuze's view, empiricism for Hume is not to be defined as a theory according to which knowledge derives from experience; empiricism is not a philosophy of the senses. What the subject is aware of in the world is a succession of perceptions, which are distinct and independent. Such is the 'principle of difference', and the principle of difference is the 'fundamental principle of empiricism'. As human subjects we have to believe in a principle of identity, that things and bodies are indeed invariable and continuous; we have to believe that there is continuous existence through time and space even though our own impressions are discontinuous. Empiricism is necessarily a philosophy of the imagination, for what makes a subject a subject is believing and inventing, is inference and artifice: 'From what is given, I infer the existence of that which is not given: I believe.' I have always to 'move from the known to the unknown'. The philosopher realizes that the world as we think it is an outright fiction of the imagination. Knowledge involves an imagination which becomes constitutive and creative, so that the world is an Idea of the imagination. Even space and time are 'in the mind'. Memory, the senses and understanding are all grounded in the imagination. Imagination and fiction and 'fancy', then, are necessary to reason itself. Philosophy knows that it cannot reconcile the contradiction between imagination and reason. Philosophy is the knowledge that any reconciliation between reason and imagination is always fictional: 'I affirm more than I know.' Such awareness leads philosophy to know and reflect on itself as 'delirium and madness'.[71]

## CONCLUSION

Both Bauman and Wokler in their different ways, negative and positive, wish to constitute the Enlightenment as a Project. Bauman defines the Enlightenment in terms of a single pervading spirit: the Enlightenment disastrously created reason for modernity, a reason that was obsessed with certainty, exhaustive knowledge, categorizing and classifying, that was instrumental, and was messianic and utopian, believing it could create the future in its own image, bend the world to its will to knowledge: reason as ever-dangerous hubris; a reason that consumed sensibility and deprived it of a capacity for wonder, doubt and speculation. Wokler turns this judgement on its head, suggesting that the Enlightenment Project was cosmopolitan, internationalist and anti-colonialist, and reveals significant affinities with post-modernist theories that emphasize an anti-instrumentalist view of reason.

I think and hope I've gone a very long way to support Wokler's admiration for the Enlightenment in terms of knowledge and sensibility. I have addressed mystical aspects of Spinoza that deserve profound pondering, as well as the Spinozan position that the mind is intimately involved with body, imagination, intuition, affect, and even fiction and feigning. I have argued, especially in relation to Toland, that in the late seventeenth and early eighteenth century theologico-philosophical critiques of institutional Christianity, in their decentred conceptions of God and the universe, openness to other religions, interest in literary conventions of the return of the gaze, admiration for strong female figures and female education, and relativizing thinking about the body, represented a desire to interact with many others. The enemies of one's enemy are one's friends, or at least one's animus inspires one to be more sympathetic to those marginalized by one's enemy, in this case, institutional Christianity – the apparently forgotten, the ignored, the usually abhorred, the persecuted; and such could include women, Jews, Mahometans and the Jewish Christian sects of antiquity. Toland called new creation stories into play that could include and resume diverse religious and philosophical histories, at the same time as they might shock and provoke Europe itself. And I have evoked Hume's appreciation of polytheism because it is the reverse of a discourse of certainty, as well as suggesting affinities between Hume's speculative approach to knowledge and postmodern thinkers like Lyotard and Deleuze in terms of a philosophy of difference.

Enlightenment thinking in its abundance and diversity cannot be characterized as utopian and messianic. In a 'long eighteenth century' of great eccentricity and idiosyncrasy,[72] there could certainly be utopian visions, as in *Gulliver's Travels* with its ideal society of the Houyhnhnms, though *Gulliver's Travels* remains everywhere – as Claude Rawson points out in *God, Gulliver, and Genocide* – a bafflingly ironic text. Yet there was no overriding mode of utopian or millenarian desire projected by Enlightenment thinkers, and we should not forget that in Voltaire's *Candide* (1758) historical optimism and the view that the universe is ultimately harmonious is relentlessly satirized in the ridiculously deluded figure of Pangloss. At novel's end the chief characters decide that European or indeed any earthly institutions relating to politics, religion and war are so irredeemably a disaster that they will spend the rest of their days in the Orient, living quietly on a little farm near Constantinople, working their garden.[73] Further, formative Enlightenment intellectuals like Spinoza distrusted any kind of centralizing of power (this was a major point of his critique in *Tractatus Theologico-Politicus* of the ancient Israelite nation and of Mosaic law as represented in the biblical stories), rather urging that democracy has to base itself on a separation of powers, in particular, of church, state and intellectual life.[74] Spinoza and Toland considered that ideally intellectuals should address only each other in an international republic of letters, and that if they were forced to relate to the wider society in which they found themselves it should always be with caution, rather than messianic millenarian fervour. Spinoza and Toland did not project political leadership as the expression of the general or popular will of the people, as in the French Revolution, for Enlightenment thinkers like Spinoza and Toland were extremely wary of the multitude, the possibly tyrannical majority which they considered incapable of philosophical reason; here they were in some ways reprising the distrust of the multitude in classical Greek thought, in Thucydides, Socrates, Plato. The most that could be hoped for was that reasonable institutions might be created so that the majority could act reasonably through being influenced by such institutions. Here Wokler is surely right to suggest that the French Revolution and its Terror was a sharp historical break with the Enlightenment.

Was the Enlightenment pervaded by a single spirit of instrumental reason? No, it wasn't. Certainly in the Enlightenment we can observe the importance, especially in European pan-world voyaging, of practices of exactitude, measurement, comparison and classification. Yet Enlightenment thought also could emphasize and revel in the fragmentary and dispersed, the wayward and enigmatic, the ironic and irreverent; there was frequently a close association of reason with imagination and affect, rather than the passionlessness of categorization and classification.

Yet I don't wish admiration to be the only note with which I address the Enlightenment. Regard must be much more mixed.

What is admirable in the cosmopolitanism, internationalism, toleration and interest in difference and plurality in Enlightenment philosophy, dissident thinking about religion, and poetics is indeed in tension with the race-thinking associated with colonialism, empire and imperium; race-thinking that assumed that rather than equality between the peoples of the earth there was a hierarchy of humanity, more or less steep.[75] Whenever there is such a conception of inequality of peoples, and even more, when such a conception is entertained in societies that are colonizing, the genocidal is always a temptation, in desire or practice or both.

We can also think of the argument of Rawson's *God, Gulliver, and Genocide*, that major figures of the Enlightenment, whilst their writings contradictorily participate in both racism and anti-racism, cruelty and outrage against cruelty, the exterminatory and protest against exterminatory wishes and practices, also deploy phrases indicating velleities and desires, however teasingly ambivalent, that participate in a nexus of associations that antici-pate in relation to the Catholic Irish what occurred with the Nazis in relation to the Jews. Rawson refers for example to Swift's *Proposal for Giving Badges to the Beggars in all the Parishes of Dublin* (1737), as well as to ideas in *Gulliver's Travels* where an unsettling modern parallelism rears its head in Nazi practices of castration and sterilization.[76]

The notion of the Enlightenment Project should be rejected because it unifies the Enlightenment just as much in Wokler as in theorists of the Holocaust and modernity like Bauman. We should recognize the Enlightenment as irreducibly contradictory, hence always open to further explorations of the entwined relationships in Western history of civilization and barbarism.[77]

# 10 CONCLUSION: CAN THERE BE AN END TO VIOLENCE?

In my view, Gandhian thought provides hope for the world. Gandhi's notions of non-violence remain the key alternative to the endless recourse to violence in history and the contemporary era, whether such violence be pursued by governments or by those who oppose persecution and oppression. Gandhi's thought reveals a cosmopolitan, internationalist, pluralist and critical interest in many religions, in Buddhism, Hinduism, Jainism, Christianity, Islam and Judaism. Gandhi does not see non-violence as simply a strategy or tactic for particular occasions. Rather, for Gandhi non-violence is a way of life, a mode of spirit and being, a kind of ensoulment, a *Bildung*, a mode of moral reflection.

Gandhi's thought reprises counter-traditions of questioning of violence, colonialism, empire and genocide in Herodotus and Thucydides, Greek classical tragic drama concerned with the mythological destruction of Troy, and, in the Greco-Roman world, the counter-narratives of Cicero's *Republic*, Virgil's *Aeneid*, and Tacitus's *Agricola* and *Germania*. These counter-traditions in turn have helped shape contemporary international law, in Lemkin's definition of genocide and his writings published and unpublished, and more generally, the 1948 UN Convention on genocide and international courts devoted to combating crimes against humanity.

Yet – what could be more sadly clear! – Gandhian principles of non-violence make little headway in a world which also inherits long, long traditions of action and thought that sanction intergroup violence. In these traditions, colonization, conquest, war, empire building and imperium are viewed as honourable in altruistic purpose and kindly in intentions to do good, to protect and defend the weak and vulnerable, to spread culture and law. The ancient international rights and conventions protecting strangers, exiles, suppliants, ambassadors and heralds, to whom hospitality must always be given, were historically extended to a 'natural law' position that it is natural and right for humans to be able to go anywhere in the world and be given hospitality and be able to settle, farm and mine, and if this natural right is not met, or is broached, then just war can be waged.

In this book I have argued that concepts that appear honourable and deserving of sympathy – victimhood, chosen people, promised land, culture-bringing, support from God or the gods – often deserve intense scrutiny for the ways they become entwined with other notions that inspire intergroup violence in history: especially supersessionism, the belief that some human groups have the historical right to supersede other human groups; a belief that sanctions genocidal destruction of other human groups.

The most egregious example in the twenty-first century of such supersessionist destruction can be daily seen in the ongoing attempts by the Zionist government of Israel to destroy the foundations of life of the Palestinians. In the late 1930s and 1940s Gandhi had decried Zionist plans to take over Palestine, saying it would lead to the displacement and humiliation of the Arab peoples of that ancient region. I have argued that there are Jewish traditions in antiquity, especially in Josephus, that can be seen as anticipating Gandhian notions of non-violence, and that can be counterposed to the endless desire for violence in Zionist Israel, a violence that issues directly from Israel's history as a genocidal settler colony.[1]

Yet perhaps in history there is a profound and continuing desire for an end to violence, and what we can do is keep looking to alternative traditions of non-violence as part of a heightened historical consciousness that can help shape world history.

# NOTES

## PREFACE

1. Benedetto Croce, 'History and Chronicle', in Hans Myerhoff (ed.), *The Philosophy of History in Our Time* (Doubleday Anchor, New York, 1959), p.46.
2. See my 'In Praise of Polytheism', *Semeia*, No. 88, 2001, pp.149–72, and 'The Challenge of Polytheism: Moses, Spinoza, and Freud', in Jane Bennett and Michael J. Shapiro (eds), *The Politics of Moralizing* (Routledge, New York and London, 2002), pp.201–22.
3. John Docker, 'The Enlightenment, Genocide, Postmodernity', *Journal of Genocide Research*, Vol. 5, No. 3, 2003, pp.339–60.
4. See Mark Dorrian, 'On Some Spatial Aspects of the Colonial Discourse on Ireland', *The Journal of Architecture*, Vol. 6, 2001, pp.27–51.

## INTRODUCTION

1. Primo Levi, *If This is a Man* and *The Truce*, trans. Stuart Woolf (1958, 1963; Abacus, London, 2006), author's preface, p.15.
2. Raphaël Lemkin, *Axis Rule in Occupied Europe: Laws of Occupation, Analysis of Government, Proposals for Redress* (Columbia University Press, New York, 1944), esp. Chapter 9 'Genocide'.
3. See John Docker, 'New History and the New Catastrophe: Ilan Pappé, the New History, and the Question of Israeli Genocide', *Arena Magazine*, No. 66, August–September 2003, pp.32–6.
4. Lemkin, *Axis Rule in Occupied Europe*, pp.79–80.
5. Cf. Katerina Clark, 'M.M. Bakhtin and "World Literature"', *JNT: Journal of Narrative Theory*, Vol. 32, No. 3, 2002, pp.266–92, and

Ned Curthoys, 'The Émigré Sensibility of World Literature: Historicizing Hannah Arendt and Karl Jaspers' Cosmopolitan Intent', *Theory and Event*, Vol. 8, No. 3, 2005. Apropos Einstein see Fred Jerome, *The Einstein File: J. Edgar Hoover's Secret War against the World's Most Famous Scientist* (St. Martin's Press, New York, 2002).

6. Lemkin, *Axis Rule in Occupied Europe*, pp.91 and 91 note 51; Lemkin, 'Totally Unofficial Man', in Samuel Totten and Steve Leonard Jacobs (eds), *Pioneers of Genocide Studies* (Transaction Publishers, New Brunswick, 2002), p.377; 'Genocide: A Modern Crime', *Free World* – 'A Magazine Devoted to the United Nations and Democracy', April 1945, pp.39–43, accessed at http://www.preventgenocide.org/lemkin/freeworld1945.htm.

7. Lemkin Collection, American Jewish Historical Society, 15 West 16th Street, New York, Box 8, Folder 11, History of Genocide. Projected Book and North American Indian Correspondence, 1947–1949, 1951. Ann Curthoys sets out the list in her essay 'Raphael Lemkin's "Tasmania": An Introduction', *Patterns of Prejudice*, Vol. 39, No. 2, 2005, pp.162–6. See also Tony Barta, 'With intent to deny: on colonial intentions and genocide denial', *Journal of Genocide Research*, Vol. 10, No. 1, 2008, p.117.

8. Mikhail Bakhtin, *Problems of Dostoevsky's Poetics*, edited and translated Caryl Emerson (Manchester University Press, Manchester, 1984), pp.113, 119, 122.

By menippea I mean a form of satire which does not judge society or history or ideas from a fixed standpoint or in terms of ideal values.

9. Bakhtin, *Problems of Dostoevsky's Poetics*, pp.112–20.

10. Claude Rawson, *God, Gulliver, and Genocide: Barbarism and the European Imagination, 1492–1945* (Oxford University Press, New York, 2001); I make this point in my review in *Journal of Genocide Research*, Vol. 5, No. 1, 2003, p.163.

11. See Anthony D. Smith, *Chosen Peoples: Sacred Sources of National Identity* (Oxford University Press, Oxford, 2003).

12. See Shino Konishi, 'The Father Governor: The British Administration of Aboriginal People at Port Jackson, 1788–1792', in Matthew McCormack (ed.), *Public Men: Political Masculinities in Modern Britain* (Palgrave Macmillan, Hampshire, 2007), pp.54–72, and Julie Evans, 'Colonialism and the Rule of Law: The Case of South

Australia', in Barry S. Godfrey and Graeme Dunstall (eds), *Crime and Empire 1840–1940: Criminal Justice in Local and Global Context* (Willan Publishing, Cullompton, 2005), pp.57–75.

13. See Ann Curthoys and John Docker, *Is History Fiction?* (UNSW Press, Sydney, 2005), pp.111–14; also Curthoys and Docker, 'Defining Genocide', in Dan Stone (ed.), *The Historiography of Genocide* (Palgrave, London, 2008).

14. I am grateful to David Pritchard for discussions about the close relationship between democracy and war in the classical world.

15. See Hannah Arendt, *The Origins of Totalitarianism*, third edition (George Allen and Unwin, London, 1967), p.123; also Curthoys and Docker, *Is History Fiction?* p.47.

16. See Curthoys and Docker, *Is History Fiction?* pp.128–9; Elisabeth Young-Bruehl, *Hannah Arendt: For Love of the World* (Yale University Press, New Haven, 1982), pp.200, 203; Samuel Weber, 'Genealogy of Modernity: History, Myth and Allegory in Benjamin's "Origin of the German Mourning Play"', *MLN*, 106 (1991), pp.468–73.

17. Edward W. Said, *Freud and the Non-European* (Verso, in association with the Freud Museum, London, 2003), pp.28–9.

My thanks to Ned Curthoys for alerting me to Said's reflections on late style in *Freud and the Non-European* and also in Edward W. Said, *On Late Style* (Bloomsbury, London, 2006).

18. Cf. Hilary Rose and Steven Rose (eds), *Alas, Poor Darwin: Arguments against Evolutionary Psychology* (Harmony Books, New York, 2000).

## 1.    GENOCIDE AS ANCIENT PRACTICE: CHIMPANZEES, HUMANS, AGRICULTURAL SOCIETY

1. Jane Goodall, *The Chimpanzees of Gombe: Patterns of Behavior* (The Belknap Press of Harvard University Press, Cambridge, Mass., 1986), p.530.

2. Jared Diamond, *The Rise and Fall of the Third Chimpanzee* (1991; Vintage, London, 1992), p.266.

3. Paola Cavalieri, 'The Animal Debate: A Reexamination', in Peter Singer (ed.), *In Defense of Animals: The Second Wave* (Blackwells, Malden, Mass., 2006), p.57.

4. Hugh Brody, *The Other Side of Eden: Hunter-Gatherers, Farmers, and the Shaping of the World* (2000; Faber and Faber, London, 2002), p.127.

5. Dan Stone, *History, Memory and Mass Atrocity: Essays on the Holocaust and Genocide* (Vallentine Mitchell, London, 2006), pp.196–8.

6. Raphaël Lemkin, *Axis Rule in Occupied Europe: Laws of Occupation, Analysis of Government, Proposals for Redress* (Columbia University Press, New York, 1944), esp. Chapter 9 'Genocide'. See Ann Curthoys and John Docker, *Is History Fiction?* (UNSW Press, Sydney, 2005), pp.111–14; also Curthoys and Docker, 'Defining Genocide', in Dan Stone (ed.), *The Historiography of Genocide* (Palgrave, London, 2008).

7. Lemkin, *Axis Rule in Occupied Europe*, Chapter 9, pp.79–95; for an extended evocation of Chapter 9, see Ann Curthoys and John Docker, 'Introduction – Genocide: Definitions, Questions, Settler-colonies', *Aboriginal History*, Vol. 25, 2001, pp.5–11.

8. For my first report on this research, see my talk, 'Raphaël Lemkin's History of Genocide and Colonialism', for the United States Holocaust Memorial Museum, Center for Advanced Holocaust Studies, Washington DC, 26 February 2004, on their website.

9. See John Docker, 'Are Settler-Colonies Inherently Genocidal? Re-reading Lemkin', in A. Dirk Moses (ed.), *Empire, Colony, Genocide: Conquest, Occupation, and Subaltern Resistance in World History* (Berghahn, New York, 2008).

10. See Samantha Power, *'A Problem from Hell': America and the Age of Genocide* (Perennial/HarperCollins, New York, 2003), pp.62–3; also http://www.preventgenocide.org/law/convention/text.htm.

11. Donna Haraway, *Primate Visions: Gender, Race, and Nature in the World of Modern Science* (Routledge, New York, 1989), pp.2, 7, and Chapter 7, 'Apes in Eden, Apes in Space: Mothering as a Scientist for National Geographic', esp. pp.150–6, 158, 164–8, 170–9, 184–5. Haraway discusses *The Chimpanzees of Gombe* on p.172. In *The Chimpanzees of Gombe*, Introduction, p.4, Goodall writes: 'Man's inherent curiosity and insatiable love of adventure led to Christopher Columbus' discovery of America; in our generation it has landed people on the moon.'

12. Goodall, *The Chimpanzees of Gombe*, pp.2–3.

13. Goodall, *The Chimpanzees of Gombe*, pp.3–4.

14. Goodall, *The Chimpanzees of Gombe*, pp.488–9, 493–4, 500–1, 519.
15. Goodall, *The Chimpanzees of Gombe*, pp.500, 504–14.
16. Goodall, *The Chimpanzees of Gombe*, pp.522–5.
17. See Lyndall Roper, *Witch Craze: Terror and Fantasy in Baroque Germany* (Yale University Press, New Haven, 2004), pp.17–18, 92–3, 158, 160–2, 165, 168, 173, 177–8; persecution of older women as witches also persisted into the eighteenth century – see Chapter 10, 'A Witch in the Age of Enlightenment', esp. p.228. Cf. Robert Thurston, 'Stalinism in Context and Perspective: Sources of Permission to Hate in Europe', in James Kaye and Bo Stråth (eds), *Enlightenment and Genocide, Contradictions of Modernity* (P.I.E.-Peter Lang, Brussels, 2000), pp.194–5.
18. Roper, *Witch Craze*, pp.74–6, 101, 121.
19. Goodall, *The Chimpanzees of Gombe*, p.532.
20. Goodall, *The Chimpanzees of Gombe*, pp.525, 527–8.
21. Goodall, *The Chimpanzees of Gombe*, p.528.
22. Goodall, *The Chimpanzees of Gombe*, pp.528–30.
23. Goodall, *The Chimpanzees of Gombe*, pp.530–1. Concerning Darwin and genocide, see Tony Barta, 'Mr Darwin's Shooters: On Natural Selection and the Naturalizing of Genocide', *Patterns of Prejudice*, Vol. 39, No. 2, 2005, pp.116–37, also published in Dirk Moses and Dan Stone (eds), *Colonialism and Genocide* (Routledge, London, 2007).
24. Goodall, *The Chimpanzees of Gombe*, pp.531.
25. Goodall, *The Chimpanzees of Gombe*, p.532.
26. Goodall, *The Chimpanzees of Gombe*, pp.532–3.
27. Goodall, *The Chimpanzees of Gombe*, pp.533–4.
28. Goodall, *The Chimpanzees of Gombe*, pp.509–10, 518, 528.
29. Dan Stone, *History, Memory and Mass Atrocity*, pp.198–9, 206–9.
30. Walter Benjamin, *Illuminations*, trans. Harry Zohn, ed. and introd. Hannah Arendt (Fontana, London, 1992), p.248, and Maxime Rodinson, *Cult, Ghetto, and State: The Persistence of the Jewish Question* (Al Saqi Books, London, 1983), p.182. Cf. John Docker, *1492: The Poetics of Diaspora* (Continuum, London, 2001), p.130.
31. Stone, *History, Memory and Mass Atrocity*, p.211; Stone is quoting from Georges Bataille, *Eroticism*, trans. Mary Dalwood (Marion Boyars, London, 1987), p.186.
32. Hilary Rose and Steven Rose, *Alas, Poor Darwin: Arguments against Evolutionary Psychology* (Harmony Books, New York,

2000), esp. chapter by Hilary Rose, 'Colonizing the Social Sciences', pp.127–53, and Steven Rose, 'Escaping Evolutionary Psychology', pp.299–318.

33. See Caroline Elkins, *Imperial Reckoning: The Untold Story of Britain's Gulag in Kenya* (Henry Holt, London and New York, 2005).
34. Diamond, *The Rise and Fall of the Third Chimpanzee*, pp.277–8.
35. Diamond, *Rise and Fall*, pp.250–9.
36. Diamond, *Rise and Fall*, p.264.
37. Goodall, *The Chimpanzees of Gombe*, pp.331–3, 532.
38. Diamond, *Rise and Fall*, pp.251, 261–4.
39. Diamond, *Rise and Fall*, pp.164, 166–7. My thanks to Ned Curthoys for alerting me to this chapter on agricultural society.
40. Diamond, *Rise and Fall*, pp.163–4, 167–9.
41. Diamond, *Rise and Fall*, pp.168–9.
42. Diamond, *Rise and Fall*, pp.169–72.
43. Diamond, *Rise and Fall*, pp.171–2.
44. Jared Diamond, *Guns, Germs and Steel* (1997; Vintage, London, 1998), pp.16–17, 27, 196–7, 210–14. The relevant chapter for the imbrication of animals and disease is Chapter 11, 'Lethal Gift of Livestock'.
45. John M. Wilkins and Shaun Hill, *Food in the Ancient World* (Blackwell, Oxford, 2006), p.7.
46. Ann Curthoys, 'Whose Home? Expulsion, Exodus, and Exile in White Australian Historical Mythology', *Journal of Australian Studies*, No. 61, 1999, pp.1–18.
47. Curthoys and Docker, *Is History Fiction?*, pp.27–8. See also John Docker and Gerhard Fischer (eds), *Race, Colour and Identity in Australia and New Zealand* (UNSW Press, Sydney, 2000), 'Introduction: Adventures of Identity', pp.10–11.
48. In *Patterns of Prejudice*, Vol. 39, No. 2, June 2005, p.247, Mark Levene, opening a review of A. Dirk Moses' collection *Genocide and Settler Society* (2004), writes as his first sentence: 'Coincidentally, while reviewing this volume, I also happened to be reading *The Other Side of Eden* (2000), Hugh Brody's wonderful evocation of hunter-gatherer peoples in the Arctic and sub-Arctic regions of Canada.' Levene then goes on to point out what Yunupingu had argued, that it is those who come from an agriculturalist-pastoral tradition who are the wanderers, not the Aborigines. I was so struck by this resonance with Yunupingu and what Ann Curthoys and I had

been suggesting for a number of years, that I immediately emailed my favourite bookshop in all the world, Gleebooks in Sydney, to send a copy of Brody's book, just in time to include it in a footnote to our analysis of Herodotus's *Histories* and the Scythians: see *Is History Fiction?* p.241 note 21.

49. Brody, *The Other Side of Eden*, p.7.
50. Brody, *The Other Side of Eden*, p.145.
51. Brody, *The Other Side of Eden*, pp.158–9, 337–8 note 157.
52. Brody, *The Other Side of Eden*, pp.144, 189, 200.


## 2. GENOCIDE, AND QUESTIONING OF GENOCIDE, IN THE ANCIENT GREEK WORLD: HERODOTUS AND THUCYDIDES

1. Homer, *The Iliad*, translated and introduced Martin Hammond (Penguin, London, 1987), p.125.
2. Herodotus, *The Histories*, trans. George Rawlinson, edited Hugh Bowden (Everyman, London, 2000).
3. Thucydides, *History of the Peloponnesian War*, trans. Rex Warner (Penguin, London, 1972).
4. Hannah Arendt, *Eichmann in Jerusalem: A Report on the Banality of Evil* (1963; Penguin Books, New York and London, 1994), 1964 Postscript p.288.
5. See Ann Curthoys, 'Raphaël Lemkin's "Tasmania": An Introduction', *Patterns of Prejudice*, Vol. 39, No. 2, 2005, pp.162–9; Curthoys' reference to Lemkin and Ancient Greece is on p.166.
6. Cf. Ann Curthoys and John Docker, *Is History Fiction?* (UNSW Press and The University of Michigan Press, Sydney and Ann Arbor, 2005), pp.12–49.
7. My profound thanks to Daniel Joyce for telling me about Judge Shahabuddeen's reference to Thucydides in the judge's separate opinion to the 1999 international tribunal on the former Yugoslavia.
8. Cf. Raphaël Lemkin, *Axis Rule in Occupied Europe: Laws of Occupation, Analysis of Government, Proposals for Redress* (Columbia University Press, New York, 1944), pp.79–80.
9. Ann Curthoys, 'Genocide in Tasmania: The History of an Idea', in A. Dirk Moses (ed.), *Empire, Colony, Genocide* (Berghahn, New York, 2008).

10. Dan Stone, *History, Memory and Mass Atrocity: Essays on the Holocaust and Genocide* (Vallentine Mitchell, London, 2006), chapter on 'Genocide as Transgression', pp.198–9, 206–9.
11. Cf. Curthoys and Docker, *Is History Fiction?*, pp.22–3.
12. Jane Goodall, *The Chimpanzees of Gombe: Patterns of Behavior* (The Belknap Press of Harvard University Press, Cambridge, Mass. and London, 1986), pp.532–3.
13. Cf. Curthoys and Docker, *Is History Fiction?*, p.25.
14. Cf. Curthoys and Docker, *Is History Fiction?*, p.16.
15. Cf. Curthoys and Docker, *Is History Fiction?*, p.49.
16. Walter Benjamin, *Illuminations: Essays and Reflections*, edited and introd. Hannah Arendt (Schocken, New York, 1969), p.256.
17. Cf. Baruch Kimmerling, *Politicide: Ariel Sharon's War Against the Palestinians* (Verso, London, 2003), and As'ad Ghanem, 'Collective Rights and Education: Lessons from Quebec in Canada', in Duane Champagne and Ismael Abu-Saad (eds), *Indigenous and Minority Education: International Perspectives on Empowerment* (Ben-Gurion University of the Negev, Beersheba, Israel, 2005); see my review article in *Holy Land Studies*, Vol. 5, No. 1, 2006, pp.113–18.
18. Hannah Arendt, *The Origins of Totalitarianism* (George Allen and Unwin, London, 1967), p.123; Curthoys and Docker, *Is History Fiction?*, p.47.
19. Cf. Curthoys and Docker, *Is History Fiction?*, pp.39–41.
20. For savage satire on Cleon as demagogue and his persuading the assembly to continue the war with Sparta, see Aristophanes, *The Knights* (produced 424 BCE): Aristophanes, *The Birds and Other Plays*, trans. David Barrett and Alan H. Sommerstein (Penguin, London, 1978), p.66.
21. Isaiah Berlin, *Historical Inevitability* (1954; Oxford University Press, London, 1955), pp.15–20, 25, 32–4, 50–3, 57, 71, 75; Curthoys and Docker, *Is History Fiction?*, p.118.
22. Sophie Mills, *Theseus, Tragedy and the Athenian Empire* (Clarendon, Oxford, 1997), pp.79–86.
23. Mills, *Theseus, Tragedy and the Athenian Empire*, pp.2–6, 10, 13, 16–17, 22–5, 59–63, 66.
24. Mills, *Theseus, Tragedy and the Athenian Empire*, pp.2–14, 18.
25. Cf. in particular David Pritchard's interventions: 'War and Democracy in Ancient Athens: A Preliminary Report', *Classicvm*, Vol. XXXI, No.1, April 2005, pp.16–25; 'Athletics, War and Democracy

in Classical Athens', *Teaching History*, Vol. 39, No. 4, December 2005, pp.4–10; 'Democracy and War: the Case Study of Ancient Athens', *Polis*, Vol. 24, No. 2 (2007).

26. Cf. Curthoys and Docker, *Is History Fiction?*, p.47.

27. See Frank Chalk and Kurt Jonassohn, *The History and Sociology of Genocide: Analysis and Case Studies* (Yale University Press, New Haven, 1990), pp.65–73.

28. Cf. John Docker, 'Josephus: Traitor or Gandhian *avant la lettre?*', *Borderlands* e-journal, Vol. 4, No. 3, 2005, essays on 'Gandhi, Nonviolence and Modernity', edited by John Docker and Debjani Ganguly.

29. Samantha Power, *'A Problem from Hell': America and the Age of Genocide* (Perennial, New York, 2003), p.74.

## 3. GENOCIDE, TRAUMA, AND WORLD UPSIDE DOWN IN ANCIENT GREEK TRAGEDY: AESCHYLUS AND EURIPIDES

1. Aeschylus, *Agamemnon*, in *The Oresteian Trilogy*, translated and introd. Philip Vellacott (Penguin, London, 1959), pp.73–4.

2. Euripides, *Hecabe* in *Medea and Other Plays*, translated and introd. Philip Vellacott (Penguin, Harmondsworth, 1964), p.71.

3. Euripides, *Helen*, in *The Bacchae and Other Plays*, trans. Philip Vellacott (Penguin, London, 1973), p.171.

4. I would like here to acknowledge the suggestions and encouragement of David Pritchard. See also David Konstan's very interesting essay, 'Anger, Hatred, and Genocide in Ancient Greece', *Common Knowledge*, Vol. 13, No. 1, 2007, pp.170–87, though Konstan does not refer to Lemkin's definition of genocide. (My thanks to David Konstan for this reference.)

5. I reproduced the outline in my paper for the United States Holocaust Memorial Museum, Center for Advanced Holocaust Studies, Washington DC, 26 February 2004; see also Ann Curthoys, 'Raphaël Lemkin's "Tasmania": an introduction', *Patterns of Prejudice*, Vol. 39, No. 2, 2005, pp.164–6, and also my essay 'Are Settler-Colonies Inherently Genocidal? Re-reading Lemkin', in A. Dirk Moses (ed.), *Empire, Colony, Genocide* (Berghahn, New York, 2008). Note that sometimes additional phrases were interpolated in handwriting in

pen or pencil, including an entry 'panic and flight' crossed out and replaced in a handwritten notation as '(suicide, hiding, etc.) escape'.

6. Cf. M.A. McDonnell and A.D. Moses, 'Raphaël Lemkin as Historian of Genocide in the Americas', *Journal of Genocide Research*, Vol. 7, No. 4, 2005, pp.501–29.

7. Aeschylus, *Agamemnon*, pp.69, 72–3.

8. Aeschylus, *Agamemnon*, pp.75, 80, 87.

9. Aeschylus, *Agamemnon*, pp.91–2.

10. Aeschylus, *Agamemnon*, p.97.

11. Aeschylus, *Agamemnon*, pp.94–5.

12. Aeschylus, *Agamemnon*, pp.70–1, 75, 87.

13. Sophie Mills, 'Campaigns Without Calamities: Euripides, War and the Portrayal of Athens', paper for Sydney Democracy Forum on Democracy and War: The Case Study of Ancient Athens, University of Sydney, 31 August 2007, draws attention to how much we 'must repeatedly focus on Hecaba's disability as she limps along or sprawls prostrate, buried under sorrow'. For detailed evocation of the dramaturgy, see Judith Mossman, *Wild Justice: A Study of Euripides' Hecuba* (Clarendon, Oxford, 1995), p.57.

14. Euripides, *Hecabe*, p.87.

15. Cf. Mossman, *Wild Justice*, p.105.

16. Euripides, *Hecabe*, pp.65–9.

17. Euripides, *Hecabe*, pp.70–4.

18. Euripides, *Hecabe*, p.69.

19. Dan Stone, *History, Memory and Mass Atrocity: Essays on the Holocaust and Genocide*, pp.198–9, 206–9.

20. Euripides, *Hecabe*, pp.73, 79.

21. Euripides, *Hecabe*, pp.71, 75, 83, 85, 90–1, 99.

22. Euripides, *Hecabe*, p.102.

23. Euripides, *Hecabe*, p.94.

24. Ann Curthoys and John Docker, 'Defining Genocide', in Dan Stone (ed.), *The Historiography of Genocide* (Palgrave, London, 2008), p.12.

25. Cf. Debjani Ganguly and John Docker (eds), *Rethinking Gandhi in a New World Order: Global Perspectives* (Routledge, London, 2007).

26. Cf. Ann Curthoys and John Docker, *Is History Fiction?* (UNSW Press, Sydney, 2005), pp.18–19.

27. Euripides, *Hecabe*, p.77.

28. Euripides, *Andromache*, in *Orestes and Other Plays*, translated and introd. Philip Vellacott (Penguin, Harmondsworth, 1972), pp.146, 150.

29. Euripides, *Andromache*, p.158.

30. Euripides, *Andromache*, pp.148–9.

31. Euripides, *Andromache*, pp.149–50.

32. *The Sociology of Georg Simmel*, ed. and trans. Kurt H. Wolff (The Free Press, Glencoe, Il., 1950), pp.402–8.

33. Cf. Docker, *1492: The Poetics of Diaspora* (Continuum, London, 2001), pp.86–7.

34. Docker, *1492: The Poetics of Diaspora*, Chapter 3.

35. Docker, *1492: The Poetics of Diaspora*, pp.68–70.

36. Euripides, *Andromache*, p.150.

37. Euripides, *Andromache*, pp.151–4.

38. Euripides, *Andromache*, pp.155–6.

39. Euripides, *Andromache*, p.156.

40. Euripides, *Andromache*, pp.156–7.

41. See Natalie Zemon Davis, *Society and Culture in Early Modern France* (Stanford University Press, Stanford, 1975), Chapter 5, 'Women on Top'; John Docker, *Postmodernism and Popular Culture: A Cultural History* (Cambridge University Press, Melbourne, 1994), p.194.

42. Euripides, *Andromache*, p.159.

43. Euripides, *Andromache*, pp.166, 173, 185–6.

44. Euripides, *Andromache*, pp.148, 153, 164–5.

45. Euripides, *Andromache*, pp.165–7.

46. Euripides, *Andromache*, pp.154–5. Euripides' *Helen* reprises a story well known in the ancient world, that Helen had never gone to Troy with Paris. In her opening lamentation on her fate, Helen explains what happened when Paris judged that of the three goddesses Hera, Aphrodite, and Athene, Aphrodite was the first in beauty. Hera, resentful that Paris has not chosen her, contrives that the Helen who goes to Troy is only an 'airy delusion', a 'living image compounded of the ether in my likeness'; meanwhile, on Zeus's orders, Hermes transports Helen 'wrapped in a cloud' to Egypt. See Euripides, *Helen*, in *The Bacchae and Other Plays*, p.136.

47. Euripides, *Andromache*, p.155.

48. Euripides, *The Women of Troy*, in *The Bacchae and Other Plays*, pp.89, 108, 112–13, 125.

49. Euripides, *The Women of Troy*, pp.113–14.
50. Euripides, *The Women of Troy*, pp.115, 126–8.
51. Euripides, *The Women of Troy*, pp.90, 100–1, 116.
52. Euripides, *The Women of Troy*, pp.118–21.
53. Euripides, *The Women of Troy*, pp.123–4.
54. Euripides, *The Women of Troy*, pp.99, 114, 126–9, 131–2.
55. Euripides, *The Women of Troy*, p.133.
56. Euripides, *The Women of Troy*, p.90.
57. See Curthoys and Docker, 'Defining Genocide', p.14.
58. Euripides, *The Women of Troy*, pp.124–5.
59. Euripides, *The Women of Troy*, pp.109, 124–5.
60. Euripides, *The Women of Troy*, pp.131–2.
61. Euripides, *The Women of Troy*, pp.89, 91–3.
62. Euripides, *Helen*, pp.147, 160.

## 4.    UTOPIA AND DYSTOPIA: PLATO AND CICERO'S *REPUBLICS*

1.  Cicero, *The Republic and The Laws*, translated by Niall Rudd, introd. Jonathan Powell and Niall Rudd (Oxford University Press, Oxford, 1998), p.65.
2.  Cicero, *The Republic and The Laws*, p.89.
3.  Sophie Mills, *Theseus, Tragedy and the Athenian Empire* (Clarendon, Oxford, 1997), pp.2–6, 10, 13, 16–17, 22–5, 59–63, 66.
4.  Cf. Ann Curthoys and John Docker, *Is History Fiction?* (UNSW Press, Sydney, 2005), p.47.
5.  Cf. Curthoys and Docker, *Is History Fiction?*, pp.14, 17, 34.
6.  Mikhail Bakhtin, *Problems of Dostoevsky's Poetics*, ed. and trans. Caryl Emerson (Manchester University Press, Manchester, 1984), p.109.
7.  Bakhtin, *Problems of Dostoevsky's Poetics*, pp.107–11.
8.  Bakhtin, *Problems of Dostoevsky's Poetics*, p.110.
9.  Bakhtin, *Problems of Dostoevsky's Poetics*, p.120. See also Bakhtin, *The Dialogic Imagination* (University of Texas Press, Austin, 1981), p.187, and *Rabelais and His World* (Indiana University Press, Bloomington, 1984), pp.168–9, 284.
10. Walter Benjamin, *The Origin of German Tragic Drama*, translated John Osborne (1928; Verso, London, 1996), 'Epistemo-Critical

Prologue', pp.28–9, 35, 41, 44–7. See also Curthoys and Docker, *Is History Fiction?*, p.96.

11. Plato, *The Symposium*, translated by Walter Hamilton (Penguin, London, 1951), pp.79–95.

12. Plato, *The Republic*, translated and introd. Desmond Lee, revised edition (Penguin, London, 1987), pp.305–25.

13. See e.g. Bruno Bettleheim, *The Children of the Dream* (Macmillan, New York, 1969); the novels of Ursula Le Guin; the anti-nuclear family ethos that informed collective households of the 1960s/70s in the Western counter-cultures.

14. Plato, *The Republic*, pp.225–36.

15. Plato, *The Republic*, pp.237, 241.

16. Plato, *The Republic*, p.241.

17. Plato, *The Republic*, pp.241, 244–6.

18. Plato, *The Republic*, pp.225–36.

19. See John Docker, *The Nervous Nineties* (Oxford University Press, Melbourne, 1991), pp.116–17, and *Postmodernism and Popular Culture: A Cultural History* (Cambridge University Press, Melbourne, 1994), pp.125–6, 170–1.

20. Bakhtin, *Problems of Dostoevsky's Poetics*, pp.112–22.

21. Plato, *The Republic*, 'The Myth of Er', pp.448, 454.

22. See James E.G. Zetzel (ed.), *On the Commonwealth and On the Laws* (Cambridge University Press, Cambridge, 1999), Introduction, p.xii.

23. Zetzel, Introduction, pp.xi–xiii, xv, xx.

24. See A.E. Astin, *Scipio Aemilianus* (Clarendon, Oxford, 1967), pp. 7, 9.

25. Cf. Bakhtin, *Problems of Dostoevsky's Poetics*, p.71, where Bakhtin is criticizing a Tolstoy story for containing 'neither polyphony nor … counterpoint'.

26. Bakhtin, *Problems of Dostoevsky's Poetics*, pp.5–7, 16–17, 111–37; also Curthoys and Docker, *Is History Fiction?*, pp.30–1.

27. Raphaël Lemkin, *Axis Rule in Occupied Europe* (Columbia University Press, New York, 1944), p.80 note 3. See also Ben Kiernan, 'Le Premier génocide: Carthage, 146 A.C.', *Diogène*, No. 203 (2003): 32–48.

28. Astin, *Scipio Aemilianus*, pp.75–80; concerning the friendship of Scipio and Laelius, see p.81; there is a sketch of L. Furius Philus, a close associate of Scipio and Laelius, on pp.81–2.

29. Astin, *Scipio Aemilianus*, pp.136, 153.
30. Cicero, *The Republic*, Book One, pp.16, 19–21, 25, 32–3.
31. Cicero, *The Republic*, Book Two, pp.36–7.
32. Cicero, *The Republic*, Book Two, pp.38–9, 42–3, 45.
33. Cicero, *The Republic*, Book Two, p.41.
34. Cicero, *The Republic*, Book Three, p.61.
35. Robert P. Carroll, *Wolf in the Sheepfold: The Bible as a Problem for Christianity* (SPCK, London, 1991), p.113. See also *The Bible: Authorized King James Version with Apocrypha*, with introduction and notes by Robert Carroll and Stephen Prickett (Oxford University Press, Oxford, 1997); see Carroll's notes, esp. pp.322–6.
36. Cicero, *The Republic*, Book Three, pp.68–9.
37. Cicero, *The Republic*, Book One, pp.3–4.
38. Cicero, *The Republic*, Book One, p.14.
39. Cicero, *The Republic*, Book Three, pp.63–4.
40. Cicero, *The Republic*, Book Three, p.64.
41. Bakhtin, *Problems of Dostoevsky's Poetics*, p.116.
42. Cicero, *The Republic*, Book Three, p.63.
43. Cicero, *The Republic*, Book Three, pp.63–4.
44. Cicero, *The Republic*, Book Three, p.65.
45. Cicero, *The Republic*, Book Three, p.65.
46. Cicero, *The Republic*, Book Three, p.65.
47. Cicero, *The Republic*, Book Three, p.66.
48. Cicero, *The Republic*, Book Three, p.66.
49. Lemkin, *Axis Rule in Occupied Europe*, pp.91 and 91 note 51; Lemkin, 'Totally Unofficial Man', in Samuel Totten and Steven Leonard Jacobs (eds), *Pioneers of Genocide Studies* (Transaction Publishers, New Brunswick, 2002), p.377; 'Genocide – A Modern Crime', *Free World* – 'A Magazine Devoted to the United Nations and Democracy', April 1945, pp.39–43, accessed at http://www.preventgenocide.org/lemkin/freeworld1945.htm.
50. Cicero, *The Republic*, Book Three, p.66.
51. Cicero, *The Republic*, Book Three, p.66.
52. Cicero, *The Republic*, Book One, p.19.
53. Cicero, *The Republic*, Book Two, p.37.
54. Bakhtin, *Problems of Dostoevsky's Poetics*, pp.112–20.
55. Cicero, *The Republic*, Book Six, 'The Dream of Scipio', pp.87, 89.
56. Cicero, *The Republic*, Book Six, 'The Dream of Scipio', pp.89–92.

## 5. VICTIMOLOGY AND GENOCIDE: THE BIBLE'S EXODUS, VIRGIL'S *AENEID*

1. Virgil, *Aeneid*, trans. and introd. David West, revised edition (Penguin Books, London, 2003), Book One, p.10.
2. Virgil, *Aeneid*, Book Four, pp.79–80.
3. Virgil, *Aeneid*, Book Five, p.111.
4. Virgil, *Aeneid*, Book Ten, pp.213–14.
5. Robert P. Carroll, *Wolf in the Sheepfold: The Bible as Problematic for Theology*, second edition (1991; SCM Press, London, 1997), p.xiii.
6. Richard Waswo, *The Founding Legend of Western Civilization: From Virgil to Vietnam* (Wesleyan University Press, Hanover, 1997).
   My thanks to Barry Hindess for suggesting I read Waswo's book.
7. Waswo, *The Founding Legend of Western Civilization*, p.7.
8. Concerning a postsecular methodology, see John Docker, *1492: The Poetics of Diaspora* (Continuum, London, 2001), p.viii.
9. Edward Said, 'Michael Walzer's *Exodus and Revolution*: A Canaanite Reading', *Arab Studies Quarterly*, Vol. 8, No. 3, 1986, pp.289–303, also in Edward Said and Christopher Hitchens (eds), *Blaming the Victims: Spurious Scholarship and the Palestinian Question* (Verso, London, 1988), pp.161–78.
10. Harry Berger Jnr, 'The Lie of the Land: The Text beyond Canaan', *Representations*, Vol. 25 (1989), pp.123, 126–9, 134–6, 138 n.12.
11. Baruch Spinoza, *Tractatus Theologico-Politicus*, trans. Samuel Shirley, intro. Brad S. Gregory (E.J. Brill, Leiden, 1989), pp.84, 96–7, 118, 221; Docker, *1492: The Poetics of Diaspora*, p.134, also p.139 for Spinoza's comparison of Jesus and Moses.
12. Cf. Ned Curthoys, 'Edward Said's Unhoused Philological Humanism', in Ned Curthoys and Debjani Ganguly (eds), *Edward Said: The Legacy of a Public Intellectual* (Melbourne University Press, Melbourne, 2007), pp.152–75.
13. Regina M. Schwartz, *The Curse of Cain: The Violent Legacy of Monotheism* (University of Chicago Press, Chicago, 1997), pp.x–xi, 6, 8, 10, 16–17, 95, 121–2, 140–1, 158–9.
14. Schwartz, *The Curse of Cain*, pp.9, 16–20, 55–62, 69, 101, 134, 140–1, 165–6, 169.
15. See Carroll's impassioned preface to the second edition of *Wolf in the Sheepfold*, pp.xi–xv.
16. Ella Shohat, 'Antinomies of Exile: Said at the Frontiers of National

Narrations', in Michael Sprinker (ed.), *Edward Said: A Critical Reader* (Blackwell, Oxford, 1992), pp.140–1.

17. Ann Curthoys, 'Expulsion, Exodus, and Exile in White Australian Historical Mythology', in Richard Nile and Michael Williams (eds), *Imaginary Homelands: The Dubious Cartographies of Australian Identity* (University of Queensland Press, Brisbane, 1999), pp.1–18. See also Roland Boer, *Last Stop Before Antarctica* (Sheffield Academic Press, Sheffield, 2001), Chapter 3, and Docker, *1492: The Poetics of Diaspora*, pp.140–8.

18. Nur Masalha, *The Bible and Zionism: Invented Traditions, Archaeology and Post-Colonialism in Palestine-Israel* (Zed Books, London, 2007), pp.15–18, 269–70, 282–3; Robert Allen Warrior, 'Canaanites, Cowboys and Indians', in R.S. Sugirtharajah (ed.), *Voices from the Margin: Interpreting the Bible in the Third World* (SPCK, London, 1991), p.279.

19. Masalha, *The Bible and Zionism*, pp.265–74. In the Enlightenment Pierre Bayle, in an essay on King David, argued that the stories concerning the king revealed not only his deceit, licentiousness, and injustice, but also, in his plans to slaughter all the family and herds of Nabal as punishment for inhospitality, an indisputable criminality; in warfare David revealed great brutality, annihilating all males, young and old. See Adam Sutcliffe, *Judaism and Enlightenment* (Cambridge University Press, Cambridge, 2003), pp.93–4. (Thanks to Ned Curthoys for this reference.)

20. Cf. Jonathan Kirsch, *The Harlot by the Side of the Road* (Johns Hopkins University Press, Baltimore, 1987), p.8; Docker, *1492: The Poetics of Diaspora*, pp.118–19.

21. Spinoza, *Tractatus Theologico-Politicus*, p.63; Daniel Boyarin, 'The Eye in the Torah: Ocular Desire in Midrashic Hermeneutic', *Critical Inquiry*, 16 (Spring 1990), pp.534–43; Docker, *1492: The Poetics of Diaspora*, pp.118–19 and 128 n.16.

22. Cf. Kirsch, *The Harlot by the Side of the Road*, Chapters 8 and 9; Docker, *1492: The Poetics of Diaspora*, pp.147–8.

23. Carroll, *Wolf in the Sheepfold*, Chapter 2, 'God the Hidden Problematic', pp.38–41, 44–7, 57–8, 60.

24. Cf. Thomas L. Thompson, *The Bible in History: How Writers Create a Past* (Jonathan Cape, London, 1999).

25. Berger, 'The Lie of the Land', pp.126–7, 129, 134, writes that in Exodus Yahweh acts as a phantom double of the Pharaoh, a super-pharaoh.

26. Robert Carroll and Stephen Prickett (eds), *The Bible. Authorized King James Version* (Oxford University Press, Oxford, 1998), 'Notes to the Old Testament', p.337.

27. Claude Rawson, *God, Gulliver, and Genocide: Barbarism and the European Imagination, 1492–1945* (Oxford University Press, Oxford, 2001), pp.269, 301–2.

28. Carroll, 'Notes to the Old Testament', p.337.

29. Raphaël Lemkin, *Axis Rule in Occupied Europe* (Columbia University Press, New York, 1944), pp.xi, 79–80.

30. Baruch Kimmerling, *Politicide: Ariel Sharon's War Against the Palestinians* (Verso, London, 2003); John Docker, 'Ilan Pappé, the New History, and the Question of Israeli Genocide', *Arena Magazine* 66, August–September 2003, pp.32–6; Ilan Pappé, *The Ethnic Cleansing of Palestine* (Oneworld, Oxford, 2006).

31. Pappé, *The Ethnic Cleansing of Palestine*, Chapter 10, pp.225–34.

32. Cf. Docker, *1492: The Poetics of Diaspora*, pp.125–6.

33. Carroll, *Wolf in the Sheepfold*, pp.39, 46.

34. Waswo, *The Founding Legend of Western Civilization*, pp.21, 36.

35. Waswo, *The Founding Legend*, pp.xi, 36.

36. Waswo, *The Founding Legend*, pp.xi–xii.

37. Waswo, *The Founding Legend*, pp.xii, xiv–xv.

38. Waswo, *The Founding Legend*, pp.21–8.

39. Waswo, *The Founding Legend*, pp.22–7.

40. Virgil, *Aeneid*, p.75.

41. Virgil, *Aeneid*, pp.77–9; cf. Waswo, *The Founding Legend*, pp.22–5.

42. Virgil, *Aeneid*, p.77.

43. Cf.Waswo, *The Founding Legend*, p.27.

44. Cf. Docker, *1492: The Poetics of Diaspora*, Chapter 3, 'The Collision of Two Worlds: Sir Walter Scott's *Ivanhoe* and Moorish Spain'.

45. Virgil, *Aeneid*, pp.41, 46–7.

46. Virgil, *Aeneid*, pp.82–9.

47. Virgil, *Aeneid*, pp.106–11.

48. I saw this quote when I visited Mani Bhavan Gandhi Museum, Mumbai, in early February 2008. It is from *Young India*, 10 April 1930.

49. Virgil, *Aeneid*, pp.54–5.

50. Virgil, *Aeneid*, p.213.

51. Virgil, *Aeneid*, p.266.

52. Virgil, *Aeneid*, p.290; cf. Waswo, *The Founding Legend*, p.27.

53. Virgil, *Aeneid*, pp.76, 204, 267.

54. Mikhail Bakhtin, *The Dialogic Imagination* (University of Texas Press, Austin, 1981), pp.106–7, 111–21; Docker, *Postmodernism and Popular Culture: A Cultural History* (Cambridge University Press, Melbourne, 1994), p.225.

55. Virgil, *Aeneid*, p.117.

56. Virgil, *Aeneid*, pp.136–40; cf. Waswo, *The Founding Legend*, pp.26–7.

57. Lemkin, *Axis Rule in Occupied Europe*, pp.79–80.

58. Waswo, *The Founding Legend*, p.27.

59. Virgil, *Aeneid*, Book Two, pp.47, 50–1, 53, Book Five, p.91, Book Six, p.133, Book Seven, p.147.

60. Virgil, *Aeneid*, Book One, p.24, Book Two, pp.27–31, Book Six, pp.128, 138.

61. Cf. John Docker, '"Re-Feminising' Diaspora: Contemporary Jewish Cultural Studies and Post-Zionism', *Holy Land Studies*, Vol. 4, No. 2, 2005, pp.71–90, and 'Josephus: Traitor or Gandhian *avant la lettre?*' in John Docker and Debjani Ganguly (eds), special series of essays on 'Gandhi, Non-Violence, and Modernity', *Borderlands* e-journal, 2005/6.

62. I owe much to discussion with Shino Konishi concerning the subtleties of first contact history.

63. Virgil, *Aeneid*, pp.145–8.

64. Virgil, *Aeneid*, pp.139, 192–200.

65. Cf. Shino Konishi, 'The Father Governor: The British Administration of Aboriginal People at Port Jackson, 1788–1792', in Matthew McCormack (ed.), *Public Men: Political Masculinities in Modern Britain* (Palgrave Macmillan, Hampshire, 2007), pp.54–72.

## 6. ROMAN SETTLER IMPERIALISM IN BRITAIN: NARRATIVE AND COUNTER NARRATIVE IN TACITUS' *AGRICOLA* AND *GERMANIA*

1. Virgil, *Aeneid*, trans. and introd. David West, revised edition (Penguin Books, London, 2003), p.11.

2. Tacitus, *The Agricola and The Germania*, trans. H. Mattingly, revised translation S.A. Handford (Penguin Classics, London, 1970), section 30.

3. Cf. Mikhail Bakhtin, *Problems of Dostoevsky's Poetics* (Manchester University Press, Manchester, 1984), p.106.
4. Bakhtin, *Problems of Dostoevsky's Poetics*, pp.112–22. Bakhtin writes, p.113, that the menippea is a 'carnivalized genre, extraordinarily flexible and changeable as Proteus, capable of penetrating other genres'.
5. Mikhail Bakhtin, *The Dialogic Imagination* (University of Texas Press, Austin, 1981), pp.132–3.
6. Bakhtin, *Problems of Dostoevsky's Poetics*, p.114.
7. Cf. Patrick Wolfe, 'Against the Intentional Fallacy: Marking the Gap Between Rhetoric and Outcome in United States Indian Law and Policy' (in preparation).
8. Bakhtin, *Problems of Dostoevsky's Poetics*, pp.116–17.
9. I read this quote at the Mani Bhavan Gandhi Museum, Mumbai, in early February 2008.
10. Cf. Ann Curthoys, 'Liberalism and Exclusionism: A Prehistory of the White Australia Policy', in Laksiri Jayasuriya, David Walker, and Jan Gothard (eds), *Legacies of White Australia: Race Culture and Nation* (University of Western Australia Press, Perth, 2003), pp.8–33.
11. For Tacitus' dislike of the Julio-Claudian emperors, see *The Annals of Imperial Rome*, trans. and introd. Michael Grant, revised edition (Penguin, London, 1996).
12. Josephus, *The Jewish War*, trans. G.A. Williamson, revised edition with a new introduction by E. Mary Smallwood (Penguin, London, 1981), pp.217, 317.
13. See Robert Bernasconi, 'Will the Real Kant Please Stand Up: The Challenge of Enlightenment Racism to the Study of the History of Philosophy', *Radical Philosophy* 117, January–February 2003, pp.13–22, and Curthoys and Docker, *Is History Fiction?*, pp.57–61, 72–3. (My thanks to Ida Nursoo for referring me to the Bernasconi essay.)
14. I owe this point to Ned Curthoys.
15. Cf. George L. Mosse, *Toward the Final Solution: A History of European Racism* (Dent, London, 1978).
16. Hugh Brody, *The Other Side of Eden: Hunter-Gatherers, Farmers, and the Shaping of the World* (Faber and Faber, London, 2002).

## 7. THE HONOURABLE COLONIZER

1. See Ann Curthoys and John Docker, *Is History Fiction?* (UNSW Press, Sydney, 2005), p.184.
2. See also David Armitage, *The Ideological Origins of the British Empire* (Cambridge University Press, Cambridge, 2000), Chapter 1, 'Introduction: State and Empire in British History', pp.1–23.
3. Andrew Fitzmaurice, *Humanism and America: An Intellectual History of English Colonisation, 1500–1625* (Cambridge University Press, Cambridge, 2003), p.19, referring – extremely unfairly – to Peter Hulme, 'Nymphs and Reapers Heavily Vanish: The Discursive Con-texts of *The Tempest*', in John Drakakis (ed.), *Alternative Shakespeares* (Routledge, London, 1985), p.200.
4. Quentin Skinner, *Liberty before Liberalism* (Cambridge University Press, Cambridge, 1998), pp.101–5, 112.
5. Skinner, *Liberty before Liberalism*, pp.13, 50.
6. Cf. Sarah Irving, ' "In a Pure Soil": Colonial Anxieties in the Work of Francis Bacon', *History of European Ideas*, Vol. 32 (2006), pp.250–3, 257.
7. Concerning the cyclical view of history of the humanists, see Fitzmaurice, *Humanism and America*, pp.162 note 84, and 189.
8. Fitzmaurice, *Humanism and America*, pp.162–3.
9. Concerning 'Asiatic', see *Humanism and America*, pp.3, 20, 25, 38, 129–36, 163, 189. Cf. Skinner, *Liberty before Liberalism*, p.64.
10. *Humanism and America*, pp.164–5.
11. *Humanism and America*, pp.159–60, 166. See Tacitus, *The Agricola and the Germania* (Penguin, London, 1970), *Agricola*, Chapters 29–32.
12. *Humanism and America*, pp.1, 11, 37.
13. *Humanism and America*, pp.1, 21, 28, 39, 47–8, 190.
14. Skinner, *Liberty before Liberalism*, pp.78–9.
15. Wendy Lower, *Nazi Empire-Building and the Holocaust in Ukraine* (University of North Carolina Press in association with the United States Holocaust Memorial Museum), pp.20–1, 24–5.
16. *Humanism and America*, p.187. Cf. Patrick Wolfe, 'Palestine, Project Europe and the (Un-)Making of the New Jew: In memory of Edward W. Said', in Ned Curthoys and Debjani Ganguly (eds), *Edward Said: Debating the Legacy of a Public Intellectual* (Melbourne University Press, Melbourne, 2007), pp.313–37.

17. *Humanism and America*, pp.149–50.
18. *Humanism and America*, pp.25, 151–2.
19. *Humanism and America*, pp.152–5.
20. Larissa Behrendt, 'Genocide: The Distance between Law and Life', pp.142–46, and 'Eliza Fraser: A Colonial and Legal Narrative', in Iain McCalman and Ann McGrath (eds), *Proof and Truth: The Humanist as Expert* (The Australian Academy of the Humanities, Canberra, 2003).
21. Richard Waswo, *The Founding Legend of Western Civilization: From Virgil to Vietnam* (Wesleyan University Press, Hanover, 1997), pp.xi, xv, 57, 60, 63.
22. Waswo, *The Founding Legend*, pp.136–7.
23. Waswo, *The Founding Legend*, pp.137–8.
24. Virgil, *Aeneid*, translated by David West (Penguin, London, 2003), Book Seven, p.147.
25. Waswo, *The Founding Legend*, pp.138, 140–8.
26. H.S. Reiss (ed.), *Kant: Political Writings* (Cambridge University Press, Cambridge, 1991), pp.93–130. I must acknowledge here discussions with Ida Nursoo concerning the relationship between cosmopolitanism and hospitality in Kant's 'Perpetual Peace' essay. See also Robert Bernasconi, 'Will the Real Kant Please Stand Up: The Challenge of Enlightenment Racism to the Study of the History of Philosophy', *Radical Philosophy* 117, January–February 2003, pp.13–22.
27. Fitzmaurice, *Humanism and America*, pp.140–3.
28. *Humanism and America*, p.148.
29. *Humanism and America*, pp.19, 146.
30. *Humanism and America*, pp.143, 147. Concerning *res nullius*, see also Andrew Fitzmaurice, 'The Genealogy of *Terra Nullius*', *Australian Historical Studies*, Vol. 38, No. 129, 2007, pp.1–15.
31. *Humanism and America*, pp.144–5. See also Ida Nursoo, 'Dialogue Across *Différance*: Culture, Kant and Imperial Hospitality' (in preparation).
32. *Humanism and America*, p.140.
33. *Humanism and America*, p.147.
34. Ann Curthoys, 'Expulsion, Exodus, and Exile in White Australian Historical Mythology', in Richard Nile and Michael Williams (eds), *Imaginary Homelands: The Dubious Cartographies of Australian Identity* (University of Queensland Press, St. Lucia, 1999).

35. Virgil, *Aeneid*, Book Three, pp.54–5.

36. Apropos Elizabethan piracy, see Barbara Fuchs, *Mimesis and Empire: The New World, Islam and European Identities* (Cambridge University Press, Cambridge, 2001), Chapter 5, 'Faithless Empires: Pirates, Renegadoes, and the English Nation', pp.118–38.

37. *Humanism and America*, pp.31–2.

38. *Humanism and America*, pp.35–6, 39–41.

39. *Humanism and America*, pp.41, 43.

40. Colm Lennon, *Sixteenth-Century Ireland: The Incomplete Conquest* (Gill and Macmillan, Dublin, 1994), pp.214–15. In terms of the use of severed heads as a mode of terror and intimidation, Gilbert was reprising an at least occasional Roman practice of war.

   Brian Campbell, 'Power without Limit: "The Romans Always Win"', in Angelos Chaniotis and Pierre Ducrey (eds), *Army and Power in the Ancient World* (Franz Steiner Verlag, Stuttgart, 2002), p.169, refers to a 'stratagem of using severed enemy heads to intimidate the survivors and bring a war to a close after a successful battle'. (My thanks to David Pritchard for the reference to Campbell's essay.)

41. Ciaran Brady, 'The Captains' Games: Army and Society in Elizabethan Ireland', in Thomas Bartlett and Keith Jeffrey (eds), *A Military History of Ireland* (Cambridge University Press, Cambridge, 1996), pp.139–40, 146.

42. Patricia Palmer, *Language and Conquest in Early Modern Ireland: English Renaissance Literature and Elizabethan Imperial Expansion* (Cambridge University Press, Cambridge, 2001), pp.4–9, 13–21, 47, 111, 122.

43. Palmer, *Language and Conquest in Early Modern Ireland*, pp.69, 110, 124, 149, 154–5.

44. *Humanism and America*, pp.3, 41, 48–9, 54 note 199, 138.

45. *Humanism and America*, pp.144, 146.

46. *Humanism and America*, p.146.

47. Cf. John Docker, *1492: The Poetics of Diaspora* (Continuum, London, 2001), pp.122–5.

48. Victor I. Scherb, 'Assimilating Giants: The Appropriation of Gog and Magog in Medieval and Early Modern England', *Journal of Medieval and Early Modern Studies*, Vol. 32, No. 1, 2002, pp.59–84. My thanks to Shino Konishi for this reference.

49. Scherb, 'Assimilating Giants', pp.62–5.

50. Concerning the Britons as Trojans, and touching on the story of Gogmagog and Corineus, cf. Waswo, *The Founding Legend of Western Civilization*, pp.57–8.

51. Scherb, 'Assimilating Giants', pp.66–9, 71–6. Apropos giants and monsters, see also Walter B. Stephens, *Giants in Those Days: Folklore, Ancient History, and Nationalism* (University of Nabraska Press, Lincoln, 1989); Jeffrey Jerome Cohen, *Of Giants: Sex, Monsters, and the Middle Ages* (University of Minnesota Press, Minneapolis, 1999).

52. See Shino Konishi, 'In Search of Giants: Revisiting the Baudin Expedition's First Encounters with Aboriginal People at Shark Bay, Western Australia, 1803', *Indian and Pacific Crossings: Perspectives on Globalisation and History Conference,* Edith Cowan University, Fremantle, 12–15 December 2006, and '"Inhabited by a Race of Formidable Giants": French Explorers, Aborigines, and the Endurance of the Fantastic in the Great South Land, 1803', *Australian Humanities Review*, March 2008. www.australianhumanitiesreview.org/archive/Issue-March-2008/konishi.html.

53. Jean-Paul Sartre, *On Genocide and a Summary of the Evidence and Judgments of the International War Crimes Tribunal* by Arlette El Kaïm-Sartre (Beacon Press, Boston, 1968), pp.67–9, 74–6.

54. Lemkin Collection, American Jewish Historical Society, 15 West 16th Street, NYC, Box 8, Folder 11, History of Genocide. Projected Book and North American Indian Research. Correspondence, 1947–1949, 1951.

55. Erich Auerbach, *Mimesis: The Representation of Reality in Western Literature*, with a new introduction by Edward Said (Princeton University Press, Princeton, 2003), Chapter 13, 'The Weary Prince', pp.314–316, 328. My thanks to Ned Curthoys for this reference.

56. Cf. A. Anghie, *Imperialism, Sovereignty, and the Making of International Law* (Cambridge University Press, Cambridge, 2004), Chapter 'Francisco de Vitoria and the Colonial Origins of International Law', pp.13–31; Paul Keal, '"Just Backward Children": International Law and the Conquest of Non-European Peoples', *Australian Journal of International Affairs*, Vol. 49, No. 2, 1995, pp.191–206; Anthony Pagden, *European Encounters with the New World: From Renaissance to Romanticism* (Yale University Press, New Haven, 1993); T. Todorov, *The Conquest of America: The Question of the Other* (1982; Harper and Row, New York, 1992).

## 8. WAS THE ENLIGHTENMENT THE ORIGIN OF THE HOLOCAUST?

1. An earlier version of this chapter, entitled 'The Enlightenment, Genocide, Postmodernity', was published in *Journal of Genocide Research*, Vol. 5, No. 3, 2003, pp.339–60.
2. Ernst Cassirer, *The Philosophy of the Enlightenment*, translated F.C.A. Koelln and J.P. Pettegrove (Princeton University Press, Princeton NJ, 1951), p.v.
3. Ole Peter Grell and Roy Porter (eds), *Toleration in Enlightenment Europe* (Cambridge University Press, Cambridge, 2000), Introduction, p.1.
4. Zygmunt Bauman, *Modernity and the Holocaust* (Polity Press, Cambridge, 1989), pp.xii–xiii, 20, 184.
5. Bauman, *Modernity and the Holocaust*, pp.xiv, 68–9.
6. George L. Mosse, *Toward the Final Solution: A History of European Racism* (Dent, London, 1978), pp.xvi, 1–3, 5, 10–11.
7. Bauman, 'The Duty To Remember – But What?', in James Kaye and Bo Stråth (eds), *Enlightenment and Genocide, Contradictions of Modernity* (P.I.E. – Peter Lang, Brussels, 2000), pp.31, 36–8. I have no space here to discuss the fine final part of Bauman's essay (45–57) where he ponders the ethical consequences of ways the Holocaust has been remembered. Memory of suffering could, he feels, involve 'the life-long dedication to the fight against inhumanity, cruelty and pain-inflicting as such'. Instead, he perceives an opposite conclusion being drawn, as in much Zionist discourse and official Israeli policy and diplomacy, where the 'tendency' is to draw the lesson 'that humankind is divided into the victims and the victimisers, and so if you are (or expect to be) a victim, the point is to reverse the tables' (p. 45).
8. See Wokler, 'The Enlightenment Project on the Eve of the Holocaust', in Kaye and Stråth (eds), *Enlightenment and Genocide, Contradictions of Modernity*, pp.70–3. See also Wokler, 'Multiculturalism and Ethnic Cleansing in the Enlightenment', in Grell and Porter (eds), *Toleration in Enlightenment Europe*.
9. Wokler, 'The Enlightenment Project on the Eve of the Holocaust', in Kaye and Stråth, p.60; see also James Schmidt, 'Genocide and the Limits of Enlightenment: Horkheimer and Adorno Revisited', in the same volume, pp.81–102.

10. Wokler, 'The Enlightenment Project on the Eve of the Holocaust', in Kaye and Stråth, pp.71, 74–5, 77.

11. Wokler, 'The Enlightenment Project on the Eve of the Holocaust', in Kaye and Stråth, pp.60–3.

12. Wokler, 'The Enlightenment Project on the Eve of the Holocaust', in Kaye and Stråth, p.60. Compare Bauman's view of the continuities between the Enlightenment and the French Revolution, in Peter Beilharz (ed.), *The Bauman Reader* (Blackwell, Oxford, 2001), p.261 (reprinted 1984 essay 'Dictatorship Over Needs').

13. Wokler, 'The Enlightenment Project on the Eve of the Holocaust', in Kaye and Stråth, pp.64–9, 77.

14. Oddly, in his essay in their volume Bauman doesn't mention the Enlightenment, focusing only on modernity. See, however, Beilharz (ed.), *The Bauman Reader*, p.272: 'the kind of universe dreamed up and promised by the philosophers of the Enlightenment ... A kingdom of reason, the ultimate exercise in human power over nature, the ultimate display of the infinite human potential' (reprinted 1995 essay 'A Century of Camps?').

15. Kaye and Stråth, Introduction, pp.13–15, 19, 26–7.

16. Kaye and Stråth, Introduction, pp.14, 16. See also Dirk Moses' critique, 'Modernity and the Holocaust', *Australian Journal of Politics and History*, Vol. 43, 1997, pp.441–445: ' he [Bauman] downplays the motivating effect of ideology in the name of an extreme functionalism. ... There is, in other words, more to National Socialism and the Holocaust than instrumental reason.' Cf. Schmidt in Kaye and Stråth, pp.95, 97–8.

17. Cf. Ned Curthoys, 'The Politics of Holocaust Representation: The Worldly Typologies of Hannah Arendt', *Arena Journal*, Vol. 16, 2000/1, p.56; also his 'Hannah Arendt and the Politics of Narrative', *JNT: Journal of Narrative Theory*, Vol. 32, No. 3, 2002, pp.348–70.

18. Hannah Arendt, *The Origins of Totalitarianism* (George Allen and Unwin, London, 1967), p.123.

19. Wokler, 'The Enlightenment Project on the Eve of the Holocaust', in Kaye and Stråth, pp.65, 72.

20. See also John Docker, 'The Enlightenment and Genocide', *JNT: Journal of Narrative Theory*, Vol. 33, No. 3, 2003, pp.292–314, testing the Bauman-Mosse view of the Enlightenment in relation to eighteenth-century literary Orientalism. My thanks to Ian Higgins for leads into the labyrinth of the English Enlightenment.

21. Cf. William E. Connolly, *Why I Am Not a Secularist* (University of Minnesota Press, Minneapolis, 1999), John Docker, *1492: The Poetics of Diaspora* (Continuum, London, 2001), and Jane Bennett, *The Enchantment of Modern Life* (Princeton University Press, Princeton NJ, 2001).

22. See J.A.I. Champion, *The Pillars of Priestcraft Shaken: The Church of England and its Enemies, 1660–1730* (Cambridge University Press, Cambridge, 1992), Sylvia Berti, 'At the Roots of Unbelief', *Journal of the History of Ideas*, Vol. 56, No. 4, 1995, pp.555–75, Iain McCalman, 'New Jerusalems: Prophecy, Dissent and Radical Culture in England, 1786–1830', in K. Haakonssen (ed.), *Enlightenment and Religion: Rational Dissent in Eighteenth Century Britain* (Cambridge University Press, Cambridge, 1996).

23. Wokler, 'Multiculturalism and Ethnic Cleansing in the Enlightenment', in Grell and Porter (eds), *Toleration in Enlightenment Europe*, pp.74–82.

24. Gilles Deleuze, *Spinoza: Practical Philosophy*, translated R. Hurley (City Lights Books, San Francisco, 1988), pp.28–9; Docker, *1492: The Poetics of Diaspora*, p.90.

25. Y. Yovel, *The Marrano of Reason* (Princeton University Press, Princeton, NJ, 1989), pp.23–30; Docker, *1492: The Poetics of Diaspora*, pp.99–102.

26. Genevieve Lloyd, *Spinoza and the Ethics* (Routledge, London, 1996), pp.4–5.

27. Lloyd, *Spinoza and the Ethics*, pp.6, 121–4, 127–8, 131.

28. Lloyd, *Spinoza and the Ethics*, pp.114–16, 122, 124–5, 130.

29. Moira Gatens and Genevieve Lloyd, *Collective Imaginings: Spinoza, Past and Present* (Routledge, London, 1999), pp.1–5, 14–15.

30. William E. Connolly, *Neuropolitics: Thinking, Culture, Speed* (University of Minnesota Press, Minneapolis, 2002), p.138; Baruch Spinoza, *On the Improvement of the Understanding, the Ethics, Correspondence*, translated R.H.M. Elwes (Dover, New York, 1955), p.132.

31. Jonathan I. Israel, *Radical Enlightenment: Philosophy and the Making of Modernity 1650–1750* (Oxford University Press, Oxford, 2001), pp.7–10, 13, 22, 94–5, 160–1, 259, 523.

32. Israel, *Radical Enlightenment*, pp.7, 60, 91.

33. Israel, *Radical Enlightenment*, pp.5, 76–7, 237, 259, 265–8, 279.

34. Israel, *Radical Enlightenment*, pp.60–1, 67, 86, 91, 236.

35. Baruch Spinoza, *Tractatus Theologico-Politicus*, translated S. Shirley (Brill, Leiden, 1989), p.234; Docker, *1492: The Poetics of Diaspora*, pp.93–6.

36. Spinoza, *On the Improvement of the Understanding*, p.337, letter dated Voorburg, 28 January 1665.

37. Stephen H. Daniel, *John Toland: His Methods, Manners, and Mind* (McGill-Queen's University Press, Montreal, 1984), pp.5–13.

38. Jan Assmann, *Moses the Egyptian: The Memory of Egypt in Western Monotheism* (Harvard University Press, Cambridge Mass., 1997), pp.5, 8, 20.

39. John Toland, *Christianity Not Mysterious* (1696; Friedrich Frommann Verlag, Stuttgart-Bad Cannstatt, 1964), pp.46, 90, 97, 153, 170–1.

40. Georg Simmel, *The Sociology of Georg Simmel*, edited and translated Kurt H. Wolff (The Free Press, Glencoe, Il., 1950), Chapter 'The Stranger', pp.402–8; Docker, *1492: The Poetics of Diaspora*, pp.86–7.

41. Toland, *Clidophorus, Or, of the Exoteric and Esoteric Philosophy* (London, 1720), pp.65, 68, 70–78, 89, 94. Thales was also a favourite philosopher of Spinoza (Israel, *Radical Enlightenment*, p.174). In *Letters to Serena* (London, 1704), p.31, Toland also writes of 'Pythagoras, one of the greatest Travellers in the World … suffering himself to be circumcis'd that he might be admitted to hear the secret Doctrines' of the Egyptian Priests and Prophets.

42. Toland, *Pantheisticon: Or, the Form of Celebrating the Socratic-Society* (London, 1751), pp.13, 15, 19, 33, 58–9, 64, 66, 70.

43. Steven Nadler, *Spinoza: A Life* (Cambridge University Press, Cambridge, 1999), p.306.

44. Spinoza, *Tractatus Theologico-Politicus*, p.49; Nadler, *Spinoza: A Life*, pp.339, 344, 348.

45. Toland, *Pantheisticon*, p.64.

46. Toland, *Tetradymos* (London, 1720), Part III, *Hypatia*, pp.103–9, 118–19, 122–7, 130–3, 136. Israel, *Radical Enlightenment*, p.91, discusses Toland's interest in Hypatia and refers to the menstruation story and responses to it by his conservative critics.

47. Lady Mary Wortley Montagu, *Selected Letters*, edited R. Halsband (Penguin, Harmondsworth, 1986), p.246. See also Israel, *Radical Enlightenment*, pp.89, 91 concerning Toland, women, and education.

48. Toland, *Hodegus, Or, The Pillar of Cloud and Fire not Miraculous,* in *Tetradymos*, p.6; *Clidophorus*, p.65. See also Assmann, *Moses the Egyptian*, pp.91–6, and Champion, 'Toleration and Citizenship in Enlightenment England: John Toland and the Naturalization of the Jews, 1714–1753', in Grell and Porter (eds), *Toleration in Enlightenment Europe*, p.141. Champion here is discussing Toland's 1714 pamphlet *Reasons for Naturalising the Jews.*

49. See also Champion, *The Pillars of Priestcraft Shaken*, Chapters 5–6.

50. Israel, *Radical Enlightenment*, p.227.

51. Toland, *Nazarenus: Or, Jewish, Gentile, and Mahometan Christianity* (London, 1718), Preface and pp.4–6, 9, 12–15. Israel, *Radical Enlightenment*, pp.66, 613 also finds *Nazarenus* an 'astounding' text, and refers as well to its admiration of Islam, comparing it to that of Boulainvilliers in France (572–3); see also Champion, *The Pillars of Priestcraft Shaken*, pp.125–9, 234.

52. Toland, *Nazarenus*, pp.16–17, 22–3, 44; on p.28 Toland defines Socinianism: Jesus was a mere man, but his mother was a Virgin conceived by virtue of the Spirit of God.

53. Toland, *Nazarenus*, pp.37–9, 42.

54. Toland, *Nazarenus*, pp.44–8; *Letters to Serena*, pp.21–2, 30–3, 40.

55. Toland, *Nazarenus*, pp.52–3, 56.

56. Toland, *Nazarenus*, p.59.

57. Toland, *Nazarenus*, pp.4–5, 56, 61.

58. Ammiel Alcalay, *After Jews and Arabs: Remaking Levantine Culture* (University of Minnesota Press, Minneapolis, 1993); Ella Shohat, 'Taboo memories and Diasporic Visions: Columbus, Palestine and Arab-Jews', in M. Joseph and J. Natalya Fink (eds), *Performing Hybridity* (University of Minnesota Press, Minneapolis, 1999), pp.131–156; and Maria Rosa Menacol, *The Ornament of the World: How Muslims, Jews and Christians Created a Culture of Tolerance in Medieval Spain* (Little Brown and Co., New York, 2002).

59. Stephen Nye, *A Brief History of the Unitarians, Called also Socinians. In Four Letters, Written to a Friend* (London, 1691). See also Champion, *The Pillars of Priestcraft Shaken*, pp.109–10. In *Nazarenus*, p.25, Toland refers to 'Mr Nye's *Judgement of the Fathers*'.

60. Humphrey Prideaux, *The True Nature of Imposture Fully Display'd in the Life of Mahomet* (London, 1697); T. Killigrew (ed.), *Miscellaneous*

*Aurea: Or the Golden Medley* (London, 1720); H. Boulainvilliers, *Life of Mohamet* (London, 1752). Concerning the interest in and disputes about Islam in the 'long eighteenth century', see Champion, *The Pillars of Priestcraft Shaken*, passim.

61. Cf. Lisa Lowe, *Critical Terrains: French and British Orientalisms* (Cornell University Press, Ithaca NY, 1991); see also Lowe's chapter, 'The Worldliness of Intimacy', in Ned Curthoys and Debjani Ganguly (eds), *Edward Said: The Legacy of a Public Intellectual* (Melbourne University Press, Melbourne, 2007), pp.121–51.

62. Spinoza, *Tractatus Theologico-Politicus*, pp.264–5; Docker, *1492: The Poetics of Diaspora*, p.138.

63. David Hume, *The Natural History of Religion*, edited by W. Colver (Clarendon Press, Oxford, 1976). Toland, in his long essay on the Druids in *A Collection of Several Pieces* (1726), Vol. I, p.52, refers to the religious tolerance of the Romans, though the Romans suppressed the Druidic religion in Gaul and Britain, Toland suggests, because of the 'barbarous Tyranny' exercised by the Druid priesthood over the 'credulous people'. Concerning the cosmopolitanism of the ancient polytheistic world, cf. Assmann, *Moses the Egyptian*, pp.20, 45–54, 136, 168, 193, 209, 217.

64. Hume, *The Natural History of Religion*, pp.62–3.

65. Hume, *The Natural History of Religion*, pp.45, 49, 75.

66. Jean-François Lyotard and Jean-Loup Thébaud, *Just Gaming*, translated Wlad Godzich (University of Minnesota Press, Minneapolis, 1994), pp.15–17, 29, 32–3.

67. Lyotard, *Just Gaming*, pp.39–40, 43. Lyotard's evocation of pagan storytelling is very close to the narratology of *The Thousand and One Nights* in the eighteenth century; see John Docker, 'The Enlightenment and Genocide'.

68. Lyotard, *Just Gaming*, pp.28, 32–3, 36, 39–43.

69. Lyotard, *Just Gaming*, p.5.

70. Gilles Deleuze, *Empiricism and Subjectivity: An Essay on Hume's Theory of Human Nature*, translated C.V. Boundas (Columbia University Press, New York, 1991), pp.33–4.

71. Deleuze, *Empiricism and Subjectivity*, pp.81–7, 90–1, 108, 126–7.

72. Cf. McCalman, 'New Jerusalems …'

73. Voltaire, *Candide*, translated John Butt (Penguin, London, 1947), pp.136, 143–44.

74. Docker, *1492: The Poetics of Diaspora*, pp.134–40.

75. Cf. Kathleen Wilson, *The Sense of the People: Politics, Culture and Imperialism in England, 1715–1785* (Cambridge University Press, Cambridge, 1995).
76. Claude Rawson, *God, Gulliver, and Genocide: Barbarism and the European Imagination, 1492–1945* (Oxford University Press, Oxford and New York, 2001), pp.232, 249. See my review in *Journal of Genocide Research*, Vol. 5, No. 1, 2003, pp.161–5.
77. See also J. Schmidt, 'What Enlightenment Project?' *Political Theory*, Vol. 28, No. 6, pp.734–57.

## CONCLUSION: CAN THERE BE AN END TO VIOLENCE?

1. See my essay on Gandhi and Josephus in Debjani Ganguly and John Docker (eds), *Rethinking Gandhi and Nonviolent Relationality* (Routledge, London, 2007), pp.205–22.

# INDEX

intellectual history, xiv, 3–5, 92,
162–3, 166, 174
intent, intention, 16, 24, 63, 68,
109, 142–3, 161–2, 168, 174,
190, 218
international law, 8–9, 16, 41, 46,
58–9, 106, 122, 161, 168–72,
178–9, 186–7, 217
law of nations, 9, 106, 161,
167, 173, 187
internationalism, xiii, 2, 90, 148,
215
Ireland, xv, 31, 126, 149, 155,
157, 162, 165, 175–6, 178, 201
Islamophilia, 205–8
Israel, Jonathan I., 198
Israel, xi, xiv, xv, 1–2, 50,
116–29, 133–4, 136, 141–2,
161, 179, 180, 198–9, 208,
214, 218

**J**
Jerusalem, 40, 57, 127, 156, 190
Jews, Jewish, xv, 1, 3, 14–15,
22–3, 57, 64, 77, 92, 103, 114,
120–1, 142, 156, 180, 204–7,
214, 216, 218
Sephardic and Oriental, 121,
142, 201
Josephus, 57, 142, 156, 218
Joshua, 5, 8, 117, 122–7, 132,
134, 140, 142, 179–80, 182
Joyce, James, 77
'Judgement of Paris', 81
Judges, 5, 8, 117, 122, 126–7,
140, 142, 179, 182
Juno, 114, 133, 136–9, 155, 158
Jupiter, 113–17, 128–9, 132–40,
145, 153, 158, 178.

just war, 104, 167, 171, 174, 177,
218

**K**
Kant, 157, 171
Kaye, James, 190, 192–3
Kimmerling, Baruch, 127
Konishi, Shino, xv, 181

**L**
Las Casas, Bartolomé, 65, 172
Lemkin, xiv, 1–9, 14–7, 26–9, 40,
52, 62, 64–86, 100, 108, 115,
122–8, 140–2, 153, 184–6,
217
*Axis Rule in Occupied
Europe*, 1–2, 5, 14–5, 40,
100, 123, 127–8, 141, 184
'Revised Outline for
Genocide Cases', 3, 62–6,
69, 71–2, 75, 78, 82, 85,
126, 185
Lessing, Gotthold, 191, 193
Levi, Primo, 1
liberty, 44, 52, 149, 154–5, 163,
166, 183, 202, 209
Lloyd, Genevieve, 196–7
Lower, Wendy, xiv, 166
Lyotard, J.-F., 194, 208–14

**M**
Masalha, Nur, xiv, 121–2
masculinity *see* gender
massacre, 2, 22, 27–8, 39, 51, 57,
63, 65, 69, 126
Melos, Melians 8, 9, 10, 51–3,
57–8, 71, 82, 90, 155
Melian Dialogue,10, 50–1,
56, 58, 71

Printed and bound by CPI Group (UK) Ltd, Croydon, CR0 4YY

25/03/2025

14647331-0003